God Stories

VOLUME SIX

*"I . . . pray . . . for those who will believe in me
through their word, that they all may be one as
you, Father, are in me and I in you.
I pray that they may be one in us, so that the
world may believe that you sent me."*

John 17:20–21

The Regional Church of Lancaster County
www.theregionalchurch.com

Dedication

This book is dedicated to the people of South Central Pennsylvania.

Acknowledgments

Thank you to the many contributing authors who made this book possible.

Edited by Karen Boyd, Lisa Dorr, Jan Dorward, Sharon Neal, Susan Shiner, Kim Wittel and Keith Yoder.

House To House Publications Team: Lou Ann Good and Sarah Sauder.

Cover photos: Jennifer Raff, Ann Rodriquez, Mark Van Scyoc

Contact an author

If a particular devotional has encouraged you and you want to tell the author, please email Lou Ann Good (LouAnnG@dcfi.org) who will endeavor to pass on your message.

God Stories 6

© 2010 by The Regional Church of Lancaster County
Lancaster, Pennsylvania, USA
www.theregionalchurch.com
All rights reserved.

ISBN: 978-0-9817765-9-0

Partnership Publications
www.h2hp.com

Printed in the United States of America

Introduction

Transformation is the theme for this edition of *God Stories*—stories about changed lives. Transformation is God at work effecting lasting change in thinking and behavior at a basic level. Individual change leads to change in communities. Spiritual transformation leads to transformation of society.

Eugene Peterson in *The Message* expresses Psalm 9:11 as ". . . tell his stories to everyone you meet." We agree. Authors from throughout south central Pennsylvania are telling God's stories to those within our region and beyond. You may search for a particular author in the index near the end of the book and contact a select author by emailing LouAnnG@dcfi.org.

In south central Pennsylvania there are several organizations whose purpose is to encourage personal and community transformation for the sake of the kingdom of God. These ministries serve their respective counties, and they have cooperated to bring this volume of inspirational stories to you. To partner with others for the sake of transformation, use the contact information inside the back cover.

Transformation takes place as we refresh our minds with truth from the Word of God. Each daily story is linked to scriptural truth. Each one gives us reason to praise God, to bless the author and to pray for similar transformation to come to our region.

The purpose of *God Stories* continues to be the cultivation and celebration of oneness in the body of Christ—for which Jesus prayed. As we daily participate in worship in these pages, let us continue to long for and anticipate that we may become one in the Father and Son even as they are one "that the world may believe" that the Father sent the Son (John 17:21).

—Keith Yoder, chair, Regional Church of Lancaster County,
on behalf of the participating regional partners

January

Being Transformed

"I myself may be in them." *John 17:26*

I believe that renewal and transformation are synonyms. You cannot have one without the other. Transformation is not just a system or a belief; it is a lifestyle relationship with God. Once His unconditional love is discovered in the person of the Father, the sacrifice in the Son, and the teaching through the Holy Spirit, renewal occurs. Transformation is as Francis Chan says, "developing a compassion for the lost, the last, the littlest and the least."

My own transformation began when I was struck by a comment from a college professor. "You will never have a profound effect on people until you come out of your cinder block house on the hill and live in the village of the people you are attempting to reach for Christ."

But transformation takes a lifetime and is a learning experience of love. It is comprehending the reality of God's love and transferring that love to others. It is also learning to love those you work with, live with and serve.

The Greek word *metamorphoo* is translated as "transformed" in Romans 12:2, "transfigure" in Matthew 17:2 and is in Mark 9:2 where Jesus is changed from a human body to one that shines in glory. *Metamorphoo* means to change into another.

Verlyn Verbrugge states, "In Romans 12:2 believers are to be characterized by a continuing process of transformation which is accomplished by an inner renewal of the mind by resisting the influence of the world. A more detailed explanation of the Christian's transformation is given in II Corinthians 3:18 where the experience of Moses in Exodus serves an imperfect model. The glory brought by the gospels is not temporary, like the radiance of Moses' face, but enduring. Believers have an open relationship with the Lord of glory, which has a transforming effect."

At Water Street Ministries, men, women and children have experienced transformation in their life. This is systematic theology evidenced in a practical way. It is one life at a time being changed.

Thank You, Lord, for Your transforming power!

Phil Wrightstone is a residential assistant at the Water Street Mission.

Live or Die

"For to me, to live is Christ, and to die is gain." *Philippians 1:21 (New King James)*

I memorized this passage in my teens, but its truth was put to the test recently as an adult.

After a routine test, physical exam and biopsy, I began to realize that the lab tests would disclose cancer. Being an introvert, I talked about it very little; I thought about it a lot.

At first, the threat of death disrupted my mind when I wasn't concentrating on tasks or conversations. At the same time, I experienced a growing peace. As Paul also wrote, this peace surpassed all intellectual understanding while guarding my heart and mind (Philippians 4:7).

When the physician confirmed the diagnosis, the issue I was facing was clear, but the peace was even stronger. Shortly, I was able to fully identify with Paul's testimony: whether I live or die, my existence is securely linked to Christ. Christ is the source of my life whether on earth or in heaven—now and always.

The surety of this position refreshed my mind, sustained the peace and focused my destiny. There was no need to scramble to try to extend my life on earth in this body. There was no fear of a death process.

Like Paul, a second conviction unfolded from the life of Christ within. Soon I knew that it was more beneficial for my wife, Marian, and for those whom I may serve, that I remain.

Months passed; I was supported by a multitude of prayers, encouraging health care professionals and friends. Delays in performing surgery did not disrupt the peace. I rarely thought about cancer or prayed about it. Surgery successfully removed the cancer.

I had been transformed by renewing my mind with the word of God, and now five decades later my relationship with Christ witnesses to that eternal truth.

Lord, transform our region through Your Word and our union with Christ.

Keith Yoder, president of Teaching The Word Ministries and member of the Worship Center, serves in leadership with the Regional Church of Lancaster County.

In God We Trust

"Therefore do not worry about tomorrow, for tomorrow will worry about itself. Each day has enough trouble of its own." *Matthew 6:34*

I find it ironic that money has the phrase, "In God We Trust" printed on it. For many years I had put my trust in money, not God. I had the perception that money brought peace and joy, and the lack of money brought worry and doubt.

Putting money on such a high pedestal opened the door for anxiety and fear in my life. When times were tough, I found that I had difficulty focusing on anything but myself. I was neither being the man that God called me to be nor was I looking to Him as the source of my joy.

When I started as director of TNT (Teens Need Truth) Youth Ministry, I was responsible for raising support for half of my salary. I found this to be very difficult because I was relying on others to help me out. My provision was out of my control, and I was forced to trust in God. I found this to be a very frightening but also a faith-building experience.

I found that gifts of money always came just when we needed them, and my family was well taken care of. During my first month at TNT, I can remember sharing with God that I was scared but willing to trust in Him to provide for my family. That evening friends of ours gave us a gift that helped to pay for all of our bills that month.

It was at that moment I realized joy comes from the giver not the gift. All along I had been trusting in money for my security, but God showed me that He cares about my well-being. He will provide for me in spite of my worry and doubt.

Father, thank You for promising to provide for me and for giving me freedom from my worry and doubt.

Grant Gehman serves as the director of TNT Youth Ministry in Ephrata.

Access

". . . through whom [Jesus] we have gained access by faith into this grace in which we now stand." *Romans 5:2*

We are privileged to have access to many beneficial things in life such as automatic teller machine PIN codes, multiple bank accounts, secret family recipes, safe combinations and so forth. Have you ever thought about the people that have access to your personal information? I have.

A couple of years ago I was going fishing in the state of Kentucky and I had to give access to my Social Security number to a Wal-Mart employee. That sure seemed risky to me.

Once on a flight to California, I was privileged to sit beside the assistant secretary of commerce of the United States. That was some pretty cool access because I had a lot of questions for him. I found out he was a believer and was leading a Bible study in the White House at the time.

In the Old Testament the high priest had access to the holiest of holies once a year and hoped to survive the event. But you and I have direct access to God every moment of every day. According to 1 John 5:14–15, we can approach God and ask anything and He will hear us.

I remember *The Beverly Hillbillies*, a television program that I really liked as a kid. As the story goes, Jed was hunting for some food, took a shot and up from the ground came "bubbling crude (oil)." For generations these folks had lived in poverty when just below the surface they had access to more wealth than they ever knew existed.

We have that kind of access to our God today so that we can come boldly and confidently to Him without reservation. Will you take advantage of this access to our living God right now?

Father, give us boldness to come to You today and not be afraid of intimacy because You granted us that access through Your Son.

Steve Prokopchak is married to Mary for thirty-five years and is a member of the DOVE Christian Fellowship International Apostolic Council giving oversight to DOVE churches in various regions of the world.

Kindness Rewarded

"Blessed is he that considereth the poor. . . ." *Psalm 41:1*
(King James Version)

The parcel postman had just left a package at our door. We four children, ages ten and under, crowded around our mother as she opened it, knowing that it would be the new blanket she had ordered from the catalog. The lingering Great Depression was affecting our lives, and we had never seen a new blanket. As we admired it, each child hoped secretly that he or she would be the lucky one to receive it. Then mother folded it and put it in the box again saying, "Wait until Christmas."

A few days later, our mother received a letter signed only, "From one who knows their need."

The letter explained that a poor family had moved into town and needed almost everything. If interested, our mother should leave any gifts with our next-door neighbor who knew this family and she would take it to them.

Puzzled, mother picked up a bushel basket and went to the cellar. Here she filled it with jars of home-canned fruits and vegetables. Then taking the new blanket from the box, she draped it over the top of the basket and carried it next door to the neighbor who would deliver it.

Some weeks later, another letter came. It was from the recipient of the basket. She thanked mother and revealed her real name. She herself had written the letter because our neighbor had told her that our mother was a Christian and would probably help her. The people were un-churched but because of mother's kindness, they started to come to our little church and later became faithful members.

Thank You, dear Lord, for the valuable lesson You taught us as children that it is more blessed to give than to receive.

Wilma Musser, Brethren in Christ Church, Messiah Village, Mechanicsburg, is a retired minister's wife and school teacher. She volunteers in nursing areas and enjoys writing.

Sowing the Desires of Our Heart

"For our present troubles are small and won't last very long. Yet they produce for us a glory that vastly outweighs them and will last forever!" *2 Corinthians 4:17 (New Living Translation)*

The Bible says that unless a kernel of wheat is planted and dies, it remains alone, but its death produces many new kernels. Without sowing, no increase or transformation will come.

Today God is calling us to sow not just words or good deeds but things we value and long not to lose such as our God-inspired dreams and desires of our heart. When we see those things that are precious to us sowed into the ground of hard times, God promises to work into our character all we need for them to come alive and flourish. In trusting God with these precious areas, we will see those things we cherish multiply through this process and spring forth in ways we can't fully imagine.

The harvest we will yield will change our world the same way Abraham's world was when he was told to sacrifice his only son, Isaac. If it weren't for his faith in God to believe exactly what was promised, Abraham wouldn't have become the father of nations as the Lord had promised.

Today my life looks nothing like it did seven years ago when I was overwhelmed with what God had done and took my eyes off what I was trying to do. Yet now is the season when He is giving me those new dreams and desires which He has poured into my heart. The Lord is seeing if I will focus more on His goodness toward me than the coveting of those desires I lack in this season. Times of being plowed and planted are not fun or glorious but they do achieve a glory from God that far outweighs them all. So do not fear the One who calls you to sow for it is He who has your best intentions on His heart and causes all things, even the painful things, to work together for your good.

Father, help me not to shrink back at the fear of loss but to focus on Your goodness and unfailing love. Help me to believe in the impossible.

Jere Mellinger serves as a greeter at Life Center Ministries International.

I Am a Kept Woman

"You will keep in perfect peace all who trust in you, all whose thoughts are fixed on you!" *Isaiah 26:3 (New Living Translation)*

Many times in the midst of nagging anxious thoughts, I sought and found peace of mind by reciting this scripture. During one especially trying season when I struggled consistently with anxiety, I created a melody to accompany these words. My mind was soothed with the promise of His peace as I repeatedly sang the scripture-song. It was like a prescription to stave off troubling mind traffic that, if untreated, would erode my hope and joy.

The specific words I focused on were "perfect peace." I savored the truth that God's peace is perfect not temporal or fleeting. I recalled often Jesus' declaration to His disciples, "I am leaving you with a gift—peace of mind and heart. And the peace I give is a gift the world cannot give. So don't be troubled or afraid." (John 14:27). What a joy to know that I did not need to be troubled or anxious. I love how God's Word is alive and spiritually discerned. This became apparent when reading through the book of Isaiah and rereading verse 26:3, however, this time my heart was drawn to the words "I will keep." I suddenly realized I had bypassed a powerful crux of truth. "I will keep" means to maintain, sustain, uphold in perfect peace, rather than experiencing a periodic temporary peace. More of his transforming work became self-evident.

I have since entered into a profound state of being peace-filled, all the while enjoying life as "a kept woman."

Thank You, Lord, for Your ceaseless gift of perfect peace. Nothing in life I face or thoughts that my mind can conjure outweighs or exhausts Your indwelling peace. Lord, my trust is in You alone.

Reyna Britton serves others through her work at Lancaster General Health as director of accreditation; leadership-development and life-transitional coaching; voluntary nurse chaplaincy role; and, as cheerleader and teammate to her husband Duane. The Brittons live in Ephrata, have three children and six grandchildren.

Transformed

"And if by grace, then it is no longer by works, if it were, grace would no longer be grace." Romans 11:6

Coming from a mixed marriage (Christian/Jewish), my childhood was confusing. We were a dysfunctional family long before the term became a part of pop culture. I attended Hebrew school for nine years, but was also schooled in Christianity. As a twelve-year-old at a Christian summer camp, I became a believer. When adulthood neared, I labeled myself a Christian and began growing in faith, but quickly became mired in extreme legalism. Marriage and parenthood arrived much too soon. Like my parents, I possessed few tools to succeed as a wife and mother, so another dysfunctional family was born.

For decades my life was full and chaotic, and I liked it that way. The busyness enabled me to avoid the incredible pain that had been stuffed inside. I busied myself taking care of others and attempting to "fix" them. In search of further escape, I retired to bed early most evenings. While quieting my anxieties for sleep's numbing relief, I mentally crossed another day off life's calendar. My actions were robotic. My response to life remained somber and glum. I yearned for freedom and assumed that death alone could provide that release. Suicide was not my fantasy, but I determined never to fight the Grim Reaper. Upon diagnosis of a brain tumor in 1988, I wondered if it would be my "ticket out of here," but surgery followed and the tumor was benign.

In the early 1980s, a close Christian friend invited me to a Precept Bible Study. Our first study was the book of Romans, a declaration of the tenets of the Christian faith. *The question was posed: If God were to ask you why He should allow you into heaven, how would you answer?* My quick response was that I had done this and that. Suddenly, my pen dropped. Something clicked and I knew that it was not my work that mattered, but *His* (Romans 11:6). My life has never been the same!

Thank You, Father, for turning my darkness into life through Your grace.

Sally Kaplan Owens is a mother and grandmother of many amazing grandchildren. Sally lives with her beloved husband Don in Lancaster, where they participate in two home fellowship groups.

Love in the Other Places

"The man who loves God is known by God." *1 Corinthians 8:3*

When I'm hiking through the woods, and see a deer crashing through a thicket or the water of a mountain stream gurgling at my feet, I experience with all my senses the loving presence of the Good Shepherd. When I look into my daughters' eyes and see beauty, creativity, passion and curiosity, I feel the loving gaze of my Father in heaven. When the sun is bright and hot and the air is crisp and cool, when the water laps against me in a languid pool, the sensations on my skin whisper to me the love of my Creator. When I dance in worship and my spirit breaks free and my heart overflows, I feel His adoring gaze upon me, enjoying me with delight.

Now I see that love in places where I could not have imagined Him before. I have felt His love in the woods . . . but I also see Him in the clamor and energy of the most dreaded neighborhoods of our cities. I know His love in silent times . . . but now I also hear Him when ambulances scream: for those with knowledge and compassion derived from Him are caring for the one in distress. I sense God's pain when bullets fly…but even they do so with mathematically precise trajectories, their paths determined by laws He set into nature. I almost touch His love when the sky is blue and the sun is shining . . . but now I also find him when storms arise, for there is something astonishing in the bright flashes of light, the gift of electricity. I feel His love when all is going well . . . but now I know also that He loves me in the sadness of life, in the disappointments that inevitably surface, in the pain of my body and spirit, in the fears and anxieties that steal my peace.

Father, thank You that You love me. You really love, in all of life's circumstances, in all of my confusion, and in all of my joy. Amen.

Tony Blair is one of the senior pastors of Hosanna! a fellowship of Christians in Lititz. He also teaches for Eastern University and Evangelical Theological Seminary.

It's Too Quiet Down There!

"Be joyful always; pray continually; give thanks in all circumstances, for this is God's will for you in Christ Jesus."
1 Thessalonians 5:16–18

When my children were babies, I worried when I heard a noise from them. Once they each became mobile, I worried when I DIDN'T hear noise from them. With infants, no noise meant they were exploring something new (with their mouths, of course). So if I didn't hear anything from the other room, I would come running and pluck away anything that seemed dangerous. But, if I heard my child babbling to the toys around or playing with the musical toys, I was comforted knowing she was doing what she was supposed to be doing. Whether she knew it or not, she was communicating with me that she was okay.

In looking at 1 Thessalonians 5:17, we are told to pray without ceasing. I take that to mean that we should keep God's presence with us always. As soon as we stop communicating with Him, look away, and "explore something new," we are probably in danger. So it is important to keep communicating with Him to avoid the temptations around us.

But quiet in His presence is very welcome also. I never worried about a child who was asleep in my arms. The closer he was to me, the better I could keep tabs on his breathing and even the beating of his heart. And he is most at peace there too. So if you are tired of babbling and want to rest—rest in His arms, assured He is listening to your heart.

Dear Father, I want You to always be on my mind. Please send me reminders of Your presence every day so that I can best think of a reason to give You thanks. Amen

Tracy Slonaker, director of Christian education at Harvest Fellowship of Colebrookdale, enjoys being Jeremy's wife and mom to Hannah, Christian and Audrey.

No Need to Worry

"Do not worry about your life, what you will eat; or what you will wear. Life is more than food; and the body more than clothes. Consider the ravens: They do not sow or reap, they have no storeroom or barn, yet God feeds them. And how much more valuable you are than birds! Who of you by worrying can add a single hour to his life? Since you cannot do this very little thing, why do you worry about the rest?" *Luke 12:22–26*

All across the country, people everywhere are suffering in light of the economy. Whether or not it is caused by joblessness, prices of food, transportation or the downturn in the housing market, people everywhere are hurting.

What I was not prepared for was that the hurting would hit home. Not only our home, but the home of our children and also our extended family. There's a very good chance that you are hurting too.

I really want to paint a picture of what I saw as I gazed out my kitchen window today. Just a few feet away, eating in front of me was the most vivid and handsome red cardinal you can imagine, flanked on both sides by several other birds, with a half dozen sparrows overhead on the telephone line, a dove or two, a crow and lest I forget, three squirrels and a rabbit. All of them were either eating, searching for food or resting. None were running around crying "The sky is falling down, we have nothing to eat!" They all had places to rest their heads. God watches over them and provides.

The day before, the Holy Spirit had brought me to the scripture of Luke and led me to those verses quoted above. When I looked out the window, the scripture was fresh on my mind; my heart was prepared. God loves His children even more than the birds! He says so! He will provide for us. He says so! No need to worry, just rest in His loving care. We may not have all our "wants" but He'll cover our "needs."

Thank You, Father, You love us so! I will rest in Your capable loving arms.

Barb Shirey, Dove Westgate Church, is a retired registered nurse, disabled but enabled through Jesus Christ

His Plan, His Timing

"'For I know the plans I have for you,' declares the Lord, 'plans to prosper you and not to harm you, plans to give you hope and a future.'" *Jeremiah 29:11*

It started in the summer of 2008. We were selling our house, lost our first child and were wondering where the Lord was taking us. Three days after we accepted a bid on our house, my husband came home and told me he lost his job. In January 2009 I found out I was pregnant again. We were excited but overwhelmed wondering how God was going to help us take care of a baby while unemployed.

Our little girl was born three months early, and spent six months in the Neonatal Intensive Care Unit. She came home January 2010. She has been the blessing we have waited for! We have medical issues to deal with, but can see God's provision and how He has transformed our lives. We had a stressful and worrisome year throughout my husband's continued unemployment, but the Lord has worked in my life personally to see that **He's the one** in control. He gave us our little girl (in His time) and He would provide the right job at the right time for my husband. I needed to put this before Him and let the Lord deal with it. I see things much clearer now than before and have been able to let things go that I held on to in the past and tried to control. I have clung to Jeremiah 29:11 as my personal promise from the Great Provider and Sustainer; that He is going to take care of me and our family whatever the situation.

Lord, thank You for being the Great Provider and source of all my strength. I clearly see that You are the one in control of every situation that comes my way. Thank You for working in and transforming my life.

Helena Jenner works as accounts payable/payroll clerk at Water Street Ministries. She lives with her employed husband and plump daughter Lizzy in Lancaster.

Present with the Lord

"We are confident, I say, and would prefer to be away from the body and at home with the Lord." *2 Corinthians 5:8*

My husband answered the phone, put it down, and looked at me with the terrible look of grief. "Mike was in a car accident . . . he's gone."

My heart was ripped from my chest. Mike was our only grandson – a beautiful twenty-three-year-old in the very bloom of life. I couldn't breathe. I couldn't sob. I thought I would die.

Mike was a wonderful grandson to me. Brilliant, so soft-spoken, and funny. It took awhile to take it in. As the family met with the minister, his mother brought out Mike's Bible and found a letter he had written to Jesus. We passed it around and all cried over its sincerity and simplicity. That was the gift from God in this dreadfully hard time. We had the assurance Mike was where the Lord wanted him, in His arms. That's really all that mattered.

Now I understand why I had the weird feeling the night before the accident that I wouldn't be going to church the next day. I was dressed and ready to leave but still had a confused feeling. The phone rang just as I was about to leave.

The funeral and burial was a blur of tears and embraces. His many friends filled the church, many of them in such a place for the first time in their young lives. His only sister, a year younger, spoke at the service. She and Mike were very close, sharing adventures, friends and pretty much all of life. How could she go on?

It's been a few years now. I still mourn at times. To remind me of how good our God is, I have Mike's photo in every room of our house. Sure, I miss him, and I'm sad there will never be great-grandchildren from Mike, but when I read the front page of the paper, how very glad I am that his earthly days are over, and he is in the place of eternal rest and peace with the rest of his forebears. I wonder, do they know each other in heaven?

Dear God, may Your perfect will be done in our lives as it surely is done in heaven, and we will forever be blessed.

Jackie Bowser is a member of DOVE Westgate, Ephrata.

Why Has This Happened?

"When the angel of the Lord appeared to Gideon, he said, 'The Lord is with you, mighty warrior.' 'But sir,' Gideon replied, 'if the Lord is with us, why has all this happened to us? Where are all his wonders that our fathers told us about?'" *Judges 6:12–13*

When I was eleven years old, I was diagnosed with brain cancer. Six days later I had brain surgery. My summer turned upside down. Doctors told me I would have radiation and chemotherapy. They told my mom and dad that I would have infections, high fevers and be in and out of the hospital all the time. The surgeon told us that I probably wouldn't be able to talk after brain surgery, but I did.

During radiation, I felt tired and beat all the time. When I had chemo, I wasn't able to run or walk correctly. At times, I was really frustrated and I felt like Gideon. I thought, "If the Lord is with me, why has this happened to me?"

Now I am thirteen-years-old and cancer free. I look back and see all the Lord has done. He got me through almost two years of treatment. All the terrible side effects the doctors said would probably happen, didn't. I am not brain damaged. I can walk and run again. God protected my siblings and me from sicknesses, infections and fevers during my treatment. We were surrounded by others who had flu, but none of my family got it.

People often tell me that because of what I've been through they have been helped and inspired.

Like Gideon, I learned that just because bad things happen to us, doesn't mean God isn't with us. God can make us mighty warriors.

Lord, if bad things happen to us, make us mighty warriors.

Seth Good attends Newport Dove and is a middle school student at Manheim Central. He is the son of Todd and Marie Good.

Eternal Rest

"Lord, saving me will bring glory to your name. Bring me out of all this trouble because you are true to your promises." *Psalm 143:11 (The Living Bible)*

I kept praying for the Lord to heal my husband or take him. I watched him deteriorate for three months until he finally phased into a coma. Once I accepted the fact that it would take a monumental miracle to heal him, I started to focus on the rewards of eternal life. Greg would have complete peace, without pain or suffering of any kind, and he would be with the Lord. I almost wished I could go with him.

His last week was amazing. Dear friends came almost daily, having traveled hours just to be with him. None of us had any idea it would be our last encounter with Greg. Day in and out I would sit with my precious husband, reminiscing out loud all the way back to the day we met some forty years earlier. I silently hoped he was hearing me. Then the doctor came in for his daily visit and the words just came out . . . no doubt in my mind prompted by the Holy Spirit, "It is time to let him go."

The Lord was so gracious to take him that night, peacefully, into his arms.

Six weeks later I read this verse that saving Greg has brought glory to the Father's name. I understood "saving me" as talking about salvation, not healing for Greg, and the "glory" is my praise of thankfulness that Greg is at peace. The Lord indeed brought Greg out of all of his troubles: troubles of this world, troubles of pain and suffering, troubles of worry. Now he is free to praise and glorify the name of Jesus.

"They that wait upon the Lord shall renew their strength. They shall mount up with wings like eagles; they shall run and not be weary; they shall walk and not faint." (Isaiah 40:3).

"Have fun up there with your renewed strength my dear, precious hubby."

Dear Heavenly Father, thank You for eternal life.

Jan Dorward resides in Ephrata where she attends DOVE Westgate Christian Church.

It's a God Thing

"He rescued me because He delighted in me." *Psalm 18:19*

When my husband and I got married December 7, 1985, I weighed ninety-five pounds. When I was pregnant with our first child, I gained seventy-five pounds. Lost some, but two years later gained again when I was pregnant. For the last twenty-three years I have been struggling with my weight.

During those years, I tried losing the weight but wasn't successful. I prayed about why I couldn't and wouldn't lose it. God showed me things in my past that were contributing to my thinking about myself and my weight and also some things that I was dealing with presently, which kept me from losing weight.

It's amazing what God can show you when you seek Him. When I awoke on September 28, 2009, God said, "Today's the day."

Since then I lost almost fifty pounds. I feel better than I have in years. People say, "Your will power is amazing," but it has nothing to do with my will power. It's a God thing! Nothing else.

God wants me healthy and to feel good about myself. He wants me to forget about the past and live in the today.

God, thank You for offering us God power. Teach us to depend on Your enabling power instead of relying on ouselves.

Brenda Boll is an elder at Newport DOVE along with her husband, Steve.

Turmoil to Peace

"The thief comes only to steal and kill and destroy; I have come that they may have life, and have it to the full." *John 10:10*

Casey's mom called to see if I would pray with her son. She explained Casey (not his real name) was a person with special needs and was wrestling with things that left him experiencing doubt and anxiety.

I agreed to meet with him and see how we would get along. Casey was a delightful young man. He was full of life and loved to talk.

As we talked, it became clear that Casey had a personal relationship with God. In spite of prayer, family, friends and church, something was disturbing Casey's peace of mind.

For several weeks we had been meeting to talk, pray and ask the Holy Spirit for guidance and help. One evening Casey shared a story that greatly impacted him. A close friend called and said he was going to take his own life. Casey jumped on his bicycle and rode as fast as he could to his friend's house. He dropped his bike and raced to the house. Looking in the front window on his way to the door, he witnessed his friend committing suicide.

With tears running down his cheeks, Casey said, "It was my fault. I did not get there fast enough! If I had been faster I could have saved him!"

I was disheartened and taken aback at Casey's belief that he was responsible for this terrible tragedy.

"Casey," I said, "let's pray and ask Jesus to speak truth into this situation.

I prayed, "Dear Jesus, what is it you want Casey to know?"

We waited. After several minutes of waiting Casey raised his head, eyes shining, and said, "If I had got there earlier, he would have killed us both! Jesus saved my life."

Only the Author of Life can speak truth into our lives that will set us free. Casey found peace!

God, thank You for the cross. Thank You for not only salvation but also for life to the full. Thank You for healing us.

John Weaver works in building maintenance and prays with people God sends his way. John is a member of Ephrata Community Church.

No Options

"We know that all things work together for good for those who love God." *Romans 8:28 (New King James Version)*

On a typical Monday morning, I got ready for work and then paused to talk briefly with my husband. He looked at me soberly from across the room and said he was going to see the doctor that morning, admitting to chest pain during the night. He declined my offer to drive and told me to go to work.

As I was sitting at my desk, the call came from my husband. "I had a heart attack," he said calmly. He informed me that an ambulance had already been called and I was to meet him at the hospital.

Upon my arrival, I was met by a chaplain who assured me that my husband was alive and was having a heart catherization. When the procedure was completed, the doctor minced no words. "Your husband has blockage and will need open heart surgery." *Just like that, there were no options.*

Throughout the next weeks, we had many "God Moments" as we called them. One of those moments came on the morning of surgery. As my daughter and I waited for my husband to be taken to the operating room, in walked a man in scrubs. I immediately went to him with a tearful hug. You see, the gentleman in scrubs was someone my husband and I had babysat for, more than forty years ago. The former toddler had grown up, became a medical professional, moved into the area and was now a personal assistant to the very surgeon scheduled to operate on my husband. As our friend wheeled the gurney to the operating room, he said, "Today I will take care of my childhood hero."

What a comfort to know that God had brought this special person into our life again at just the right moment.

Thank You, Father, that You are ever watchful of Your children and show Your compassion in unexpected ways.

Marie K. Mumma, Erisman Mennonite Church, is an administrative assistant at Lancaster Dairy Herd Improvement Association, Manheim.

God Loves All Sinners, Even Me

"I needed clothes and you clothed me, I was sick and you looked after me, I was in prison and you came to visit me." *Matthew 25:36*

A few years ago I was invited to participate in a women's prison ministry program. I really struggled with my decision. I was an active, good "church lady" but what did I have to offer to girls behind bars? How could I relate? What could I say? What could I do which would make a difference?

Day after day I prayed for God's guidance but didn't seem to hear anything. My time was running short and I needed to decide. As I made my decision to say, "no", I was led to the above scripture.

"Wow, you really want me to do this, Lord?"

I then said "yes" in obedience to God. By being a part of this ministry team, I was able to be Jesus to girls who had made some wrong choices but who also had little opportunity and little love. I was a pen pal and later a mentor to one inmate which enabled me to stay connected as she served her term in three different prisons. During her time of need, I was able to share the love of Christ.

God showed me that all my works as a "churchlady" were really unimportant unless I listened and responded to Him.

Can we do that? Can we let go of our preconceived notions about ourselves and others and allow God to work through us? Can we let go of our works and open ourselves to Him?

I went to prison each week showing God's love to others even when I thought they had no common bond with me. As I did, I found Jesus in them. What an amazing time of prayer! What a presence of the Holy Spirit! What amazing healing for me!

Thank You, Jesus, for amazing me. Thank You for showing up in surprising places, in surprising ways. Thank You for loving all sinners, even me.

Laurie Sabol serves as a life leader with Tapestry Church, Lancaster.

Go First

"But seek first His Kingdom and His righteousness. . . ."
Matthew 6:33

As children, we are taught that "going first" is rude and selfish. As a result, we often consider going first to be a negative thing. However, if one reads and applies the words of Jesus, we recognize that many times Christ calls us to "go first."

Consider Matthew 5:23–24 when Jesus said, "If you are offering your gift at the altar and there remember that your brother has something against you. . . first go and be reconciled to your brother." Jesus calls His children to be the first to reconcile. This is not easy since our tendency is to wait until others come to us.

Another example is in Matthew 18:15, "If your brother sins against you, go and show him his fault . . ." Here Jesus calls us to be the first to restore a relationship. Most often we wait hoping that someone else will do the confronting, but Jesus says we are to "go first" in restoring a relationship.

A final example is from Matthew 28:18–20. "Then Jesus came to them and said, "All authority in heaven and on earth has been given to me. Therefore go and make disciples of all nations." In this passage, Jesus calls His church to keep evangelism as first priority. For most of us many fears and excuses keep us from sharing Christ's amazing grace. However, Jesus calls us to "go first" into the entire world.

Today is there a relationship that needs to be restored? Go first! Is there another brother, sister or friend who needs support or admonishment? Go first! Is the Lord presenting you with opportunities to mentor, disciple or simply invite someone to your church? Go first!

Lord Jesus, forgive us for often putting off until tomorrow that which You have called us to do today. Enable us to lay aside our pride, our fears and our limitations. Fill us with a fresh anointing of Your Spirit, so that this day, we boldly "go first" in carrying out Your Kingdom priorities! Amen.

Wesley D. Siegrist pastors Erb Mennonite Church, Lititz.

Set Free Again and Again and Again

"And you shall know the truth and the truth shall make you free."
John 8:32 (New King James Version)

As I journeyed in my relationship with God, John 8:32 has been a reality in my life. Each time I embrace God's truth, it sets me free – free to be who He created me to be. This truth has transformed me starting with the knowledge of salvation, and was my very first intervention with God.

I had significant other encounters with God's word since then. I was chosen by God. This was a big truth for me. You see, I always believed that people were stuck with me, including God. With that mind set I wasn't willing to step out fully as to who I was. At times I would shrink back. Also, I was a people pleaser so people would be happy with having me around.

One day I was reading Psalm 139 and God's words jumped off the pages: God did not have to create me–He chose to. I was here by His choice. Nobody was stuck with me. I had the right to be here. That changed how I viewed myself which changed how I related with others. I didn't have to shrink back; I could walk in a godly confidence. Because I laid down my people-pleasing ways, I didn't have to get approval to be here.

I have embraced more of God's truth, too many to list in a one-page devotional. I can say that with each one I have been changed – changed more into who God created me to be.

God's truth will do the same for you. It will change you. Change you to be who God created you to be. Oh, what freedom there is in that! And as we change, God will use us to help make a difference to those around us.

Father, thank You for Your truth. May we continue to seek Your truth, be changed by Your truth, and be set free by Your truth. Use us to bring about transformation to others.

Kathy Nolt lives in Lititz with her husband Gary and is administrative assistant for Regional Church of Lancaster County.

Christ My Redeemer, My Friend

"Come to me, all you who are weary and burdened, and I will give you rest." *Matthew 11:28*

At the age of fourteen, after the death of a friend, I was told that God would not tolerate my "lack of faith." I wanted nothing to do with a god who couldn't handle my questions, so I started running from Him.

Alternatively, I built my life around my husband, taking on unhealthy views of love that included begging him to love me like I loved him. After all *he* was the center of my universe. At the age of twenty eight, after ten years together, he left me. I was destroyed and lost my desire to live.

During this ordeal, I often fantasized about driving my car off the road, and I told myself that if things became too overwhelming I would just end it all. One day while driving home from an outpatient hospitalization program, I finally gave up. In desperation I cried out to God; "If you're really there, I need to hear from you . . . NOW!"

Right then and there, the God of the universe spoke to me in a way that only I could understand.

Although it was a long road to truly choosing life, that moment was the beginning. Five years later, I can say that I have traded my sorrows for a life of joy. God made me a new creation, and all that I had lost He has redeemed. Today I live each day with Him as the center of my universe.

Father, thank You for loving me so much that when I was desperate, You ran to meet me exactly where I was.

Nichole Gatten, River of God Church, serves as ministry assistant at Good News Church.

Good News File

"But remember the Lord your God, for it is he who gives you the ability to produce wealth, and so confirms his covenant, which he swore to your forefathers, as it is today." *Deuteronomy 8:18*

I have been challenged by the Lord to be more positive. I know that may seem simplistic, but I assure you that it is not easy. When I consider Jesus said every word that I speak in secret will be shouted from the rooftops, it helps me to work at refining my speech. Even though I don't pretend to know exactly what that means, it implies we should be very careful about what comes out of our mouths.

You can generally size up a person simply by listening to him speak. One can say that he or she is a happy person, but if their speech betrays them then they are only fooling themselves. I can hear the scriptures in my head saying *this is the day that the Lord has made and I will rejoice and be glad in it* (Psalm 118:24) and other similar Scriptures. Until I focus on being positive I generally will not be. If you are one of those people that were born with a permanent smile, I am happy for you, but I wish it was easier for me.

The book of Deuteronomy says repeatedly to remember the great things the Lord has done. I started writing my own "Good News File," which is a list of the good things in my life. If you keep a journal, that is a great place to put your list. If you don't, consider starting one. If you are like me, you will be surprised at the length of your list. Reread your list and add to it daily for your first few months and at least weekly after that.

Lord, help us to remember the good that You do for us each new day so we can write on our hearts the goodness of the Lord.

Patrick Wilson is the senior pastor at Living Truth Fellowship. Patrick has a passion for teaching and learning. He and Mary have been married twenty-five years and have two grown children.

A Welcoming Home

"'For I know the plans I have for you,' declares the Lord, 'plans to prosper you and not to harm you, plans to give you hope and a future.'" *Jeremiah 29:11*

We had learned the routine by now. It seemed like every time a bed emptied in our house, God sent someone to fill it. Lisa, then Reba, then Sherenne. As the time drew closer for our second daughter Andrea's wedding, the family began to joke: "I wonder who God will send to take Andi's place." The week of the wedding, Brenda came up to me with a stunned look on her face. She said, "I just got a phone call. The woman asked me if it was true that we take in girls." Brenda's response was "Please not this week." Dani arrived on Tuesday of the following week.

We have taken the dangerous step of turning our lives over to God's working, whether it be convenient to us or not. In a span of ten years, God has sent us twelve girls from California to Maine. From Indiana to Philadelphia. At one point we had twelve people living in our five-bedroom house. They have come from abusive families, from loving families, from no families at all, but all have come from God as certainly as if God had stamped them with His return address. It is not something that we have ever dreamed or planned, but we arrived where we are one step at a time as God has opened the way before us.

Father, You know the path You have set for my feet. Give me the peace of knowing that no matter my circumstances now, You know the beginning from the end.

Steve Hershey is a teacher and speaker at White Oak Church of the Brethren. Steve and his wife Brenda have opened their home to young adults.

The What-If Syndrome

"For I am the Lord your God, who takes hold of your right hand and says to you, Do not fear; I will help you." *Isaiah 41:13*

My life has been affected by the "What-If Syndrome." Its symptoms go like this: What if I make this decision and something happens, or something doesn't happen, then what? A bad case of the "what-ifs" causes great stress! Defeating this has not been easy. Even though I know God has a plan for my life, it seems to me, when I face decisions, that it is my responsibility to help the Almighty by sorting through the alternatives!

One day when I was bogged down in "what-ifs," I decided to take a break from stress at a nearby family lake. Bible in hand, I sat by the water's edge where a father was teaching his little girl to swim. She was clearly afraid of the water and her little hands clung to her father while asking, "What if you drop me? What if I get water up my nose?" Her father answered her concerns with, "I will be right here if you need to hold my hand." Finally the little girl took a big gulp of air and disappeared underwater. Splashing her way back to the surface she shouted, "I did it," and grabbed her father's waiting hand.

I looked at my Bible and opened it to Isaiah 41:13 and let that wonderful verse wash over my heart. I knew God was giving me a key to my struggles against the "what ifs." So simple and yet so profound is the reminder that God's hand is always there for us. Decision making may never be comfortable for me, but I will never forget the little girl's struggle and her father's waiting hand. We can reach out to find our moment of victory!

Dear Father, thank You for Your promise of help just at the right moment. When we get stuck in the "what-ifs" of our lives, let us seek Your hand and trust You to help us.

Karen Knight, Lancaster, is a former actress with Sight & Sound Theaters and an inspirational speaker and concert artist.

Angels All Around

"... I will protect him, for he acknowledges my name." *Psalm 91:14*

It was a normal class day at the Christian school where I taught high school Spanish and French. The bell rang to dismiss a class and through the door walked my husband. He looked a bit pale and had a few small cuts on his face. He said, "I had a car accident and I wanted to tell you about it before you heard it from anyone else."

As my incoming class gathered, Joe told me what had happened. He had been driving on the inside lane of the interstate highway when he saw an eighteen-wheel truck coming on the inside lane from the opposite direction. The trailer was out of control and was headed over the guardrail in Joe's direction.

Joe was unable to move into another lane due to heavy traffic. Before impact, Joe leaned across the passenger side and ducked his head as he tried to accelerate out of harm's way. He almost made it, but the right rear corner of the trailer hit the left front windshield of Joe's car and crushed the driver's side of the car from front to back. The police officer said that it was the worst accident he had ever seen where no one had been seriously injured.

I was extremely grateful to the Lord for protecting my husband. That evening I saw the car that had been towed to the junkyard. I almost hyperventilated as I noticed that the bar between the front and back doors was flattened into the top of the seat and there was no glass left in any of the windows.

God had graciously spared my husband, and we were reminded again that God provides protection even when we aren't praying for it. That experience reminds me that we often go about our daily lives unaware of the angels that God has sent to protect us.

Oh how we thank You, Lord, for the protection of Your mighty army of angels!

Linda Barnes worships at Quarryville Reformed Presbyterian Church where she directs a class for adults in English as a second language.

An Explosion of Joy

". . . the Mighty One has done great things for me—holy is his name!" *Luke 1:49*

Over the past year, God has been doing a transforming work in my life. As I minister to women, God has been ministering to me in significant ways. I grew up learning that God loved me, but I had a difficult time believing that He *truly* loved me. I desperately needed this head knowledge to move deep into my heart. As a single adult I believed the lie that "something was wrong with me" because I was not married. Because I believed that "something was wrong with me," I also believed that others and God viewed me the same way.

One day while I was walking in the park I sensed God speaking to my heart. I felt a certain anticipation that something new was about to happen. The image that captured the anticipation was an explosion. Explosions can be dangerous and scary, but I did not sense any fear. This explosion was good! Explosions bring things down! My prayer and desire that day was that God would bring down barriers in my life that keep me from abundant life in Him. I want an explosion of joy, of God's peace and love, of God's acceptance of me, seeing myself through God's eyes. There was a hole in my heart, and I needed God to fill it.

As God was bringing healing in my life, He again spoke to my heart through a mental picture. I am no longer holding an umbrella, which were the lies that I was holding onto to shield me from God's love and acceptance of me. Now I am fully able to receive God's rain on me—His love and grace, His acceptance and approval.

Father, thank You for Your amazing love for each of Your children! Bring down barriers in my life that keep me from my abundant life in You.

Lisa Good, West End Mennonite Fellowship, is a counselor at Lydia Center, a division of Water Street Ministries.

Porous Souls!

"My soul finds rest in God alone; my salvation comes from Him. He alone is my rock and my salvation; He is my fortress, I will never be shaken." *Psalm 62:1–2*

I read a phrase in an article that caused me to pause and think more about what the author was really saying. In his article, he stated that our "souls are porous." Porous is not a word I would have thought to use to describe my soul, but the definition of it: things that pass through, things that are absorbed, really does fit. In today's world, our souls take in a great deal on a constant basis. Among other ways, live media coverage gives us instant information, and far too often what we hear is not good news. Many times we take it to heart and it is absorbed in our souls. Fears and concerns can very easily "soak in" and cause us to be shaken.

There are a number of ways that we seek to find release and comfort from the heaviness of our souls. There is, however, only one true way to have our souls saturated with life-restoring hope and peace . . . and that way is through Jesus Christ. There are many passages in the Scriptures that speak to this, but in the Psalms it is a frequent theme. Psalm 62:1-2 expresses this truth well. Now those are words of comfort and assurance!

Truthfully, it is easy for me to become overwhelmed and to feel as it says in Psalm 6:3 that "my soul is in anguish." And I also know that it is a lifetime pursuit for me to "be anxious for nothing" (see Philippians 4:6). I am confident, though, that God understands my weakness and is patient with me as I seek to be, once again, filled with renewed hope and peace that comes from Him.

Lord, I thank You that the most important commandment is "Love the Lord your God with all your heart and with all your soul and with all your mind and all your strength"(Mark 12:30).

Patti Wilcox serves with Good Works, Inc.

Unlearning the Lies

"And we know that in all things God works for the good of those who love Him, who have been called according to His purpose." *Romans 8:28*

Raised in a Christian home, I accepted Christ as my Savior at an early age in our little country church. I was sheltered and naïve, not understanding the cruelty that existed outside my safe, secure world. Love flowed, forgiveness abounded, and prayers were always answered. Even when my mother had her first mastectomy on my thirteenth birthday, I was sure that God would heal her and my world would continue to remain safe and comfortable. As time passed, my mother's health deteriorated and her body shrank to nothing, but I still believed God would restore her health.

Then, one night my world came to a crashing halt as my mom, the center of my world, took her last breath and went to be with Jesus. Devastation, sorrow, anger, fear, a raging river of tumultuous emotions filled the months that followed settling into a pool of unworthiness. Surely, I had failed; my love was not strong enough; my prayers were not diligent enough; I was not good enough for God to heal my mom.

Lessons learned can also be unlearned. The great thing about having a relationship with a gracious God is that He will help us unlearn the lies, making change and freedom possible. The added blessing is discovering that He loves us for ourselves and values our love in return. He asks of us only that which He has already given. We become a lodging worthy of the guest, when we invite Christ into our lives, not just as Savior, but also as Lord.

Father, thank You that You love me and cherish me as Your daughter. I praise You for reminding me that I am a part of Your heart's plan. I want to know You more and to see myself as You see me.

Paula Sentgeorge, Chiques Church of the Brethren, serves as kitchen manager at the Lydia Center of Water Street Ministries.

What Fear Can Teach

"Praise the Lord, O my soul . . . he who . . . heals all your diseases."
Psalm 103:2–3

I watched my husband carry our son to our bed—his limp legs dangling off the pillow where his body lay. I'd never seen a fever so high. We knew the emergency room was imminent if we couldn't get ahead of this climbing fever.

Our family had endured illnesses and poor response from the medical community, but in recent years, God blessed us with a new doctor and health approaches that resulted in healing multiple chronic issues. We were healed so well, I'd ceased praying about health anymore. Anything new that came up was so aptly handled by our new doctor; there was no need to ask God for miracles.

Suddenly, while reapplying the cool cloths to my little boy's skin, obsessively watching for his temperature to drop a couple degrees, I found myself praying—because nothing else was working. Astonished, I realized how I'd put all my faith in our doctor, giving her all the credit and forgetting God. Because I knew she prayed for our issues, I became comfortable leaving the prayer responsibility to her.

As fear for my son gripped my heart, I recognized how completely I'd stopped seeking God because all was well. I pleaded with Him to help, despite my failures.

As I touched my son's cool skin in the morning, fever broken, I took back my responsibility as a parent to go to His throne for my kids, hoping I would not need to be reminded again through fear that God is the Great Physician. Since that night of panic, I've been consciously reminding myself to see God's hand behind all the people who bless us, lest I forget and credit them alone.

Lord, help me not to take Your blessings for granted to the degree that I cease to ask You for them, counting on other sources, even Christian ones, to be my source of provision.

Renee Lannan, New Cumberland Church of the Nazarene, previously a director of children's ministries, now serves as a stay-at-home mother to two small ones.

The Lord Is Your Shepherd

"Cast all your anxiety on him because he cares for you." *1 Peter 5:7*

If there was a moment that I truly needed "God to show up" it was now! I had just experienced the worst night in my life and was about to experience the worst day of my life—so it seemed. The beautiful six-hour landscape from Alba lulia to Bucharest, Romania, paled in comparison to what was going on in the landscape of my mind. I had become a mother to two little orphaned girls and had accepted multiplied trials and added afflictions.

It was at my deepest need when I turned from the landscape of my troubled mind to the landscape outside my window. My eyes perked in amazement at what I was seeing. It was the same picture on the front of a note card that a friend sent to me right before I left for Romania. There on the hillside was a shepherd dressed in a heavy wool coat with a staff in his hand. He was watching over his flock of sheep. That picture suddenly became the frame in which my life would constantly depend on. As the card said, "How strange that we should carry tomorrow's load of care when our loving Lord has promised tomorrow's load to bear!"

I am continuing to trust my Shepherd—the one who gathers His lambs in His arms and carries them close to his heart according to Isaiah 40:11.

Is tomorrow consuming your mind? Do not give in to carrying tomorrow's burdens. God has already made provision for them.

Heavenly Father, there is someone today who needs to see the evidence of You being their Shepherd. Speak to the one who desperately needs Your assurance that tomorrow's load has already been lifted. Thank You, Jesus, for the truth of Psalm 23:1. You are our Shepherd and that is all we need.

Rosene Hertzler worships at Valley View Alliance Church in Hellam.

February

Father to the Fatherless

"A father to the fatherless, a defender of widows, is God in his holy dwelling." *Psalm 68:5*

Three years after my husband of twenty-three years died from a brain tumor, my children and I were camping with friends at Camp Hebron. Three out of five of my children had come along and were having fun with the others. Before we adults started a Rook tournament, I had a chance to walk down to the lake by myself and meditate.

It was so peaceful. I watched two squirrels playing and suddenly one scurried up a tree, out of sight. I saw fish jumping in and out of the water. But the scene that made the most impact on me was watching a mama and daddy goose and their three goslings. The mama was swimming ahead while the daddy was bringing up the rear overseeing things. They swam to shore and walked up on the lawn area. Mama goose and the goslings were busy walking around unafraid, looking for food while Daddy Goose held his head high looking to the right and to the left watching for danger.

At that moment, I sensed the Lord saying, "This is what I am for you and your children. I am looking out for you. I am your protector and provider."

What a comfort spread through me as I felt the Lord's abiding presence and care.

God, Thank You for Your care and protection over us, especially when we feel so weak and vulnerable. Thank You for speaking to us and giving us word pictures we never forget. Thank You for being so faithful.

Sharon Kurtz is a widow, mother of five, grandmother, a member of Petra Christian Fellowship.

Groundhog Day

"One person esteems one day as better than another, while another esteems all days alike." *Romans 14:5 (English Standard Version)*

"This is the day which the Lord hath made; we will rejoice and be glad in it." *Psalm 118:24 (King James Version)*

At the sound of reveille, General Beauregard (Beau) Lee emerges from his burrow. It's February 2 and Beau is called upon to predict the weather. If he does not see his shadow, tradition predicts an early spring. If Beau does see his shadow, six more weeks of winter are forecast.

In spite of the Atlanta, Georgia, hoopla, for most it is just another day, but to others, Groundhog Day is exciting.

Years ago, I allowed others to determine my mood for the day. If a family member or friend voiced a struggle or exhibited an unpleasant mood, I, in turn, took on his dilemma or disposition. At that time, one look in the dictionary for the word codependency would have shown an illustration of my face. With work from the Potter's hand and great eagerness to change, my life gradually improved. I learned that I could choose to be pleasant in spite of people and circumstances.Philippians 4:4 commands us to "rejoice in the Lord always." Later in that same chapter, Paul exhorts us to entertain only positive things in our minds. "…whatsoever things are true, honest, just, pure, lovely, good report, virtue, praise, think on these things."

By God's grace, I have resolved to follow these admonitions. No, I don't do it perfectly, but I'm learning and growing. And I choose to appreciate every day the same, to enjoy each one as God's gift . . . even Groundhog Day.

Lord, thank You for teaching me Your ways.May I rejoice and be glad every day.

Sally K. Owens lives with her husband Don in Lancaster, where they participate in two church fellowship groups. They share many children and oodles of amazing grandchildren.

The Mighty Power of God

"Now unto him who is able to do immeasurably more than all we ask or imagine, according to his power that is at work within us."
Ephesians 3:20

I have spinal bifida and have walked with crutches all my life, which is why the following events happened. The first week of March, 2010, I came down with a respiratory infection. I went to the doctor who gave me medicine for it, but I didn't get any better on the medication. Because of my weakness, I received an injury that became infected and turned into Fournier Gangrene.

Early Sunday morning, I was rushed to Baltimore Shock Trauma Center in critical condition with 20 percent chance of survival. That morning they performed a serious surgery that they really didn't expect me to survive. However, I survived that one and five additional surgeries.

I am healing at a pace that completely amazes the doctors. The surgeon said it's incredible how much my wound has healed in such a short time. He later told my wife that he didn't think the wound would ever heal well enough to do a skin graft, but now it is healed to the point where he wants to do the graft.

This experience has shown me again that we serve a miracle-working God who cares deeply about us. There is nothing that is too hard for Him. When it seems like there is no hope, we have a mighty God who delights in showing us His power and glory.

Loving Father, You are constantly showing us that there is nothing that You can't do. Help us to daily proclaim your mighty works to the world around us. In Your strong and mighty name we pray. Amen.

John Miller and his wife are members of Carpenter Community Church in Talmage. Mary is active in children's ministries and together the Millers serve as care group leaders.

The World Is Not Worthy

"These all died in faith, not having received the promises, but having seen them afar off, and were persuaded of them, and embraced them, and confessed that they were strangers and pilgrims on the earth. For they that say such things declare plainly that they seek a country. And truly, if they had been mindful of that country from whence they came out, they might have had opportunity to have returned. But now they desire a better country, that is, an heavenly: wherefore God is not ashamed to be called their God: for he hath prepared for them a city." *Hebrews 11:13–16 (King James Version)*

The news appears as a one-minute report as I get ready for work. A team of eye care professionals is robbed and killed as they return from establishing a clinic in a remote part of a war-torn country.

I hold my breath as I listen for details. Finding none, I go directly to my computer to Google the latest information. As I wait for the search to produce results, I think of one of the families that our fellowship helps to support. Their service has led them to that part of the world. There are no names given just yet, but the confirmation that some of the dead were Americans.

My heart goes immediately to prayer for the families and co-workers of the deceased while my mind begins to play back the passage above, long ago memorized with my children. Those who serve the Lord on foreign fields choose to trade residency in the lands of their births for the opportunity to see others become citizens of the kingdom of God. They give up the comforts of their homelands to comfort those in need, leaving their families to see others brought into the family of God.

These workers are our present-day heroes of the faith "of whom the world is not worthy."

Father, we are pilgrims on this earth. We seek to please You as we look to You to bring us to our heavenly home.

Peachy Colleluori and her husband Domenic have served on the staff of the National Christian Conference Center for more than twenty-five years.

Angel Wings

"He will give His angels charge of you to guard you in all your ways. In their hands they will bear you up, lest you dash your foot against a stone." *Psalm 91:11–12 (New King James Version)*

Hours after I arrived at work that day, I still felt shaky and on the verge of tears. Thankfully, I had gotten into the habit of asking God for His protection as I slipped behind the wheel of my car each morning. Previously that week had brought me into "sideswipe" position with cars whose drivers were overly eager to exit expressways and make record dashes into left-turn lanes without bothering to check oncoming traffic. I had barely gotten over the amazement of these happenings when I was totally awed by the presence of God's "angel wings."

Rush hour on a typically narrow part of Route 23 outside Valley Forge National Park was the staging ground for God's miracle. Here, where one line of traffic heads north and the other south, the car directly in front of me suddenly veered to the right as if headed into the parking lot. But no! To my horror, he was making a U-turn and crossing back in front of me!

I never had time to brake, yet our cars never touched. The stream of oncoming traffic was endless, yet no horns blared or gut-wrenching sounds of metal twisting split the air. Returning to the scene a bit later, I saw no signs of disruption to roadside foliage, no skid marks, nothing to suggest anything out of the ordinary had occurred.

For years I have envisioned what I call angel wings, which are whisper thin but stronger than steel. They slice between me and disaster. Perfectly childlike and exceptionally effective! I have seen God provide this time after time. His Word tells us that He gives us angels to guard us, to protect us at all times. They can appear in human form such as when Abraham and Sarah entertained three strangers outside their tent or the angels can be invisible. But God's angels are always on guard, carefully watching over His chosen ones.

Thank You, Lord, for caring enough to surround me with Your precious angels. Thank You for Your awesome protection and immeasurable love.

Janet Medrow is a deacon at Great Valley Presbyterian Church in Malvern.

I Can Only Imagine

"Your love for one another will prove to the world that you are my disciples." *John 13:35 (New Living Translation)*

In many ways it was the anti-American Idol. It was also a night that l I will remember for years to come.

Families gathered from several surrounding states for a week-long retreat sponsored by Joni and Friends. Each family was entrusted by the Lord with at least one member with special needs and had come for much needed rest, renewal and recreation in a supportive environment.

Billed as a "talent show," it was, in reality, a glorious celebration of life. There were no judges and no one was assessing the level of talent in those who performed onstage. From the first "act" to the last, the audience cheered and clapped. The spirit present was one of honor and blessing. There was a powerful dynamic of mutual inspiration that led to worshipping the One who created all and was in all.

The final presentation proved to be the climax of the evening. A wheelchair-bound young man with multiple disabilities moved to the center. After years of not being able to communicate, he and his family discovered he could learn and use sign language effectively. There wasn't a dry eye as he joyfully signed "I Can Only Imagine" as the song played over the sound system. The glory of the Lord was evident in His countenance and filled the gym.

As I wept and worshipped the Lord with overwhelming gratitude and love, I clearly heard Him speak to my heart. "*This* is My design for My Church. *This* is what I desire whenever and wherever My people gather."

The thought gripped me: What if the love, unity and mutual edification I experienced was present in everyday church life? I can only imagine and believe.

Jesus, make us one in love as You and the Father are one in love.

Don Riker, a member of Manor Church, serves congregational, ministry and business leaders with Teaching The Word Ministries.

Coming Home

"Do not withhold good from those who deserve it, when it is in your power to act." *Proverbs 3:27*

My mom, aunt and I have had a twenty-five-room farmhouse on the outskirts of Lancaster for twenty-one years. We rent rooms to those considered "unlovable" or "not trustworthy." Due to my involvement in prison ministry, we rent to men coming out of prison, rehabs or going through rough divorces.

It has not all been peachy but the blessings are uncountable. Until about two years ago, we lived with the tenants. We shared our kitchen, living room and bathrooms. Every holiday we had a meal and invited anyone who had no family or had nowhere to spend the holiday. Sometimes there were a few, other times more than we thought we could accommodate, but God knew differently. We always had enough room, enough food, enough events and enough ears to listen to the struggles and the victories of one another.

Memorial Day took on new meaning for one tenant who has lived with us for five years. He came to us angry, hurt and discouraged. Three years ago I offered him my pickup truck. This year he will have it paid. He has been an awesome help to us at the house. He appreciates that we trust him. A couple of months ago, he asked to talk to us. We were thinking he was going to move. Here is the miracle: For more than twenty years he had thought the love of his life and their son were killed in an accident. Through Facebook, he was contacted by his son, and soon, his son's mother. Within days, they were married. They were planning to move into their own apartment, but instead decided to stay and help us run the ministry.

He was a changed man before this, but now he glows. Only God!

Father, thank You for the hundreds who have been through our house. Only You know how they have touched our lives and how our light may have shined on them.

Darlene Adams works with Backpack Outreach and Prison Ministry through Ephrata Church of the Nazarene.

Tapping into Transforming Power

"Be strong and of a good courage, fear not, nor be afraid of them: for the Lord thy God, He it is that doth go with thee; he will not fail thee, nor forsake thee." *Deuteronomy 31:6 (King James Version)*

My wife and I have been through some very deeply sorrowful times in the past few years. The deaths of her father, my youngest brother and my oldest sister's husband have shaken us. These have been hard to endure, but our faith in God and the love of our families and friends have sustained us.

Everyone suffers loss in their lives. Some people are never able to get over a loss, rejection or disappointment. Sadly, one event serves to forever define the rest of their lives. How blessed we are that by God's grace we can overcome grief and move on to bless others. When I first gave my life to the Lord, I was transformed from my old self to a new being in Christ.

Over the years, I have experienced God's grace and mercy in my life; and even witnessed His miracles. However, there have been things that have rocked me to my core. I felt abandoned, almost forsaken by not knowing where God was in the midst of my trials. I felt sorrow, pity, anger, frustration, helplessness and despair. It isn't until I reached the end of my understanding, until I gave up trying to handle things in my own strength when the Holy Spirit was able to work.

It isn't until I tap into the transforming and unchangeable power of the Holy Spirit that I am able to overcome.

Hasn't He promised that He will never leave me or forsake me? When I am able to let go, God is there to uphold me. His Spirit is steady and sustaining; in Him there is no wavering.

Thank You, for Your mercies are new every morning and Your love is never ending.

Domenic Colleluori *and his wife Peachy are on staff at National Christian Conference Center and have been serving the Lord for more than twenty-five years.*

Ten Weeks and the Word

"For the word of God is living and active. Sharper than any double-edged sword, it penetrates even to dividing soul and spirit . . . it judges the thoughts and attitudes of the heart." *Hebrews 4:12*

I was a happy young Jewish adult. I had just graduated college with a bachelor's degree in science. I had an excellent job, great friends and had moved back into my parent's home. A year later, I decided to go for ten weeks of certification training to become a secondary education teacher.

During that time, a fellow student asked me out on a date. He discovered that I was of the Jewish faith. He informed me that he was a Christian, and on all subsequent dates, he read verses to me from the Bible. I felt like I was being tormented by the verses that had been read to me from the Bible. Was Jesus real? Was He the Messiah? Would I be denying my Jewish faith to believe that He was?

After months of anguish, I screamed out to my Jewish God to help me. I asked Him to give me total peace if this Jesus was the Messiah, and if not, I never wanted to think about Him again. Immediately, I felt enveloped by a peace that passed all understanding. I was instantly transformed. I did not understand what had happened to me, but I knew I was a new person. I had no idea what church to attend because I knew nothing about Christianity. I would spend time devouring the Bible. God and His Word became my best friend. I married the student that had been reading the Bible to me. We have eight children; all have asked Jesus into their hearts. It is our family's greatest desire to fulfill God's purpose for us on this earth. I am one example of the power of the spoken Word. It changed my heart, my life and my destiny.

Lord, please help me to honor and recognize the power and the life-changing ability of the Word of God.

Bonni Greiner, Ephrata Community Church, is an inspirational speaker.

No Mountain Too Big

"For the Lord grants wisdom. His every word is a treasure of knowledge and understanding." *Proverbs 2:6 (The Living Bible)*

"Wait up, Ted!" I called to my ten-year-old son. What possessed us to climb the largest granite mountain in the country at Georgia's Stone Mountain State Park was beyond me. We were just about to tackle the last quarter mile when my body gave way. "Your poor old mom can't climb this mountain the way you can," I protested. "Let's rest a minute."

As Ted's fingers traced the cracks in the mountain's surface, I could see he was deep in thought. "Mom, can you imagine if we were tiny people, I mean like ants, how big this mountain would seem?"

"Not at all," I responded. "Those tiny people would have such small eyes that all they could see would be right in front of them. When ants are at work, they are never bothered by what's above them. The bigger we are, the more we can see above and around us. That's when this mountain can appear big and beautiful, or downright frightening!"

I was satisfied with my response, but then God showed me a parable: The tiny people are those who are spiritually narrow-minded and unwilling to grow. They simply see situations which are right in front of them and deal with them. Their visions are small and their spiritual growth stunted. The bigger we are spiritually, allowing our faith to grow, our ears to hear, our minds to seek and our spirits to be tested and matured, the larger our visions will become. Our wisdom will be as grand as a mountain, our character as beautiful as God Himself and our perspective in dealing with monumental situations will come within God's grasp.

"Hey Mom!" Ted's voice interrupted my thoughts. "Let's get going." Renewed, refreshed and having gained something more than muscles, I completed the climb to the top.

Lord, help us not to be afraid of the mountains we climb. Allow our security to be in You and our visions to be as vast as heaven itself.

Jan Dorward resides in Ephrata where she attends DOVE Westgate Church. Jan loves to write and presents Messianic Passovers.

Words of Encouragement

"Season our speech with grace that we will speak life that brings encouragement." *Colossians 4:2–6 (The Living Bible)*

Words of encouragement can be life-giving words and can bring new vision to our lives. Even Mark Twain said that he could live a whole month on one good compliment.

Encouragement is a kind of expression that helps someone strive to be a better Christian even when life is rough.

As a child I was very insecure and never felt like I could be quite good enough. As an adult, I felt I did not have any special gift. I liked to sing, but I wasn't outstanding.

One Sunday morning many years ago in my adult class, the Sunday school teacher entered the room and said to me, "I really appreciate that you are in the class because you have a real gift of making people feel comfortable and relaxed."

My heart soared. I did have a gift—a special gift that was appreciated in my Sunday school class.

Since then, I have stepped out many times to make people feel welcome because my Sunday school teacher took the time to point out the gift God gave me.

Lord, help me always remember not to compare myself to others but to value the gifts and abilities You have given me.

Sandy Weaver is a licensed practical nurse and member of Ephrata Community Church.

Walking Together

"This is the account of Noah. Noah was a righteous man, blameless among the people of his time, and he walked with God."
Genesis 6:9

My first date with the person who became my wife was a five-hour walk. We had a lifetime of memories, interests and experiences to share, so we took the opportunity to walk, talk and get to know each other in the quaint community of Mt. Gretna. As we were talking, our relationship was taking a step forward into a deeper friendship.

We still enjoy casual walks in our neighborhood today, though admittedly they have not lasted five hours since that very first date.

Generally speaking, we choose to take leisurely walks with friends. This gives us an opportunity to share matters of the heart with each other. Walking together is a picture of a friendship moving forward in a meaningful way. That is what our journey of faith with God can look like. As we walk with God, our relationship with Him moves forward. The book of Genesis tells us that Enoch walked with God. Also, Noah walked with God. As we think of having a relationship with God, we can think of the picture of walking with God as His friend. We would be wise to follow one step behind. After all, Jesus did tell His disciples, "Follow me." As they followed, they stepped right into the will of God to proclaim the Good News of Jesus to the world. That is a productive place to be.

Dear God, thank You for Your offer of friendship, even when I was in sin as Your enemy. You have won me over by Your grace. Your kindness leads me to repentance.Please walk with me every step of the way every single day. While we walk, teach me to follow You faithfully.Show me where to go. In Jesus' name. Amen.

John Shirk works for WJTL radio.

Mark of Grace

"And God is able to make all grace abound to you . . ."
2 Corinthians 9:8

No one has influenced my spiritual life more than Grandpa Creech. Grandpa exuded grace as few people I've ever known. He pastored a church in southern Ohio for more than sixty years, spent his life preaching, visiting the sick, conducting funerals and weddings and taking the gospel to homes throughout the county in his fulltime work as a lineman for the telephone company. He never missed an opportunity to display God's grace.

As he and Grandma grew older, she was afflicted with Alzheimer's and had to go to a nursing facility. But Grandpa's love ran so deeply for his bride that he refused to let her go alone. At ninety-one years old, he left both his independence and the house he had built on Maple Street in order to be by her side. It seemed, however, that from that time on his own health deteriorated rapidly. In his last year, he could no longer walk, read his Bible or clearly communicate. Yet the same kind, generous spirit would still shine through to all those who visited him.

Even in death, the grace that had prevailed throughout his life expressed itself in one final work. In the last months before Grandpa died, he had been unable to speak at all. That's what made the end so powerful. The nurse who was with him told us what happened before he took his last breath. The restlessness and labored breathing suddenly stopped and a great look of peace came over his face. He lifted his head up from his pillow, and as his eyes focused on some great unseen reality, Grandpa uttered clearly, "Lord God in heaven!"

The nurse, a backslidden Christian, was shaken. She confessed that Grandpa's witness caused her to realize it was time for her to rethink some things.

Thank You, Lord, for the transforming power of grace.

Becky Toews serves at New Covenant Christian Church. This is an excerpt from her recent book, *Virgin Snow: Leaving Your Mark in the World.*

Magnificent Love

"[That you] may have strength to comprehend . . . what is the breadth and length and height and depth, and to know the love of Christ that surpasses knowledge, that you may be filled with all the fullness of God." *Ephesians 3:18, 19 (New American Standard Version)*

After counting down for a month, my seven-year-old heart couldn't believe my birthday was finally here. It was going to be an amazing day: I had a special dress to wear, my favorite supper would be cooked and everyone would (as only a young child can imagine) shower me with presents.

I skipped out to breakfast, ready for the "Carolyn Fest" to begin but stopped dead in my tracks. In horror, I saw that on each of my siblings' chairs, wrapped in heart-filled paper, was a gift.

I couldn't bear the injustice of it all. Valentine's Day or not, it was *my* birthday!

I burst into tears and ran to my mother. After calming me down, she very lovingly broke the news to me that just because it was my birthday didn't mean that she didn't want to celebrate the special love she had for my siblings. She explained that today was a day that was bigger than me, and while we would still have our birthday party that evening, I needed to understand that today was about greater love, too.

All these years later, Father God still has to gently remind me each day that life isn't about me. True fulfillment and contentment in life comes from understanding a love that is so deep and immense and perfect that it can cover sins, offer grace and undeserved mercy, and allow us to be reconciled with the One who longs to dwell with us intimately. Today is about walking in, understanding more, accepting and offering others His love.

Thank You, Father, for reminding us that Your love is deeper than we can ever understand. Today, help us to remember Your love is unconditional and everlasting, and help us to love You as You deserve.

Carolyn Schlicher enjoys celebrating her Valentine's birthday by leaving presents at her children's breakfast places.

My Father Is King

"Then you will know the truth, and the truth will set you free."
John 8:32

In 1991, my twenty-four-year marriage to a nonbeliever ended. I entered psychotherapy, participated in a women's support group, journaled regularly. I compelled myself to face horrific sorrow and intense pain, which refused to remain buried any longer. The work was excruciating, and at times I thought it would be the death of me. But my resolve did not waiver, I would find truth and freedom or die in its pursuit! There was no middle ground for my life had been one of living death, and I wanted no more of it.

Gradually my heaviness lightened. A smile formed in the core of my being and crept across my face. Life was different. The mundane was now delightful. Simple pleasures became great joys. Joy and praise flowed automatically.

I was more than a little curious about this transition. What was this new manner of living?How did it come to be?

I narrowed the possibilities to three: Was the dawning freedom a result of my recovery process? Was it recovery enhanced by knowing God? Or, was it knowing God?

It seemed illogical that God would choose to do this for me. Why? I didn't deserve this release, this freedom. What about others who remain in chains? Why me?

One Saturday, the truth became clear, like a lightning jolt from the crackling sky. Neither voices nor signs, yet I understood. At first subtly, then with greater and greater intensity, I knew—I just knew. My Father is the King! My Father is the King! And He can do whatever He chooses!

Simple, yet profound. I leaped with vigor and excitement. I skipped and jumped from room to room. At last, truth! Freedom, sweet freedom!

Thank You, Father. I rejoice that I am free from my self-imposed prison. By Your grace, the shackles have been removed and the prison door unlocked.

Sally Kaplan Owen is grateful that the names Sally and Sarah are synonymous in Hebrew and mean "princess."

Mine!

"For of him, and through him, and to him, are all things: to whom be glory forever. Amen." *Romans 11:36 (King James Version)*

Most of us know the challenge of helping young children learn the social skill of sharing while hearing the clear protest, "Mine!" It doesn't end there. We continually face the choice of ownership or sharing.

I remember very vividly a lost opportunity to share that occurred when I was a barefooted, pigtailed child on a small farm.

A new family moved to our small farming community. Unlike most, their family did not attend church. Ever ready to share, my parents reached out by giving tomatoes, beans and corn from our garden. We invited Bertha and Linda, girls about my age, to go with us to Vacation Bible School.

On this memorable summer evening, my new friends and I were walking by the small stream in our meadow when we saw something unusual. A large white goose egg lay in the shallow water. As I went to retrieve the egg, I discovered something even more unusual. A five-dollar bill was under the egg.

I remember well the strong impression I had to give it to my new friends. But five dollars?

That was a lot of money for a ten-year-old in 1953.

I remember drying the money on the warming rack of our coal stove and my feelings of sadness and guilt for keeping it for myself. I have absolutely no idea what desired object that five dollars purchased for me. But I do know the anticipated satisfaction was totally missing. Instead, I received a valuable lesson: "It's not mine to keep. It's His to share."

Father, forgive me for thinking that what I have is "Mine." Help me to give back to You by giving to others.Help me to honor You by using Your possessions for Your purposes, Your honor and Your glory.

Ruth Ann Stauffer, Lititz, is wife to Al and with him enjoys their four children, seven grandchildren, leading a house church and prayer counseling.

Our Extraordinary Trip

"Many, O Lord my God, are the wonders you have done. The things you planned for us no one can recount to you; were I to speak and tell of them, they would be too many to declare." *Psalm 40:5*

We went to see our daughter and her family in Holmes County, Ohio. The first week in June was a lovely time to go. However, the first day was hot and muggy. Our first stop in Ohio was at the Walnut Creek Cheese store. As we entered the store it began to rain very heavy with some light hail. By the time we were ready to leave the store, the rain had stopped. We arrived at our daughter's house and unloaded our car. Minutes later there was heavy, torrential rain, which created a flash flood. Flooding water soon covered the lane to our daughter's house. It was impossible to drive through it. Soon the sun came out and gave us a double rainbow. It was God's promise of protection.

The next morning the sky was cloudy with threatening clouds. We did some shopping and went to a Kidney Fund Benefit Auction and came into the village of Berlin, where the sirens were blowing, indicating the threat of a tornado. We learned the next morning that a tornado touched down several miles from where we were. Thunderstorms with crashing lightning and thunder continued into the weekend. During our moving about, every time we needed to get out of our car, it had stopped raining. We surely felt God's protection.

We knew we served a God who is faithful. God gives peace in the midst of uncertainty. How blessed we are when we fully trust Him.

Lord, You are a merciful God. You know our comings and our goings. You protect us according to Your will. Thank You, God.

Miriam Witmer, a prayer intercessor, lives with her husband Howard at Landis Homes.

From Mountaintop to the Valley

"'Test me in this,' says the Lord Almighty, 'and see if I will not open the floodgates of heaven and pour out so much blessing that you will not have room enough for it.'" Malachi 3:10

A few years ago, I lost my job. With no income for a family of four, I was down in the valley and doing a lot of praying. Ten months later, God blessed me with a wonderful job.

Soon I started thinking I was in control of my job, the start-up company I was trying to get off the ground and my family. During all my arrogance and cockiness, I was growing distant from God.

I was attending church but not listening to the sermons. God started working on me by planting a little seed about tithing. Since I had an arrogant attitude, I decided to challenge God: "OK, God, you want me to tithe? I'll tithe ten percent on every penny that comes my way. In return I expect a miracle in three months."

Two weeks before my ninety-day trial period with God, my world came crashing down. What I thought was a good life and good marriage blew up in an instant. I was enraged and said things in anger.

That night, God spoke to me as clear as day. He said, "You want me to bless you? Really? Why should I bless you when you can't even take care of what I have already given you?"

The next day, I went to church and listened to the message, which was directed at me.

I prayed, "God, make me genuine, none of this artificial stuff anymore. I want to be real in everything I do and completely filled with Your Spirit."

Since that day I gave everything over to God, I have praised His name. All the worldly activities that once possessed my life are now gone completely. I am helping around the house and spending as much time as I can with my family. Turning into the man God has wanted me to be started with tithing.

Dear Lord, many people claim it takes ninety days to break a habit. Completely wrong. It takes You only a few minutes at an altar with a humbled individual handing everything over to You.

Ken Klopp II attends Ephrata Church of the Nazarene with his wife and two children.

Guilt? No More!

"Which of you, if his son asks for bread, will give him a stone? Or if he asks for a fish, will give him a snake? If you, then, though you are evil, know how to give good gifts to your children, how much more will your Father in heaven give good gifts to those who ask him!"
Matthew 7:9–11

Did you ever want to get into Jesus' head? (As if we could!) Wonder what He is thinking? I often do. Sometimes I feel guilty that He came and died for me. I imagine Him having to do this big chore that He shouldn't have to do, like picking up trash that someone else dropped, only on a much greater scale.

Giving birth helped me see a tiny glimpse of God's love for me. (Tiny to Him, overwhelming to me) . Suddenly, I saw the connection between the experience and my redemption. Jesus did not look forward to dying on the cross, much like I did not look forward to the process of labor (Matthew 26:39). But when it was finished, the joy was insurmountable.

As soon as I held a baby in my arms, I saw that the pain was worth anything I could have gone through for this reward. I am thinking that this is the way Jesus feels. He does not begrudge us for having to go through His torture, because the reward is to have His beloved brothers and sisters spend eternity with Him.

As days pass and the reminders of labor are fewer and dimmer, my love continues to grow for each of my children. I am glad I have them and forget somewhat what it took to get them. Imagine how long Jesus has had to love you if He began at the dawn of time.

Dear Lord, I am Yours! I cannot even begin to thank You for what You have done for me, but let me live as Your reward. Amen.

Tracy Slonaker, director of Christian education at Harvest Fellowship of Colebrookdale, enjoys being Jeremy's wife and mom to Hannah, Christian and Audrey.

Outward Conformity Versus Inward Transformation

"The sacrifices of God are a broken spirit; a broken and contrite heart, O God, you will not despise." *Psalm 51:17*

Years ago, in one Lancaster County Anabaptist family, there were four brothers. Each of the four was "all boy." One evening at bedtime, the mother sent all four boys upstairs with the firm instructions that they were to get to bed promptly. Tomorrow was a school day, she reminded them, and they needed their rest.

But boys will be boys, and they had other plans—things like romping, pillow fights, jumping up and down on the bed, scrapping—whatever! Finally the mother could no longer stand the commotion, so she grabbed the yardstick and made a beeline up the steps. But the boys heard her coming, and by the time she entered the room—yardstick in hand—all four were kneeling piously by their beds ... saying their prayers!

Outwardly, the four brothers were certainly in a posture of prayer, but in their hearts, they were still romping and having pillow fights.

It's very possible for you and me to be the same. In an outward way, we may verbally express sorrow for our sins, but God desires an inward transformation. When we sin (and we do sin—sometimes willfully) our repentance needs to be real, our hearts need to be broken and our spirits need to be crushed.

O, God, grant that my confession of sin may be genuine—from the inside out. In the name of Him who gives victory, even Jesus the Christ. Amen.

Paul Brubaker serves on the ministry team of Middle Creek Church of the Brethren, Lititz.

Our Country

"The foundations of law and order have collapsed.What can the righteous do? But the Lord is in his holy temple; the Lord still rules from heaven.He watches everyone closely examining every person on earth." *Psalm 11:3–4 (New Living Translation)*

Our great country was founded on principles of God's law and order. Our forefathers, although not perfect, sacrificed greatly to build a foundation of respect for God and each other. As I listen to the news, I can see the enemy at work to destroy the great foundation our forefathers laid for us.No longer is there respect for law and order. Wickedness appears to be taking over. I am tempted to get discouraged and depressed, feeling helpless; there seems nothing to do to reverse the trend.

David expressed similar feelings in Psalm 11:3 as he says "The foundations of law and order have collapsed.What can the righteous do?" But David doesn't stop there. He goes on to say "But the Lord is in his holy temple; the Lord still rules from heaven. He watches everything closely examining everyone on earth."

David reminds me that I can find comfort in the fact that the Lord is watching closely and rules from heaven.

As we listen to the news, may we look to the Lord, who rules from heaven and be encouraged.

Heavenly Father, thank You for ruling from heaven.Thank You for watching everything and everyone closely here on earth. I pray, Our Father in heaven, that Your name be honored. May Your kingdom come soon. May Your will be done here on earth just as it is in heaven.

Sue Breckbill and her husband John are life group leaders and coaches at Lives Changed By Christ.

Held in My Heart

". . . just as He chose us in Him before the foundation of the world . . . ." Ephesians 1:4 (New American Standard)

When saying good-bye to my two-year-old niece who lived in Florida, I said, "Angie, I won't see you for a while, but you will be in Aunt Linda's heart."

With fearful perplexity as only a two-year- old could, she looked at me with bulging eyes and immediately said, "Aunt Linda, I can't fit in your heart!"

In order to dispel her underlying fear that she would somehow be "eliminated" by my putting her in my heart, I explained that since I would not be able to "see" her once I got on the airplane, my heart would think about her, picture her and love her!

She understood. Angie now lives near me and is an intelligent four-year-old girl.We talk about how she "pops out of Aunt Linda's heart" when I see her and she "goes back into Aunt Linda's heart" when I leave her.

Angie loves that description and now tells me that the people she loves are in her heart when she is not with them!

Years ago I prayed how to teach the truth that we have been "in Christ" since before the foundation of the world. I captured a glimpse of this truth by realizing that when I am absent from my nieces and nephews, I hold them *in* my heart.

Yes, Christ held you *in* His heart "before the foundation of the world" thinking about you, seeing you and loving you!

Father, thank You that we have been in the heart of Christ before the world was created!

Linda S. Ingham is director of Life Awakening.

No More Regrets

"Oh, what joy for those whose disobedience is forgiven, whose sin is put out of sight! Yes, what joy for those whose record the Lord has cleared of guilt, whose lives are lived in complete honesty!"
Psalm 32:1–2 (New Living Translation)

I tend to be very hard on myself for failures and mistakes I made in the past. I have let people down or given up too soon, all the while wondering what might have been. I find myself looking backward, wishing I could undo decisions that I have come to regret.

What a waste of time and energy! I have come to see that floundering over past mistakes is really a lack of trust in God—a lack of trust in His grace and forgiveness. It is failure to trust God to redeem those mistakes and to weave both good and bad choices into a beautiful design that will bring honor to Him. Making mistakes is sometimes a humbling experience but it also helps me have empathy for others in their weaknesses and to realize my need to depend on God and to trust Him to work all things for the good.

God's love and acceptance do not depend on my performance or my perfection. I am human and will continue to make poor choices sometimes. I am encouraged, though, by Jesus' story of the prodigal son. The father ran to embrace his son and offered forgiveness even before he was asked.God's love and forgiveness are unconditional. Why should I not accept His forgiveness and grace?

If anyone knew what it meant to have regrets over the past, it was the Apostle Paul. According to Philippians 3:12–14, Paul was able to forget the past, to press on and to look forward to what lie ahead. I pray that God will enable me to do the same.

Thank You, God, for Your unfailing, unconditional love.I accept Your forgiveness through the blood of Jesus and trust You to use even my mistakes and failures to bring about something good, something that will bring honor to Your name.

Marv Smoker is employed by Berean Christian Stores and attends Petra Christian Fellowship.

Jesus in the Workplace

"No eye has seen, no ear has heard, and no mind has imagined the things that God has prepared for those who love him."
1 Corinthians 2:9 (God's Word Translation)

I always wondered how you present Christ and his saving power in a professional workplace. Intellectuals oozing self-sufficiency never struck me as the kind of people to walk up to and say, "Do you know Jesus?" Nor did just living out your Christian life in front of them seem to have drawing power. One day when I sensed openness in a colleague, I invited her to a women's monthly breakfast group. She came and later thanked me for inviting her, mentioning that she felt something powerful radiating from us.

Over the next eight months she came three times and as we shared our lives, she asked, "How do you get like that? Why do I not experience life like that?" While she had religious upbringing, she did not have a personal walk with Jesus.

We told her that Jesus is within us and we walk in daily relationship with Him. She then asked with tears in her eyes if you must be in a church to accept Jesus. We assured her it can be done anywhere, even in a restaurant.

After about fifteen minutes of discussion, she wanted to ask Jesus' forgiveness for her sins and give her life to Him, but she didn't know how. We led her into the kingdom right there in the restaurant.

On the way out she said, "You might think I'm crazy, but it seems to me like the whole room got lighter."

We shared that her eyes and ears are now open to things she never saw or heard before, and it will look like a new world. She was truly changed and deeply grateful.

I guess that's how you share Jesus in the professional workplace.

Father, thank You for Jesus who makes all the difference in our daily lives.

Marian Yoder, an assistant professor at Harrisburg Area Community College, leads a Worship Center small group breakfast discussion for women in the marketplace.

When Was the Last Time You Prayed? What Did You Pray?

"Pray without ceasing." *1 Thessalonians 5:17 (New King James Version)*

I was sitting in the prayer room at City Gate, beginning my prayer watch, when I heard these questions. "When was the last time you prayed? What did you pray for?"

All sorts of answers came to mind. I had prayed for my family, my husband, the ministry, the city. But still the question came. I began to realize perhaps there is something I was missing.

As I read the above scripture, it hit me that if I am really to pray without ceasing, there must be more to prayer than asking for things. Not that things are bad, but perhaps my focus had been on things and not on the Creator of the things.

If prayer is a continuous conversation with God, what is filling that conversation? My wants and needs, or seeking the One who gives. Jesus' own words are the example of a life of prayer. "Abide in me." How do we abide? By seeking first the kingdom of God and drawing near to God.

My Father already knows the things I need according to Matthew 6:8. The closer I draw to His heart, the more I realize how good and extravagant He is. How awesome a Father I have that if my prayer life is focused on seeking first the kingdom of God, all these things shall be added unto me.

How many times have I prayed for the things, and because He loves us, he still provides for us. But how extravagant if I seek Him, His name, His will (My Father, My God, Holy is Your Name, Your kingdom come) that He responds in love by providing, pardoning and protecting (daily bread, forgiveness and leading).

Jesus, You are still teaching us to pray. Find me praying without ceasing, in a devotion of prayer, seeking You.

Kim Zimmerman and her husband Brian are the founders and directors of City Gate Lancaster and the CG Prayer room in Lancaster City. They attend The Lord's House of Prayer.

Spiritual Legacy

". . . we will tell the next generation the praiseworthy deeds of the Lord, his power and the wonders he has done. . . . Then they would put their trust in God and would not forget his deeds but would keep his commands." *Psalm 78:4, 7*

These instructions to pass along a spiritual legacy to the next generation are reiterated throughout scripture. As God guided and provided for his chosen people, the Israelites, He instructed them to build memorials so that His mighty works would continue to be celebrated by the next generation. This legacy-passing is one of the greatest responsibilities of believers.

How is this accomplished? Through living out God's principles and truths in the routines of everyday life and wholehearted devotion to Jesus and obedience to God's commands. In this way, spiritual truths are received by children as they experience life with their parents.

After my children were grown and married, I sensed God leading me to continue investing in the next generation by mentoring young women who are spiritually lost and confused. When Rebecca walked into my small group one Sunday morning, I immediately discerned her need for spiritual parenting. Her background was full of abuse and pain, and she had been rejected by her mother. She was a single mother and was in recovery from drug addiction. Her young son had behavior problems and she felt distressed and hopeless about her situation.

I began to meet with her to encourage and pray for her. She began to trust me enough to share the secrets from her past. And I was able to share what I had learned about God's faithfulness in my difficulties and dark times of the past.

Rebecca came to know the goodness of God and answers to her prayers. Her faith grew and she dedicated her life to the Lord.

Passing on a spiritual legacy to Rebecca resulted in a life transformed and the opportunity for her to pass on the legacy to her son.

Father God, You are holy, all-knowing and wise. Thank You for opportunities to share Your greatness with those who need You.

Sharon McCamant serves at Susquehanna Valley Pregnancy Services as director of the Lebanon Pregnancy Clinic and at the Ephrata Nazarene Church Celebrate Recovery ministry.

God Stories 6

God of Details

"God saw all that he had made. . . . " *Genesis 1:31*

The sky was clear and the sun was bright as I drove across the prairies of western Canada. That's when I realized I had forgotten my sunglasses. Squinting my eyes against the glare, I drove on deciding that there were more important things to spend my "missionary money" on than sunglasses.

Arriving in British Columbia, I flew by plane over the mountains to an isolated Native village to spend time with friends I had previously ministered to. After several days of visiting, the time came to depart. As I walked down the trail to the plane, one of my young friends, a nine-year-old boy, walked beside me.

Reaching into his pocket, he pulled out something, and asked, "Do you want these?"

Looking down, I told him he should keep them, because he'd probably need them. That wasn't what he had in mind. Again he asked, "Do you want these?"

Putting my reasoning aside, I replied, "Yes, I could use a pair of those." Thrusting them in my hand, he concluded, "Here, friend, take them."

"Thank you, just what I need," I replied. Trying them on, they fit perfectly. A pair of sunglasses!

There, in the Coastal Mountains of Canada, God took my faith to a deeper level. He affirmed, in a personal way, that he is a "God Of Details" (GOD). My friend was not aware that I had forgotten my sunglasses. Yet the only thing that he gave me, small as it was, was exactly what I needed. As I settled into the plane for the outgoing flight, I thanked God for the life lesson that He is a God Of Details and cares about the little things of life.

Father, when You created the world You saw all that You made. This tells us that You are interested in details.Thank You for being a God of details, caring about the little things in life.

Dave Siegrist is a member of River Corner Mennonite Church and has spent sixteen years in Canada ministering to the Native Canadians.

Fulfillment Comes from the Giver

". . . I pray that you, being rooted and established in love, may have power, together with all the saints, to grasp how wide and long and high and deep is the love of Christ, and to know this love that surpasses knowledge—that you may be filled to the measure of all the fullness of God." *Ephesians 3:17–19*

Years ago I attended a writer's conference at Montrose Bible Conference in North Central Pennsylvania. In one of the sessions, Shirley Brinkerhoff, a well-known fiction writer, made the point that it is easy for us to get caught up in what we are working on that we feel unfulfilled if we are not working on a project. I realized, that was me— seeking fulfillment through my work, through a ministry, through a friend, and when that is completed or leaves, I'd feel dejected, lost or unfulfilled . . . until the next project.

A quote this writer used that day has stayed with me, "Do not confuse the job with the giver of the job. Fulfillment comes from the giver." This hit me. I was looking for fulfillment in my ministries, in people, in projects, instead of the real source of contentment.

This realization transformed my approach to "the giver"— our precious Lord. I began to focus more on the person of God, letting Him be real, letting Him be a friend, a husband, a papa. . . . it is then that contentment, joy, peace, fulfillment begins to seep into every corner of my world. People come and go. Ministries come and go. Projects come and go, but the Lord remains intimately connected to me.

Papa, You are so dear to me. Thank You for desiring to be intimate with me. In You I am fulfilled. I love You.

Lisa Hildebrand, Valley View Alliance, works for Susquehanna Valley Pregnancy Services and ministers as a teacher and speaker in local churches.

Photo by Lauara Allen

March

Problems Caused by a Few Staples

"And we know that in all things God works for the good of those who love him. . . ." Romans 8:28

We were adopting our daughter from China and there were loads of forms to fill out that needed to be perfect. The whole packet of papers is called a dossier.

I received an email from our agency about our dossier. She had some bad news. Our documents were rejected at the consulate because I had taken the staples out! I was so upset I could have spit staples. No one told me I couldn't remove the staples! It was just easier to make copies if I took them out. This meant that we would have to pay to get them recertified again. It was going to cost at least $180 for the recertifications just because of silly staples.

Here is where God showed up: Two days after I got the bad news from our agency, we received this letter in the mail from my cousin who had no idea about our "staple incident."

I'm sure this (check) will go to good use on your journey. I felt led to clean out some boxes in the attic. In the first box I found a bunch of two-dollar bills and half dollars. I sold the half dollars on craigslist that day (they were worth two to six dollars each). It came to a total of $193, which I had no idea we had! I know God will provide everything you need to get your sweet daughter.

Did you get "God" bumps? I sure did along with tears of amazement. In our hearts we knew God would take care and provide for every little detail in this journey, but to see Him provide to redo our paperwork because of a few silly staples was simply amazing!

If we never had problems in our lives, we would not see God at work.

Father, thank You for being in control and caring about every detail of our lives. Amen.

Lynnea Hameloth cherishes being a mom to (soon) five blessings from God and being married to her best friend.

What Are You Waiting For?

". . . they who wait for the Lord shall renew their strength; they shall mount up with wings like eagles; they shall run and not be weary; they shall walk and not faint." *Isaiah 40:31 (English Standard Version)*

I hate to wait in lines. On the other hand, I have found that waiting has its rewards. I had to wait almost seven years to marry the girl who is now my wife for more than forty-five years. I had to wait almost thirty years to see the dreams and expectations of what I believed was God's call to ministry. Didn't the Apostle Paul tell us that the same power that raised Jesus Christ from the dead lives in you and me?

God doesn't need to wait. Actually the concept of waiting becomes meaningless for One who is timeless and who is both the beginning and end all at once. The waiting happens because I need it. Waiting provides the time and space for the people and circumstances around us to converge. "In the fullness of time" God acts to reveal things, move mountains and advance His purposes.

The past four weeks are a case in point. Let me just say that waiting for the Lord has renewed my strength, helped me to soar, run with fresh energy and not feel faint in the walk I am on. OK—I don't run quite as fast as I used to, but I am experiencing something of the spirit of Caleb. If you don't know who he is, check out Joshua chapter 14.

Father, thank You that You reveal yourself and show up just at the right time. Even though my impatient and sometimes restless spirit has difficulty with the wait, You continue to prove that You are well worth the wait. You, Yourself, are the end that satisfies the longings of my heart.

Bruce Boydell and his wife Joan equip and empower individuals and emerging leaders of businesses and ministry organizations through Lifespan Consulting and Coaching Services. Bruce is president of The Haft, Inc. and serves there with Joan as on-site ministry director.

When God Shows Up

"... for the Lord your God goes with you; he will never leave you nor forsake you." *Deuteronomy 31:6*

One morning I was having my devotions and talking with God. My mind went to my biological mother whom I had lost two years prior.

I had been adopted as an infant and was able to find my biological parents before my wedding. It was been a huge blessing. So on this particular day, my mind wandered to my mother. Missing her, I started crying so hard I just clung to my Bible. I was trying to talk to God out loud, but I could hardly speak.

I was missing my mother so desperately! I guess I was having a pity party for myself. Just then, I got a text out of the blue from my neighbor. It was a "forward" that said, "God sees you struggling, He hears your cry." I can't remember the remainder of the message, but I sensed that God was with me, holding me in His arms and sending me hugs from her.

This text message reached me in a way that made me realize God really does hear us when we cry out to Him. He made Himself known to me in that very moment to reassure me that He was there and that He cares.

What an awesome Father, to take a time like this to "show up" in such a mighty way. It's just another one of those times when we feel so alone and isolated just for a few moments, and He finds a way to comfort us and use those moments to reassure us of His glorious presence. He will never leave us or forsake us! Even in my own little pity party, He used that moment to show His undying love for me.

Thank You, Lord, for the small ways in which You make Yourself known to us when we so desperately need it. You are so faithful and I love You! Amen.

Susan Kornhaus is a wife, mother of four boys, volunteer for SVPS in Lebanon and attends Lebanon Area Evangelical Free Church.

When God Speaks We Listen and Obey

"Trust in the Lord with all thine heart." *Proverbs 3:5 (King James Version)*

My husband Marlin and I were traveling back home from a vacation in North Carolina. We were looking forward to driving through the scenic Skyline Drive. Early in the morning my husband was awakened by God's voice saying to him, "Marlin, do not go on the Skyline Drive."

He sat up in bed and asked God if that was a dream or if He was speaking to him. He lay down again and the same words came again. So he said, "OK, Lord, we won't go there."

Two days later in a motel in Winchester, Virginia, my husband became violently ill and extremely weak. In the emergency room we learned he had suffered a ruptured bowel for two days, not knowing anything was wrong. The doctor said Marlin would have lived only hours without care.

He almost died during surgery from loss of blood, and for the next two days his life hung in the balance as *E coli* bacteria had taken over his body. As I prayed over him those nights in the ICU, I asked God to heal him according to His will. I had lost two husbands in earlier marriages and totally trusted His sovereignty for Marlin's recovery. At that point, I sensed the power of God so beautifully and powerfully all around us, it seemed we were lifted up into His awesome presence on a higher plane. Marlin did recover after thirty days in hospitals. This was truly a miracle from our loving Father.

We thank our Lord continually for this and are so glad we trusted his direction.

Do we trust Him much more now? You bet we do and always will!

Heavenly Father, thank You that You love Your children so much that You warn us of danger ahead. We trust Your words completely and want to always listen and obey.

Rosalyn Givens is a counselor at Lebanon Pregnancy Clinic and is involved in music ministry at the Community Bible Church, Palmyra. She also provides music for two ministries at Lebanon Valley Brethren Home.

Close Calls

"See, I have engraved you on the palms of my hands; your walls are ever before me." *Isaiah 49:16*

It is easy to take routine events for granted. I set off for a day of shopping with my friend's daughter accompanying me. I actually like to shop alone, but wanted to invest time in this fourteen-year-old girl and build a relationship with her. She is sometimes elusive and quiet, but this day the "on" button was pushed before we got out of the driveway. As she paused for air, I prayed out loud to ask God to give us a safe and productive day. Everything went smoothly and we loaded two carts with goods. We were in a rural area, and every hour-long drive to the major stores needed to count for something. We chatted on the way there, through a quick lunch and most of the way back.

At a stop sign just six miles from home, I sat patiently behind the wheel as a huge rig made a left turn toward me. I suddenly realized he was not going to make it, but there was nowhere to go. I felt concern about my young companion, who was talking to her mom on her cell phone. The trailer caught the left front fender and opened up the side of the car like a can opener in slow motion. There was no whiplash, no broken glass, and no injury. There was little drama and no trauma. It took about a minute for my young friend to even realize what had happened, then she said, "I think we just had an accident, Mom."

The Lord held us safely in His hands, and the walls around us were secure. I wonder how many close calls occur in our lives when we are not even aware of them.

Thank You, Lord, for Your vigilant care and protection. You know every twist and turn, and nothing can happen without Your permission.

Joan Boydell works with her husband Bruce in leadership development and refreshment at The Haft, Inc., in New Albany.

A Perfect Father

"Our fathers disciplined us for a little while as they thought best; but God disciplines us for our good ... *Hebrews 12:10*

"I HATE you!" The words hung in the air. The last words spoken into the cordless phone before she threw it across the yard.

"But I love you," I whispered back into my now dead cell phone "and everything I do, whether you understand it or not, I do because I love you."

Being closely involved with the young people whom we have taken into our home has given me a new appreciation for the role of a father. Many of them have no father or have a bad relationship with the father that they do have. One of the hardest jobs I have is teaching them that there is nothing that they can do that will make me stop loving them. Our view of God is influenced greatly by our view of our earthly father. If we have a good relationship with our father, it is easier to understand the love of the Father. If we have a bad relationship with our father, it tends to translate over to our view of God.

How often do we not give to God as much confidence as we give to our own father? Is the perfect father patient? How much more our Father? Does the perfect father have the best interest of his child in mind? How much more our Father in heaven?

I was still contemplating the words I had heard, when the office door opened, and she flung herself into my arms, sobbing, "I am so sorry. I don't hate you. I love you. I just have a lot on my mind right now."

Is it time for you to throw yourself into the arms of your Father for the forgiveness that He is holding out for you?

Be in me the perfect father. Live in me that I might be a more perfect child.

Steve Hershey is a teacher and speaker at White Oak Church of the Brethren. Steve and his wife Brenda have opened their home to young adults.

Turning a Corner in My Life

"... He has sent me to bind up the brokenhearted, to proclaim freedom for the captives and release from darkness for the prisoners, to proclaim the year of the Lord's favor. . . ." *Isaiah 61:1–2*

This year I turned the "BIG Five-O." To some this may be a sad, sad day that they fear throughout their forties. To me it was a day of great anticipation and excitement! I couldn't wait to be fifty because I believed it came with the earned privilege of joining the Red Hat Society. Throughout my forties, I secretly tried on various styles of red hats wondering which one I would purchase on the big day. Well, my fiftieth birthday came and went and my closet still lacks a hatbox with a red hat inside. I may not have a red hat but God gave me a birthday gift that I am blessed to have.

For years I've carried a passion for women to know who they are in Christ and to walk out their purpose in wholeness. This year I shared the vision of this women's ministry possibility with several friends during one-on-one lunches and meetings. As I shared, I witnessed a spark come alive in their spirits. These seven women have joined me on our new women's ministry venture called "REAL Women 4 God." We are working toward our first conference in April 2011. At long last, I will see my vision become reality as real women minister to real women. Women that experience brokenness from divorce, abuse, loss of employment, adoption, offenses and more will have the opportunity to become whole in Christ. Those of us that have walked this walk will turn to other women and say, "If God changed my life, He can and will change yours too!"

I anticipated a simple red hat but God had a life-changing mission for me instead. As I gather around the table with my leadership team, I am humbled at God's love for not just me, but all women. This is the best birthday gift I've ever received! Blessed be His Holy Name!

Thank You, Father, that wisdom is gained through our life experiences. Help us to be willing to share our strengths and struggles with each other. By being vulnerable we can help lift others up and help them be the person You've created them to be.

Karen Pennell is founder of Real Women 4 God ministries.

Seeking First the Kingdom

"But remember the Lord your God. . . gives you the ability to produce wealth . . . ." *Deuteronomy 8:18*

I was quite certain that God was leading and providing some simply amazing guidance, which was taking my company and me in the direction of a very significant new venture, requiring a major financial commitment. At the very last minute, just before signing an obligation to an international vendor, we were informed that they had nearly *doubled* the amount of equity required to do the deal. I was devastated! All the effort, all the plans, all the grandiose expectations—"up in smoke," with one seemingly heartless phone call.

Over the next several days, I experienced some of the most intense and life-changing challenges to my decision-making and implementation processes that I have ever imagined. I was clearly in need of some serious spiritual correction. One after another the questions came: "Why are you anxious?—be anxious for nothing!" "Who is building your business anyway? Is it you or is it Me? Do you really think that is by your might, your power or by My Spirit that this business is established? Oh, you of little faith—speak to this mountain and it will be removed..Are you leaning on your own understanding or do you trust completely in Me?"

I repented on numerous fronts. I sensed and embraced a new impartation of grace toward my unwholesome approach to conquering difficult tasks. My typical approach was to work longer and harder. I began to see the importance of "seeking first the kingdom." We regrouped as a company and approached the issue again. By God's grace and amazing provision, we were able to meet the equity threshold and have been blessed to do significant business with this vendor for more than five years.

Thank You, Father, for Your patience with us and Your provision for us. We testify of Your faithfulness. May Your kingdom come and Your will be done in and through our businesses. Help us to steward wisely the opportunities You entrust to us for Your glory. Amen.

Don Hoover is committed to serving Christ in the marketplace of agribusiness.

Broken but More Valuable

"Let us throw off the sin that so easily entangles, and let us run with perseverance the race marked out for us." *Hebrews 12:1*

Today is known as Ash Wednesday, recognized by Christians as the first day of Lent, which prescribes forty days of preparation for experiencing the Holy Week of Christ's death and resurrection. Ash Wednesday derives its name from the practice of placing ashes on the forehead as a sign of repentance.

My understanding of repentance has become deeply enriched through my lifelong intrigue that I have with horses. I enjoy horseback riding as a recreational hobby and continue to learn life applications while working with horses. Training a horse to become useful and develop into its fullest potential is a process in horsemanship known as "breaking." There is a time in this "breaking" process that a horse reaches a place that a trainer can clearly recognize it as being "broken". When a horse becomes fully broken, it accepts the reality that the master loves it and believes the master can be trusted. It also surrenders its own will and submits to the master's plan which is a far better plan.

Ash Wednesday is a special day set aside to consider the importance of being broken and to humbly yield ourselves to the Master and the plan He has for us. Jesus humbled himself and became obedient to the "Master's Plan"and paid the price for our redemption by giving His life for us on the cross. He became a powerful example for us to see that as we die to our old life and surrender to the Master, we can also experience a hopeful and purposeful future through the power of the resurrection.

O God, forgive me for the mess I make of things by doing them my way. Cleanse me of wrong attitudes, wrong motives and areas of sin that want to rule in my life. Forgive me for my selfish ambitions and accept my invitation to lead me in the way You know is best.

Lloyd Hoover is bishop and overseer in the Lancaster Mennonite Conference and expectant of great things through God's reconciling and transforming ministry.

God Stories 6

The Sun Broke Through

". . . the people who sat in darkness have seen a great light . . . ."
Matthew 4:16 (New Living Translation)

It was a cold, cloudy Sunday afternoon in 1945, one of those gray winter days that makes one wonder if spring would ever come. Daddy was lying down for some much-needed rest, and my mother was down in the kitchen, putting together a little supper for our family. The warmth from the kitchen filtered up through the open register in the floor of my bedroom. I suppose I was feeling sorry for myself as I sat there gazing out the bedroom window.

Suddenly, the sun broke through the clouds, and the most beautiful sunset I had ever seen swept across the sky, into my room and deep into my soul. We would be leaving for Sunday evening services in a few hours, but this was a moment that should last forever. I picked up a pencil and some paper. I tried to preserve my feelings in poetry, but the words never came. The magnificence of that moment could not be translated into mere human expression.

That afternoon I experienced something I had never before known. Perhaps I was growing up. Perhaps God said, "There's a boy who needs me right now." Whatever the reason, the experience was burned indelibly in my mind. No, I never captured the moment in poetry, but it really wasn't necessary. I can still go back to that little room above the kitchen and revel in my first real encounter with God. His grace was sufficient even for an eleven-year-old boy. My soul experienced a much-needed rebirth. That afternoon, for a brief moment, God reached down and touched me, and I will never forget it.

Thank You, God, for those moments that reveal Your magnificent grace. You are with us always if we but have eyes to see. Amen.

Jay D. Weaver, a member of the Lancaster Church of the Brethren, is a retired mathematics professor at Millersville University.

Lesson from Sophie

"You have made known to me the ways of life; You will make me full of joy in Your presence." *Acts 2:28 (New King James Version)*

Sophie, along with her human entourage, resides upstairs. Supposedly, cats are very independent and have the attitude that humans are nothing more than a means to fulfill all *their* selfish desires.

One particular Saturday morning, quietness pervaded both upstairs and down. The household majority was out attempting to subdue the ever-present list of errands. All that remained at home were Sophie, me and my service dog.

Forlorn cries emanated from this independent feline. Realizing it was not an expression of, "Great! Now I can do anything I want. No one is home to stop me," my soft voice assured her she was not abandoned.

A few minutes passed, which must have been an eternity to her, and once again the air was transporting mournful cries of abandonment from the next room. This time I not only assured her with my vocal response but also revealed my location. The sound of racing paw steps replaced her fearful crying. Her flying leap onto the sofa back joining us released her anxiety. She slept at my shoulder basking in the lamp's warmth.

We as God's children are so much like Sophie, living independently in our selfish stupor. Then we awaken, suddenly realizing our lonely condition, and send plaintive cries searching for the Lord. When hearing His still small voice reassuring and reminding us that He will never leave us, we snuggle in His arms, warming our frail spirits and being comforted by His love.

Lord, thank You for never abandoning us even in our fickleness. Your still small voice reminds us. You will never leave us or forsake us. You comfort us in Your warmth. Our joy is full in You.

Joan Patterson is a writer, speaker and member of Lancaster Christian Writers.

The Lord *Is* My Helper

"I am crucified with Christ and I no longer live, but Christ lives in me. . . ." *Galatians 2:20*

My husband Barry and I were spending a long weekend away when I came across a Triazzle puzzle in the common room of our bed-and-breakfast suite. I was intrigued with the puzzle's shape and design. Taking it back to our room, I worked on it over the next three days. I enjoyed the challenge and it seemed it would be rather simple to do because there were only sixteen pieces. As easy as it seemed, I was becoming frustrated because I wasn't able to complete it.

Our room was large and pleasant with bright windows. Soft music played while my husband read and I worked at the table by the fireplace. Suddenly, the Lord made His presence known to me in a way I had never experienced before. My first response was to ask if He was here to help me with this puzzle!

The Lord said to me, "Yes, I will help you complete the puzzle because apart from Me, you can do nothing."

Well, right away I became fearful that I would not be able to complete the puzzle because I had been working on it for many hours! But my next thought was, "The Lord said He would help me!" Within the next ten to fifteen minutes, it was completed!

Wow! I told my husband that I was finished and explained how the Lord helped me to complete it.

Two weeks later I bought my own Triazzle puzzle and discovered that the puzzle box states there are "Thousands of possibilities, but only one solution!" I would never have been able to complete the puzzle on my own—never!

This was a wonderful lesson from the Lord. He is interested in us, in everything we do, and He longs to be a part of our lives in a real way. Now, I actively consider His presence with me every day, realizing that He lives in me to accomplish His plans and purposes through me!

Dear Father God, thank You for Your Holy Spirit living in us; leading and guiding us in everything we do. I pray that we will simply yield and surrender to Your Spirit and behold with wonder what only You can do through us! Amen.

Carol A. LeVan is a member or the Worship Center.

Doing the Good Things He Planned for Us

"For we are God's masterpiece. He has created us anew in Christ Jesus, so we can do the good things he planned for us long ago."
Ephesians 2:10 (New Living Translation)

One day as I was walking through the house, I heard a voice say, "God resists the proud."

Unfortunately, my husband wasn't home and the dog didn't count, so I assumed the Lord must have been talking to me. How annoying! Alarmed, I went to God to find how I was walking in pride. A little later in the day, the Lord spoke again, "The weapons of our warfare are not carnal."

I realized that I had been trying to change myself (again) in my own strength and walk in a way that I thought would please the Lord. The heart was right, but the source (my flesh) was not. So, I repented for walking in the works of the flesh, instead of trusting and allowing the Spirit to lead me in paths of righteousness.

I have seen others live in this same place of bondage that I've personally experienced. A place where Christian life is hard because we are not leaning on our Beloved and His grace, but trying to finish in the flesh what God started in the Spirit.

We need to continually strive to enter the rest of God in this area of life. Rest in this fact: God is bigger and stronger than we are and knows how to complete and perfect the job He began in us. He has every intention of leading us into His perfect plan and in His perfect timing.

Father, in Jesus' name, please forgive us when we walk in an independent way, without allowing You to lead the way. You told me we are not here to impress You, but to express You and Your ways to others. That, I realize now, will be done in faith by Your grace.

Dorinda Kaylor is an intercessor and minister at Gateway House of Prayer.

Presence of Angels

"... For he will command his angels concerning you in all your ways ...." *Psalm 91:9–1 (King James Version)*

I was home alone, very sick and my heart was racing. I called 911, and arrived at the hospital by ambulance. The nurse in emergency room was an acquaintance from my church. Her presence reassured me, as I pondered, there are no coincidences.

After tests, I waited for a room. The nurse dimmed the lights in my triage room. It was two weeks before Christmas.

I lay still and felt at peace, but tears filled my eyes and ran down my face. I thought of my daughter and grandsons. I began to pray, asking God to allow me to live and to be with me through the night.

I saw the image of a small child appear on the wall. She was dressed in white. She had platinum blonde hair and was wearing a white dress and white gloves. On her head was a silver crown and she held a sword. Bright light surrounded her.

I saw a male figure standing with his back to me. A glowing light surrounded him. He wore a long robe and sandals. He was holding a shield. I did not move, but I felt no fear.

Staring at the male figure, I started to feel the presence of the Lord. I said in a soft voice, "Thank you, Jesus. Thank you, Lord. How beautiful Father. Thank you."

Believing my Lord and his angel personally guarded my bedside that night, today I live with *no fear* of dying. I trust when my Savior does call me home, I will have life with him ever after.

Dear Loving Father, I thank You and praise You for Your grace and Your mercy. Thank You, Lord, for healing me and for commanding Your angels concerning me, today and always. Great is thy faithfulness.

Barbara Ann Morgan attends the Worship Center. She has one daughter and two grandsons.

Working Too Hard?

"Be still, and know that I am God; I will be exalted among the nations, I will be exalted in the earth!" *Psalm 46:10*

Several years ago I was experiencing a particularly stressful time at work. My supervisor had resigned, and I was trying to cover both my responsibilities and what I could of hers. At the same time, I was dealing with some emotional struggles in my personal life. As you might imagine, it was not a very peaceful time.

God knew my need and used a Sunday school lesson to get my attention and give me much encouragement. As we studied Psalms 46:10, our teacher told us that in his study, he had found another aspect of the command "be still." Those words, he said, could also be translated "cease striving." That was exactly what I needed to hear; I could stop struggling to do it all, to make it on my own strength.

I learned that day, and am still learning that I must take myself out of the way and instead rest in God's strength. I made this phrase the screen saver on my computer at work. When the stressful days come (and they do seem to show up way too regularly) I am reminded to stop my struggling, take my stress to God and let Him bring calm and peace to my heart and mind.

Father God, You are a God of peace and order. When I am struggling with the stress and chaos that so often takes over, remind me to "cease striving" and focus on You. Flood my heart and mind with Your peace so that my life will exalt You everywhere I go.

Diane Kirkpatrick is a nurse, homemaker, scrapbooker, photographer and the wife of Pastor Kevin Kirkpatrick of Berean Bible Fellowship Church in Terre Hill.

God Comforts in Many Ways

"But those who hope in the Lord will renew their strength. They will soar on wings like eagles; they will run and not grow weary, they will walk and not be faint." *Isaiah 40:31*

It was a cold Saturday in February 2007. I had just returned from visiting my terminally ill mother and my stepson had just gone to his heavenly home less than a month before.

My heart was heavy and my spirit quenched. I was downtrodden to say the least. However, my dog Trudy needed a walk in the woods. I pulled on my boots and trudged away up the path. Ordinarily I would sing praise songs and hymns as I walked and then pray. That day I could not even look up but watched the snow-covered ground as I walked. My heart hurt so badly. No praises and prayers would come.

We arrived at the end of the path, and I turned to go back home. As I stood there looking to the sky, I saw in the distance, up over the barren trees, a large bird flying toward me. First I saw the white head, the black body and then the white tail as it soared over me. It was the most beautiful eagle I have ever seen. Immediately the passage from Isaiah 40 came to mind. My spirit lifted, and I knew that God was right there with me. He sent that eagle to remind me of his faithfulness and goodness. He knew my heart was so very heavy that I needed that great reminder.

I had been walking in the woods for thirty years, but it was the first time I had seen an eagle fly overhead.

Recently my husband went home to be with the Lord. God has been faithful to be my comfort, to provide for my every need and to bless me in so many ways.

Thank You, Lord, for always being there for me, for never leaving me or forsaking me. Even in my darkest days You are there to comfort me and restore my spirit. Amen.

Jean S. Hassel attends Millersville Bible Church and has been a counselor for fifteen years at Lancaster Pregnancy Clinic.

St. Patrick: Man of Reverence, Not Revelry

"... For he will command his angels concerning you to guard you in all your ways ..." *Psalm 90:11*

In my hometown everyone is Irish once a year. St. Patrick's Day provides an excuse to "party hearty" for thousands of residents and visiting revelers. Savannah, Georgia, hosts the second largest St. Patrick's Day parade and festivities in the nation. My childhood memories include the annual parade and plenty of kelly green—from shamrocks—to clothing—to the dyed-green Savannah River. As an adolescent, I became aware of the greater excitement available to those so inclined. Anyone could wander into the Knights of Columbus Hall where beer flowed freely and partygoers spilled into the street. In fact, such activity was commonplace throughout the downtown area. St. Patrick must have been a wild "party animal"— or was he?

Anne Fremantle writes that as a sixteen-year-old, St. Patrick (389-461) was kidnapped from his family's English farm and taken into Ireland as a slave. Escaping six years later, he made the journey home where he entered a monastery and dedicated himself to God. St. Patrick eventually became a bishop and returned to Ireland as an evangelist.

I recently discovered "The Lorica of St. Patrick," an exquisite prayer attributed to this same man in whose name so many celebrate. You may know that lorica, as defined by Webster, is "a hard, protective shell or other covering." The prayer beautifully illustrates a heart dependent upon God's protection. Also referred to as "St. Patrick's Breastplate," both titles evoke a similar image, for he "binds" or shields himself with Christ: "Christ with me, Christ before me, Christ behind me, Christ within me, Christ beneath me, Christ above me, Christ at my right, Christ at my left . . . . "

Father, I ask for your protection in every area of my life.

Sally K. Owens lives with her husband Don in Lancaster, where they participate in two church fellowship groups.

Breastplate of Righteousness

". . . put on the breastplate of righteousness." Ephesians 6:14; ". . .
the breastplate of faith and love." *1 Thessalonians 5:8*

The breastplate metaphor, of course, is not original to St. Patrick.
The Apostle Paul exhorts us to put on the breastplate of righteousness
and of faith and love. How else may we be defended, body and soul,
except by the armor and grace of God? Obviously St. Patrick believed
this. Seeking not only physical protection, the author covets God's spiritual defense: against the snares of demons, the seduction of vices, the
lusts of nature, the incantations of false prophets, the black laws of
heathenism, the false laws of heresy, the deceits of idolatry and against
every knowledge that binds the soul of man.

Limited space prohibits a thorough examination of his prayer. I
invite you to plumb its depths for yourself. You may then agree that a
man inspired to compose such a prayer is unlike one who espouses
"eat, drink and be merry" (with emphasis on the drinking and merri-
ment). Allow St. Patrick to defend himself. How? By his own words,
words which reveal the true man. As Christ taught, "out of the abundance of his heart the mouth speaks" (Matthew 12:14). St. Patrick would
undoubtedly not feel honored by the annual festivities which bear his
name. For St. Patrick was a man of reverence, not revelry. His prayer
continues: "God's power to guide me, uphold me, teach me, watch
over me, hear me, give me speech, lie before me, shelter me and secure
me."

As we see reminders of the holiday March 17, let us reflect on St.
Patrick's legacy—the true legacy from his heart, his pen. As we consider his prayer, and if it reflects our hearts' cry, may we make it our
own.

Father, I accept Your protection, my only sure defense.

Sally K. Owens lives with her husband Don in Lancaster, where they participate
in two church fellowships.

Motivated by Father Love

". . . for the joy set before Him He endured the cross. . . ."
Hebrews 12:2

What motivates you to stretch beyond your pain threshold?

In the spring of 2010 , I observed my son miraculously recover from a life-threatening accident. On March 19, he hit gravel along a curved road. Although he was going the speed limit, his motorcycle launched him into the guardrail injuring his spinal cord, pulverizing four vertebrae in his neck and breaking various bones in his body. This was plenty of pain in plenty of places.

Prayer from family and friends all over the world and a strong advocacy on the part of his wife, the right surgeon at the right time and the motivation of his Father's heart put him on a path to the best possible chance of recovery.

When we are traumatized by life's changes, we need to establish what will motivate us to seek life. We have been given the love of a Father who sent His Son to endure that we might know the power of our Father's love in a tangible transforming way in all our situations on earth as it is in heaven.

Every time my son was given a choice for physical therapy or time out to rest, he picked therapy. He wanted to lift his son and hug his wife. He wanted it at the cost of enduring the pain to have the best chance to obtain it.

There was one day when the therapists gave my son a heavy bundle: the weight of his sixteen-month-old son. He carried that heavy bundle in his arms around and around the gym at Magee Rehabilitation Center without dropping it even though it hurt. The next morning my son was positioned to assist his child to get dressed. Suddenly his son took hold of him wanting to be carried. Confidently, my son lifted him and walked just as he had practiced!

Dear Lord, what a precious prize exchanged for the pain endured! I am inspired to let Fatherly love motivate me beyond my threshold.

Nancy Clegg is the Father's child.

Finding God

"Do not be conformed to this world: but be transformed by the renewing of your mind, that you may prove what is good, acceptable and perfect will of God." *Romans 12:2 (New King James Version)*

I never wanted children. Sounds terrible, doesn't it? My parents divorced when I was a baby, and I have few memories of my father. I would say it was just me and my mom against the world, but she was in the Air Force and was never around. We moved constantly, and I always felt unwanted—a burden. I didn't want to inflict that pain on a child of my own.

However, we are not the ones in control and through some choices I made I became a mother. He was my absolute joy! I had never known such love. Sadly, because I was a troubled person, he was taken from me before his first birthday.

My mother had been forced to go to Catholic School all her life so she didn't take me to church at all. With my grandmother I had to go, but there was no joy. It all seemed so foreboding and ritualistic. So I also chose not to go as an adult.

After I lost my son, Aiden, I cursed, raged and drifted down a path of self-destruction. I never knew that such emptiness existed.

Four years later found me not only pregnant but on the verge of eviction. Desperate, I contacted a Christian program. I now believe these trials led me to The Lydia Center. During my time here, I have learned to recognize and cast away old lies I was acting on. Every day I remind myself that my identity is not in my past behaviors, who my family says I am or anything else of this world. My identity is in Jesus alone.

My second son Jakob is my heart. I know that we will both be with Aiden and our Father in heaven.

Father, thank You for this path, for it led to You.

Sheila is a resident at Lydia Center, a division of Water Street Ministries.

Resist the Devil

"Submit to God. Resist the devil and he will flee from you."
James 4:7 (New King James)

The devil crept into my family's genes disguised as divorce and control. As I look at my daughter, a high school graduate, I ask myself is her future worth the sacrifice? The sacrifice of choosing sin.

I have lived in active addiction for nine years after a twelve-year reprieve. It was a slow fade and subtle, starting for me at a riverside bar sipping a drink as a middle-class divorced woman. It ended like post-hurricane Haiti as a middle-aged depressed, homeless woman who smoked a burnt pipe in her abusive boyfriend's home. This time I was a Christian, disabled by shame.

God, why did you save me during my divorce ten years ago only to see me struggle like this? Why does the pain of abandonment from my father, husband and the loses from my addiction keep me going back to sin again and again and wanting to die!

But God told me life is passing you by and I'm not through with you yet! You're not ready to die! I want to give you abundant life! Get up! Don't give up! Don't look back! I forgive you! Resist the devil and surrender to me! Time to face up and clean up! Time to breathe in and release all your held back tears!

God, I am tired of the life I'm living. I'm going to surrender. I know why You let it all happen. You are a jealous God. I know I was worshipping others and myself before You!

It was time to get on the potter's wheel. I traveled to the Lydia Center. Now my goal is to live a godly life for my daughter and others as an example of His love and transformation.

Lord, I surrender to You. Strengthen and sustain me. Thank You for giving me the strength to follow through with taking the first step.

Karen is a resident at the Lydia Center, a division of Water Street Ministries.

God's Spring Season

"So don't get tired of doing what is good. Don't get discouraged and give up, for we will reap a harvest of blessing at the appropriate time." *Galatians 6:9*

Spring

The rose blooming after its winter sleep is truly a miracle from above;

The robin singing its song of praise shares with all the Father's love.

The flowers blossoming so full and bright are a sign of the Master's love.

Oh, the miracles that bring in spring with all its majestic wonders.

The rebirth and renewal of Nature's beauty causes the heart to ponder on the Master of the handiwork as in Him we grow fonder.

One of the things I enjoy about living in Lancaster County is experiencing the four seasons. Spring is my favorite season. Everything comes to life after the winter where life is slowed and in some cases dormant.

The weather seasons remind me of the seasons of my own life. I have experienced winter seasons where there was no evidence of life such as the time I had to walk through the death of my marriage. I thought that "winter" season would never end. Sometimes in my life, I have been praying, believing, waiting, standing and waiting some more for God to move in a situation. Those times also felt like winter!

But living in Lancaster County gives me the wonderful experience of springtime. The season reminds me that spring always comes no matter how long the winter seems to last. My hope is renewed because with God I know that spring will also come in my personal situation. It is during springtime that God's handiwork is seen in our lives.

Father, thank You for the seasons of life. Thank You for being in each season changing us, refining us, crafting us by Your handiwork.

Kathy Nolt is a wife and mother living in Lititz. She also serves as administrative assistant for the Regional Church of Lancaster County.

Don't Quit

"Believe in the Lord Jesus, and you will be saved—you and your household." *Acts 16:31*

After becoming a Christian in 1971, I not only confused my friends, I confused my family as well. I was so zealous that most likely I turned them from Jesus rather than attracting them to Jesus. Thirty-eight years had passed and I was unsure if my father would ever discover the reality of personal faith and forgiveness of sin.

Last summer, a day before our planned family vacation, my mother had a major heart attack followed by quadruple bypass surgery. We had the time off, so we could travel south where they lived and serve them through the life-changing days ahead.

A month or so later, I was traveling for my work and my evangelist wife traveled alone to see my parents. Early one morning, she made breakfast for my father and began to gently question him, "What if the heart attack was you, Dad, and you didn't make it?"

He answered that he hoped that his orthodox upbringing would help. After my wife shared the gospel very simply along with several appropriate Scriptures, my father said he was ready to "pray and accept Jesus."

A text message hit my cell phone half way around the world one morning and then a second one. My dear wife wrote, "Grandpa accepted Jesus today." And then from my daughter, "Daddy, your father will spend eternity with his Father. And the heavens shook with their rejoicing."

I know you're contending for some loved one(s). Do not quit praying. Never, never, never stop praying. Your heavenly Father is working on their behalf to draw them to Himself.

Father, we trust You and we know that You know what You are doing to bring our household to Yourself, in Jesus' name.

Steve Prokopchak is married to Mary for thirty-five years and is a member of the DOVE Christian Fellowship International Apostolic Council giving oversight to DOVE churches in various regions of the world.

Privilege or Responsibility

"Son of man, I've made you a watchman for the family of Israel. Whenever you hear me say something, warn them for me. If I say to the wicked, 'You are going to die,' and you don't sound the alarm warning them that it's a matter of life or death, they will die, and it will be your fault. I'll hold you responsible. But if you warn the wicked and they keep right on sinning anyway, they'll most certainly die for their sin, but you won't die. You'll have saved your life." *Ezekiel 3:17–20 (The Message)*

You are the only Christian some people know. Your mission is to share Jesus with these people. It is a privilege to share Jesus with them: "God has given us the privilege of urging everyone to come into his favor and be reconciled to him." (2 Corinthians 5:18).

If your neighbor had a deadly disease and you knew the cure, it would be inexcusable to withhold that information. But it is worse to keep secret the way to forgiveness and eternal life. We have the greatest news in the world, and sharing it is the greatest kindness you can show to anyone.

Persons who have been Christians for a long time often forget how hopeless it felt to be without Christ. No matter how contented or successful people *appear* to be, without Christ they are hopelessly lost and headed for eternal separation from God. Jesus is the only One who can save people.

Why did God leave us here after we accepted him? In heaven we can worship, fellowship, sing, pray and hear God's Word, but we won't be able to win people for Jesus and make disciples. Nothing you do will matter as much as helping people find Jesus. Why is that? Because it is a matter of life and death. Your work, your friendship, your finances will all be gone in a few years. The consequences of your mission will last forever.

Jesus, thank You for the privilege of sharing the Good News with those who don't know you. Amen.

J. David Eshleman is a church consultant who has served as pastor and church planter for numerous Mennonite churches in the past fifty years. Recently he published a devotional, *Living with Godly Passion*.

My Real Cheerleader

"Therefore, since we are surrounded by such a great cloud of witnesses, let us throw off everything that hinders and the sin that so easily entangles, and let us run with perseverance the race marked out for us." *Hebrews 12:1–2*

Someone, somewhere, convinced me I was a distance runner. She set a goal for me—the Philly Broad Street ten-miler—which may as well have been a chocolate bar dangling in front of me. So the treadmill, trails and I became good friends.

After a while, I began to enjoy having two hours to myself on each training run. A lot of thoughts and prayers were sorted out and the miles seemed to pass quickly.

But when the day of the race arrived, no one had really expected it to exceed 90 degrees in the early morning hours on May 2. And this asthmatic had not trained outside in any kind of humidity. Surrounded by thirty-thousand other people, I did not keep my thoughts to myself. I had to share them with everyone else who was trying not to step on the heels of the person in front of them. Discomfort followed me in each step of the ten-mile run.

As mile nine passed, I was miserable. There was quite a crowd at this point. The crowd possibly had more experience than I had, as they seemed to understand my struggle. Many called out encouragement such as "you can do it" or "dig deep." Well-meaning words, maybe, but demon-laced to me. You see, I was convinced I could not do it. I did not have my inhaler and my lungs were closing.

As soon as I shut out those calls and reminded myself that with Christ all things were possible, I suddenly got an extra kick. I finished the last half mile strong (although with a lousy time), carried only on the wings of His strength.

To whoever made me enter the race, I would like to remind you that I am a short-distance sprinter. Let's see what God can teach me in a hurry.

Dear Lord, thank You for creating fun opportunities that cause us to focus on You. I ask You to reveal Yourself in all aspects of my life.

Tracy Slonaker is a short-distance runner—only!

The Rope Swing

"Be not forgetful to entertain strangers: for thereby some have entertained angels unawares." *Hebrews 13:2 (King James Version)*

In early 1972 we moved to our secluded farm of twenty-seven acres. It was a perfect place to raise four children. The road was only paved to our driveway and then continued on as a dirt road. There were no neighbors along that dirt road, and the closest family along the paved portion was more than a half mile away.

There was an old walnut tree just across the road that was situated perfectly for a rope swing as the land sloped downward. I chose a branch to use where the children would be able to get a running start from the road and swing out and up as the land dropped beneath them.

One day we were at the rope swing with our tomboy daughter Laura who was three or four at the time. Often the children would swing two at a time because it seemed a little more daring. Laura and one of her older brothers were swinging as high as they could when she fell to the ground. We were kneeling over her when a young man, who had been walking, suddenly appeared. He asked if he could pray for her. He knelt, laid hands on her and asked for healing in the name of Jesus, and then he was on his way. It seemed very unusual that we had never seen that man before and have never seen him since. We never knew how seriously Laura had been injured before that man prayed, but in no time she was up and playing again.

It's been many years since Laura fell from that swing. She's a woman of strong Christian faith, married and has four children of her own. As we think back on the perfect timing of that young man's appearance during that incident and his prayer, we count it a privilege that we may have been in the presence of an angel.

Lord, thank You that You are so faithful to us in times of need, even if we are blind to the urgency of them. Amen.

Terry Hodecker and his wife Priscilla, Lititz, attend Dove Westgate Church and have four children and nine grandchildren.

Worrying Is Useless

"So do not worry about tomorrow; for tomorrow will care for itself. Each day has enough trouble of its own." *Matthew 6:34 (New American Standard)*

A few years ago, I was hurrying to get ready for our older son's high school graduation party at our home. The day was very hot, and I was worried about not having much shade for guests who wanted to be outside or that people would be crowded inside. I rushed around taking care of the last-minute details, stressing about having enough food or forgetting something.

Guests began to arrive and I opened the door to greet one of our neighbors. As soon as I saw her face, I knew something was terribly wrong. She told me she had just heard that the four-year-old boy who lives a few doors from us may have drowned in a hot tub while visiting friends in Connecticut with some of his family. He had been taken to the hospital, but the outcome did not look good.

In that moment, God drastically put things into proper perspective for me. The things I'd been worrying about were all so trivial. It didn't matter how hot it was, if there was enough food, or if people were enjoying themselves. . . . Here was a family facing the loss of their child (something my own family had experienced when my older brother drowned when I was eight years old). We all felt sick and could think of little else waiting to hear any update. Tragically, news came that this family had lost their dear son.

Now, when I start to worry, I am reminded that all is in God's hands and my worrying is useless.

Dear Lord, when I start to worry or stress about trivial things, remind me that You have everything under control and fill me with a sense of peace. Amen.

Lois Rhoads, Pequea Brethren in Christ Church, is blessed to have a wonderful husband and two great teenage sons, and is enjoying working as a secretary for Susquehanna Valley Pregnancy Services at the Columbia Pregnancy Center.

Looking for Love in the Wrong Places

"... I have loved you with an everlasting love; I have drawn you with loving-kindness." *Jeremiah 31:3*

My father and mother divorced when I was very young. Due to my mother's work schedule, I lived with my grandparents. They lived a distance from her, so she visited twice a month, but would only spend a brief time with me before going out with her friends.

I begged her to spend more time with me, but it seldom happened. Whenever I displeased my mom, she screamed, "You don't deserve (whatever the issue happened to be)."

Her behavior greatly affected my view of God even after I was an adult. Although I believed that Jesus died for the sins of the world, I had great difficulty understanding that He loved me personally and desired a close relationship with me.

For years, I tried to fill the void in my life by seeking love through various friendships. However, those friendships never satisfied or lasted. Instead they left me feeling empty and alone.

Eventually the Lord used several sermons and articles to address the source of my emptiness and to reveal His unconditional love to me.

His amazing love has drawn me to His side and given me an abiding peace so that I have no desire to look for fulfillment elsewhere.

Even though God continues to show me areas in my life that need changing, He doesn't scream, "You don't deserve . . ." Instead, God's discipline is part of His great love that He uses to make me more like Jesus.

I am in awe that God could love me so deeply and completely in spite of my years of sinfulness.

Lord, thank You that the blood of Jesus Christ has cleansed me from all my sin and for so great salvation!

Sandra Kirkpatrick, DOVE Westgate Church, tutors children with learning disabilities.

Gratitude Journaling

"In everything give thank: for this is the will of God in Christ Jesus concerning you." *1 Thessalonians 5:18 (King James Version)*

I keep a gratitude journal. Every morning (well, most mornings) I write five things for which I am thankful. My lists are extremely varied and over time have included things such as my husband's liver transplant, the health of our children and granddaughters, hot peppers and petunias growing in my garden and my personal favorite—Dunkin' Donuts coffee!

Recently, I've been faced with some very challenging circumstances in my life. As I read scripture and devotionals, my spirit and my intellect grasp readily at the encouraging words of our Lord and the saints that have gone before me. I claim the verse that assures me of God's covenant-keeping character, the promise of peace that passes all understanding and my Lord's guarantee that He is working all things together for my good.

Sometimes, my emotions lag behind what I know to be true. I get hit with the appearances of a situation and my countenance bears witness to that struggle.

Yesterday, as I worked at the front desk, I was also trying to "work through" my emotions. One of our guests came up to me and asked how I was doing. I assured her that I was fine and trusting the Lord.

She then said, "You know, I just went through a trial with my daughter's health. I was beside myself with concern and the Lord told me that this was when I needed to thank Him. I must say 'thank you' for this thing."

What a blessing this was to me—a sort of spiritual nudge from the Lord. I am to give thanks in everything, for this is God's will for me and my life. Starting this morning, I am including things that have never before made it to my gratitude journal, my burdens, my heartaches, my faith challenges. But first on my list is the faithful sister who spoke these words of encouragement. How thankful I am for the Body of Christ!

Thank You, Lord, for Your provision and care.

Peachy Colleluori and her husband Domenic have served on the staff of the National Christian Conference Center for more than twenty-five years.

When Odds Are Fifty to One

"Do you not know that those who run a race all run, but one receives the prize? Run in such a way that you may obtain it."
1 Corinthians 9:24 (New King James Version)

If you are a sports enthusiast and follow horse racing, you might remember a little horse that won the Kentucky Derby in 2009 named Mine that Bird. There was nothing spectacular about this little horse. In fact, he was smaller than the rest of the field, was purchased for a mere $9,000 and was not expected to win. In fact, he was written off by most as a long shot at fifty to one.

Mine that Bird went on to win the Kentucky Derby, soundly beating the field by a six and three-fourth-length victory, the greatest margin since 1946. His jockey was credited with masterfully guiding this little horse through the packed crowd on to victory.

Fifty-to-one odds? That's what I think when I reach out to the homeless, the hopelessly addicted, the wounded and offended. From that number I have been privileged to have witnessed a transformation in the lives of some who have struggled against impossible odds but have taken God at His word.

These individuals who, in spite of great difficulty and lack, have allowed the Master's hands to bring great change into their lives, to mend their broken heart, to heal their battered and diseased body and to restore their fractured family while facing fifty-to-one odds.

Each individual is a rare and blessed testament to the unfailing power of His grace in our lives and His love that sees us through to the end. Each victory reminds me of the impossible that becomes possible and of a race that is being finished when our sights become set on Him.

Thank You, Lord, for eyes of faith to Your hand at work.

Mary J. Buch is senior pastor of Breakout Ministries and serves on the boards of the Conestoga Valley Christian Community Services and Light of Hope Ministries.

Just a Simple Touch

"His left hand is under my head and with his right hand he embraces me." Song of Solomon 2:6 (Living Bible)

It was a year I would like to forget. My husband was out of work, and I was working three jobs just to keep afloat financially. The tension was high and we weren't getting along. We tried everything: talking (arguing), getting away (with money we didn't have), selling our house (which took forever) and finally just not speaking (that wasn't as peaceful as one might think).

There was only one thing left to do: go to a marriage counselor. We argued back and forth until finally the counselor said, "Stop! I want to ask you each one simple question: On a scale of one to ten, how much do you want to keep your marriage alive?" The question stunned me. I had given up long ago and in my mind I wanted to say ZERO.

"Jan, what is your answer?"

With my face in full blush and with a lot of hesitancy, I pushed out the number four. Then she turned to my husband and asked him for his answer. Without hesitation, he said "eight."

I was stunned. Looking at both of us, her next question was another stunner. "Do you ever hold hands?"

We both shook our heads.

Our assignment was to hold hands wherever we went. At first it felt awkward, but then it became natural almost to the extent that if we weren't touching, we felt a void. That assignment changed our relationship. Our romance came back. It was a lot easier to talk, and he saved my life three times when I wasn't watching to cross a street.

The simple task of holding hands stayed with us for the rest of our thirty-eight years of marriage. Even when he became comatose, I longed for that touch by massaging his hands. God got us through a near divorce with an effortless touch of holding hands.

Dear Heavenly Father, You made woman from man and You put the desire in our hearts to behold one another. Thank You for teaching me that a simple touch can save a life.

Jan Dorward is a messianic Jew who resides in Ephrata where she attends DOVE Westgate Church. Jan loves to write. She presents Messianic Passovers.

Photo by Mark Van Scyoc

Nobody's Fool

"At one time we too were foolish, disobedient, deceived and enslaved by all kinds of passions and pleasures . . . . But when the kindness and love of God our Savior appeared, he saved us, not because of righteous things we had done, but because of his mercy . . . . so that, having been justified by his grace, we might become heirs having the hope of eternal life." *Titus 3:3–5, 7*

Being a pregnant teenager labeled me the fool of the town, the school and my family. I used to love April Fool's Day and the hope of fooling people, but after the many jokes I had tried to play, it seemed nothing was funny anymore. Now I was the joke.

After my pregnancy, no one expected I would become anything of significance. After a few more years of allowed foolishness, God stepped in and began to reveal His plan to do great things with me. Undeserving of anything, I saw God open doors and lead my eventual husband to my doorstep— something I never thought I was worthy of. What an awesome man of God is he!

I share these details to encourage you to trust. When you think life can't get any worse, God has a plan. Everyone, especially the enemy, thought the worst for my life. God came in and turned it upside down. I can say today, I am living the best life imaginable! I have won the victory through Christ Jesus! He is doing in me all He has planned out for my life just as He had destined before time!

I no longer live a fool's life, but one of abundant blessing! No joke, no pun, just plain life in Christ!

Lord, You have taken the junk of my life and made it beautiful! Let me never think of myself as a fool, but as someone who has been shown grace and mercy. Help me to always see me as You see me— Your child! Thank You Jesus!

Joy Ortega is an associate pastor of Living Word Fellowship, an urban church plant whose purpose is to reach people and change lives.

Grace and Mercy

"The Lord *is* gracious and full of compassion, slow to anger and great in mercy." *Psalm 145:8 (New King James Version)*

When I was a little girl, my favorite place to be was on my father's lap. He would wrap his seemingly gigantic arms around me and I would put my ear against his chest. I liked listening to his heartbeat but I loved listening to his booming voice resonate from the inside. I always felt so safe and secure in that spot.

One day, to my parents' annoyance, my little sister and I could not stop giggling. They were trying to have an "adult" conversation and we just would not stop running around being noisy. Finally, my dad yelled, "Girls! Line up and be quiet!" We quickly obeyed, since his booming voice, when used at maximum volume, is quite intimidating! My sister and I tried our best to suppress our laughter but it had shifted to nervous giggling. I believed we were going to get the spanking of our lives because my dad had given us several chances to obey but we didn't listen.

"Come here," he gestured toward me. I trudged over to his side and braced myself for the worst. Before I knew what was happening, my father had scooped me up in his arms and placed me on his lap. He calmly said, "We're just going to sit here until I squeeze the giggles out of you."

I was dumbfounded! The weight of my fear just slid off my back! At that moment I clearly understood mercy.

Our heavenly Father longs to wrap His arms around us and pull us into His lap. Far too often, we resist, thinking that we're going to get it. But, God has shown us His mercy by giving us His Son.

Dear heavenly Father, thank You for Your amazing love and help me to remember Your infinite grace and mercy.

Leah McKelvey is married to Ed and is mom to two amazing preschoolers. Leah is a volunteer counselor at the Columbia Pregnancy Center and a youth leader for New Christian Fellowship in Marietta.

True Worshippers

"But the time is coming—indeed it's here now—when true worshipers will worship the Father in spirit and in truth. The Father is looking for those who will worship him that way." *John 4:23 (New Living Translation)*

My heart was deeply moved as I observed those who were seated on the hot, dusty ground before me. Some were deformed while others had open sores that rarely healed. Yet the look of expectancy on their faces belied the reality of their world: a leper colony in South India.

My reflections and intertwined prayers were interrupted by a question. "Will this do?" My host had forgotten to bring the elements for communion and after a search of the nearby huts, they brought me what they had: a small, stale roll and a bottle of Indian cola (think flat, hypersweet Coke). My first reaction was negative, but as I looked at the faces of my brothers and sisters I knew how to answer. "I believe the Lord would be delighted."

I was unprepared for what followed. As each received barely a crumb and mouthful of what had been set apart for the Lord, tears flowed, eyes sparkled with joy and voices expressed gratitude. In awe, I watched Jesus visit His poor, suffering flock and witnessed the life His presence imparted. The harsh realities of life disappeared as heaven came to earth.

Communion has always been special to me, but since that day, it has come to mean much more. Each time I partake I remember not only the Lord but a faithful band of true worshippers.

Father, make me the kind of true worshipper You are looking for— one who will worship you in spirit and in truth at all times and in all places for Jesus' sake and in His name. Amen.

Don Riker is a member of Manor Church and passionately serves congregational, ministry and business leaders with Teaching The Word Ministries in Leola.

God's Touch

""When all the people saw him walking and praising God … they were filled with wonder and amazement at what had happened to him." *Acts 3:9–10*

During a ministry trip overseas, we had the opportunity to pray for a pastor who was in so much neck pain that he was hospitalized. He had degenerative disease due to heavy labor of carrying large rocks, and also chipping away at boulders to make gravel road beds. He lay on the hospital bed, unable to raise his head to greet us.

We laid hands on the pastor and prayed that God would meet, bring hope and life, touching him with His healing touch and strengthening him with His almighty power. We then turned to his wife to pray for her as well. As we finished, we realized that he had raised his head and was lifting himself to a sitting position. Then, without help, he rose to a standing position and moved his head to the right and to the left! We praised God for His work.

As the news spread throughout the ward, people were crowding into the room requesting prayer. Though none understood what we prayed, they knew they wanted a touch from God and prayed not only for their physical challenges, but prayed for their hungering hearts. As one after another came, the doctor sent word that she wanted us to come to her office—not to chastise us, but to request prayer for herself!

I realized that this was truly a divine appointment and was thankful for the privilege to pray. We were not sent out to the chapel or to the sidewalk as might have occurred in this country, but we were welcomed in the name of the Lord.

Thank You, Lord, for using ordinary people in everyday situations to be instruments in Your hands, to the praise of Your glory.

Cindy Riker is involved with Teaching the Word Ministries with her husband Don and enjoys being a wife, mother, homeschooler and leader at Change of Pace Bible study.

Shifting the Focus

"You are worthy, O Lord our God, to receive glory and honor and power. For You created all things, and they exist because you created what you pleased." Revelation 4:11 (New Living Translation)

I was assigned to develop an action plan to increase the number of clients making a personal commitment to Jesus. How could counselors at Susquehanna Valley Pregnancy Services better communicate people's need for a Savior in a way that encouraged individuals to respond?

To find answers, I began researching the current culture. I read about postmodernism, visited emerging church Web sites and investigated evangelism methods. I also immersed myself in God's Word. Throughout the pondering, one question remained the loudest: "We can get more people to say the sinner's prayer, but what if their lives never change? Will they go to heaven?"

The honest questioning resulted in me being turned upside down by the Word and God's Spirit. I realized I was asking the wrong question. Is salvation about people getting into heaven? Not primarily. We are saved so that God can receive glory from our lives—both as we walk with Him on earth and spend eternity with Him forever. The shift in focus from a human-centered gospel to a God-centered gospel has drastically impacted how I view life, people and evangelism.

That shift in focus is also impacting how Susquehanna Valley Pregnancy Services shares the gospel. Rather than encouraging individuals to pray a salvation prayer in order to receive the gift of heaven, we more intentionally help people get to know—through Bible study and short-term discipleship—the One who is giving the gift. We also communicate that receiving the free gift will cost them their very lives and that a life given over to God brings Him glory.

Papa, please continue to shift our focus so that You are always at the center. May You receive great glory as we receive Your love, return love to You, and reveal Your love to others in our lives.

Kati Swisher is a wife, mother and grandmother. She serves as vice president of discipleship at Susquehanna Valley Pregnancy Services.

From Rejection to Acceptance by God

"I beseech you therefore, brethren, by the mercies of God, that you present your bodies a living sacrifice, holy, acceptable to God, which is your reasonable service." *Romans 12:1 (New King James Version)*

I was accepted by my family and doted on by my godmother until I turned twelve and gained weight. My family was distraught at my weight gain and took every occasion to criticize me.

I wasn't eating any differently, so I didn't understand their verbal attacks. Their criticism caused emotional confusion within me, and I turned to food for comfort and began eating secretly. The only way I could get positive attention from my family was when I lost weight. This caused yo-yo dieting for many years.

Every time I looked in a mirror, I felt disgust and guilt. After many years of despair, my heavenly Father showed me that in order to achieve permanent weight loss, I was to be obedient to His Word. In January 2008, I started a weight-loss program that uses the point system.

With God looking over me, I actually enjoyed eating correctly. Two and a half years later, with the Lord's help, I have lost ninety pounds. I don't ever want to go back to my old ways of eating.

It took fifty-five years for the Lord, using many people and circumstances, to demonstrate His love for me and thus prepare me to learn how to honor Him with my eating. He has taught me a new way to eat and a new way to look at food by eating properly and in moderation. Most amazingly, I enjoy it!

Dear Lord, I praise You for loving me and setting me free after fifty-five years of bondage to despair and wrong eating habits.

Sandra Kirkpatrick is a special needs school teacher and a Sunday school teacher at DOVE Westgate Church.

Not as We Planned!

"For My thoughts are not your thoughts. Nor are your ways My ways, says the Lord." *Isaiah 55:8 (New King James Version)*

At the pregnancy center where I work, one of the services provided for our clients is a free first trimester ultrasound. We do this to educate the client as to what is developing inside of them. The words fetus, tissue, specimen and so forth do not truly define what is taking place in the womb. Between eight or ten weeks gestation, some of these little babies can put on quite a show. Other reasons we love to do the ultrasounds are to provide a due date and determine viability.

One evening a young girl, who was considering aborting her baby, came in for a scan. We hoped that she would be able to see her baby and make a connection with the great miracle taking place inside of her. Instead, we were unable to complete the scan. Our instructions to her were to call her doctor in the morning and schedule an appointment with him for follow-up. How discouraged we were that she would not see that little baby.

The next afternoon the client called our nurse to say that the doctor ordered a scan, which discovered that she was farther along than she thought. She also said that after being unable to scan her the previous evening, she was concerned about what might be wrong with her baby and could not sleep. In the midst of her worry she realized that if she felt that concerned for the baby's well-being, she could never choose abortion.

Just when we thought she had to see that scan in order to change her mind, God used not seeing the scan to show her how much she already cared for this little one.

God's ways are not our ways—I am so thankful they are not! Lord Jesus, I am so glad that You see things from a much different perspective.

Lisa Hildebrand, Valley View Alliance, works for Susquehanna Valley Pregnancy Services and ministers as a teacher and speaker in local churches.

Grace Alone

"For it is by grace you have been saved, through faith—and this not from yourselves, it is the gift of God—not by works, so that no one can boast." *Ephesians 2:8-9*

I consider myself an overachiever. Most of my life I have spent working hard to get good grades, performing well at my job, going above and beyond expectations to help others.

I remember sharing my old high school yearbook with some friends a few years back and being teased about the long list of accomplishments below my photograph. As I reflected on my current list of community activities, it was even longer! When did I do all of this? Why did I do all of this stuff?

The more I achieved, the more "together" I thought I was. I know now that I was trying to obtain personal fulfillment and self-worth. I worked hard at gaining respect from others.

Although I developed some medical issues, that didn't stop me. I kept pushing on. I began to realize that perhaps there was something more, Someone much greater to rely on for help to slow me down.

I found it hard to believe that I hadn't already known this because I had been actively involved in church for many years yet I was caught up in all of the busyness of good deeds and work accomplishments. I was relying on my works to pull me along.

It was not until I actually stopped all of my busyness that I turned to God for help. Instead of doing everything for everybody, I allowed others to do their part. Instead of just doing things for God, I began to take time to be with God. I am now able to receive love from others and love myself as God made me. I know that God has given me this gift, through His grace alone.

Lord, I am sorry that I try to do it all myself. Thank You for Your grace and mercy. May I trust You to care for me, allow You to guide me and know Your love.

Laurie Sabol serves as a life leader at Tapestry Church, Lancaster.

Lost and Found

"Find rest, O my soul . . . ." *Psalm 62:5*

Lost is no good. Lost is unnerving and panic. Lost is dismay. Found, on the other hand . . . found is very good. Found is relief and comfort. Found is safe.

I mostly understand *lost* in relation to space. *Where am I and how do I get home?*

I'm the one who gets lost in revolving doors! My husband doesn't understand this kind of lost. That man is a human homing pigeon. Recently he experienced the unnerving, panicked feelings when his home and office keys went missing overnight. Sweet relief came in the morning, as light revealed glistening copper in the dew of our yard.

Ah, *found* . . . there is nothing quite like it!

Today's verse encourages us to find something more essential than our keys or our sense of direction or glasses or remote controls. The verse encourages us to find rest. Have you ever lost that? Lost is no good.

Rest is defined as freedom from everything which wearies or disturbs. To find rest is to find freedom from the stresses that have no problem finding us. If it feels like troubles type your name and address into a GPS on a daily basis, it's seriously time to run and hide. Find rest! But where? Psalm 62 answers, "in God alone."

The Psalmist David speaks of being hidden, sheltered and covered by God. David found a place of deep rest for his soul, where the troubles of life just could not break through. Find rest, O my soul! Stop living continually in that which wearies or disturbs; that which troubles and encumbers. Find rest, O my soul! *Find* it! It awaits you deep in the heart of God.

Daddy, I can't find my rest just now. I am weary. Will You pick me up and hide me? In Your arms, I am home. I am found. And found is very good.

Jenny Gehman, on a good day, can be found resting in both God and her hammock in Millersville.

An Unshakable Kingdom

"Therefore, since we are receiving a kingdom that cannot be shaken, let us be thankful . . . . seek first the Kingdom . . . and all these things will be added unto you." *Hebrews 12:28 and Matthew 6:33*

A few weeks ago I had the privilege of ministering to Christian business persons in six different cities in Chile. As we drove up the coast from city to city, we saw signs of the recent earthquake everywhere. Bridges had been destroyed, roads were ruined and buildings were flattened. When I asked the Chileans what it was like to experience this earthquake that was five-hundred times as intense as the earthquake in Haiti a few months earlier, they told me it felt like they were walking on the waves of the sea, only they were on dry land.

It was so amazing for me to witness the faith of these new believers . . . faith in an invisible kingdom that cannot be shaken . . . the kingdom of our God. So many busines persons were new in their faith, yet so grounded in the reality that they were a part of the unseen kingdom of God that cannot be shaken. They were so thankful for life itself. For the Lord's deliverance in their lives has brought them freedom from addictions and sins that had previously overcome them, until they completely committed their lives to Christ as Lord. The natural earthquake seemed to be secondary to them.

So then, as things shake around us, in our nation or in any area of our lives, may we also be thankful. Grateful to our God we are part of an eternal unshakable kingdom, trusting Him to give us all that we need.

Lord, I am so grateful today that I am a part of a kingdom that cannot be shaken . . . the kingdom of our God. And as I seek first Your kingdom today, I am thankful that You will give me all that I need. In Christ's name, I pray. Amen.

Larry Kreider loves being a husband, father and grandfather and serves as international director of DOVE International.

Quieting of the Soul

"But I have stilled and quieted my soul like a weaned child; with its mother, like a weaned child is my soul within me." *Psalm 131:2*

As I turn to a new chapter in the seasons of life, I join the ranks of parents who have launched their firstborn into the world upon high school graduation. Although this is an extremely busy time, I am aware of what a difference it makes by practicing centering prayer. The quieting of the soul every day for twenty minutes is something I've sensed God inviting me to do these last four years. It is a daily practice that characterizes my relationship to my loving heavenly Father.

When my firstborn came into the world eighteen years ago, I knew the Lord differently than I've grown to love him now. Then, I lived a hectic pace and without the practices of silence and solitude. I paid the price as did the relationships I hold most dear!

Quieting my soul is not in itself a difficult task and yet it is the most difficult thing I've ever done. I accept that as truth and simply live in God's grace in order to continue with this practice. My intention to worship God, quieted and stilled, bears itself out in daily living in one important way. As it characterizes my relationship with God so too it begins to shape what I bring into my relationships with others: A non-anxious presence. Even in tumultuous seasons of life, I see God's love in this paradoxical invitation to know him more in the silence.

Thank You, Lord Jesus, for Your grace to me as I daily make my prayer of silence known to You and I consent to meet You in that space. You are holy and I willingly choose to be still before Your holiness.

Susan K. Shiner, mother of four boys and married twenty-two years to Jeff, serves as a Songs for the Journey minister to the actively dying and as an intake volunteer for Love in the Name of Christ.

Don't Quit

"I will give them a heart to know me. . . ." *Jeremiah 24:7*

It had been twenty-five years of praying for four high school friends. Their names had been on my prayer cards ever since I began using index cards as bookmarks in my Bible. accepted Jesus in 1971 in the middle of my senior year. That change in me confused my friends, who politely listened to my "born again" story but shrugged it off as a passing fad.

In that twenty-fifth year, I was making new prayer cards and questioned whether or not I should continue to transfer their names onto new cards. Seeing their names seemed to be merely a reminder that nothing was happening. While I still had a relationship with my friends, they did not seem to show a visible movement toward God. I asked my wife if I should just remove the names and not transfer their names to the new prayer card. Her answer was a resounding, "Absolutely not."

She was right. That very year Ron called me and said he was getting water baptized. Some friends at his workplace were sharing the Word of God with him and he surrendered his life to Jesus. I told him I was blown away by answered prayer. His response? "I knew you were praying for me."

Within a year, a second friend committed his life to Jesus. I was even given the opportunity to water baptize him! A little time passed and I heard from Ron that a third friend was playing guitar in his local church worship band.

Okay, Lord, one to go.

Don't give up. Keep praying for that friend or that relative. Even when we don't see any visible sign, know that the Holy Spirit is "giving them a heart to know Him."

Father, I thank You that You love the ones we love and are calling them to Yourself.

Steve Prokopchak is married to Mary for thirty-five years and is a member of the DOVE Christian Fellowship International Apostolic Council giving oversight to DOVE churches in various regions of the world.

Sincere but Sincerely Wrong

"There is a way that seemeth right unto a man, but the end thereof are the ways of death." *Proverbs 16:25 (King James Version)*

"Aren't we soon there?" I asked the driver.

"Keep your eyes open. Any minute now you will see a sign pointing to Buffalo."

The ladies' chorus of a small Christian college in eastern Pennsylvania was on an Easter tour including appointments in Pennsylvania, New York and Canada. We had given our last program in Canada and stayed in various homes overnight. Now in separate cars, we were happily on our way back to the U.S.A. via Buffalo where we were scheduled to give the Easter program. Then I saw it—the sign to Buffalo. But it was pointing in our direction. It said "Buffalo, 70 miles." We had traveled seventy miles in the wrong direction!

Panic set in. Our gas was getting low. This was in 1942. A war was going on, gas was rationed and no gas stations were open on Sunday. What should we do?

Eventually we pulled into the parking lot of a church. Our driver went inside and talked to an usher who came out and siphoned gas from his car into ours. When we finally arrived at our destination in Buffalo, the morning service was over, the other chorus members, having performed without us, were eating lunch and our director was frantic with worry.

We had been sincere in thinking we were on the right road. In fact we were on the right highway but going in the wrong direction.

Dear Lord Jesus, thank You that You are The Way, the only way to heaven. Thank You for Your word to direct us. Help us to obey and follow Your direction so that we will not be lost.

Wilma Musser, Brethren in Christ Church, Messiah Village, Mechanicsburg, is a retired minister's wife and school teacher. She volunteers in the nursing area and enjoys writing.

Life Lessons from Nature

"The heavens declare the glory of God; the skies proclaim the work of his hands." *Psalm 19:1*

As I spend time with nature, I am filled with the awesomeness of God. My family and I vacation at the beach, and I never tire of the sound and sight of the waves that continue to crash to the shore. They are beautiful and destructive at the same time. With that same consistency, the love of God comes to us both to bless and to discipline. Another thing about the beach is the sun which is beautiful and its rays are good to feel on your body. But we all know that too much of a good thing can cause pain.

In our region, the farmers pray for the early spring rain that needs to come at the right time and the right amount for the abundant harvest. But too much rain causes flooding and loss of crops. I believe that nature cries out, "There must be balance." In our lives we must work our jobs but not live our jobs. We must spend time in prayer and play. We must learn from good books but also learn from experience. We must stand on the promises of God and also trust His sovereignty.

I believe that the main lesson from creation is to trust in the ebb and flow of God. He said that there will be times of rain and times of harvest until He returns, so we trust Him in the rainy season as well as in the harvest season.

Father, Help us to trust in You whether we are in a season of plenty or lack, knowing that You are still working all things out for good. Amen.

Patrick Wilson is the senior pastor at Living Truth Fellowship. Patrick has a passion for teaching and learning. Patrick enjoys reading, chocolate and spending time at the beach and with his family. He and Mary have been married for twenty-five years and have two grown children.

Before We Ask

"Before they call I will answer; while they are still speaking, I will hear." *Isaiah 65:24*

After leaving an abusive marriage, our daughter moved to our home with her four-day-old twins. In the ensuing months, the care for the babies and the stress of the situation was often overwhelming for all of us. But the Lord was so faithful in providing all the physical, emotional and spiritual needs we all felt.

As the months went by, our daughter returned to college to finish her degree. Walking the babies daily became part of my regular routine. Prior to the babies' arrival, I had spent my walking time with the Lord as part of my daily devotional. Now I spent the time praying over the babes and declaring God's love for them and speaking out destinies with hope for their futures.

In November, they were at a point where I knew they would really enjoy playing with a ball. I had been shopping for a small beach ball for them to enjoy but soon realized that beach balls were a seasonal item. I had no success in locating one.

While walking our three-mile loop through a nearby state park on a windy day just before Thanksgiving, I was laying out all my little needs before the Lord. This prayer was not completely spoken as we turned the corner of the park, where out of a big pile of leaves blew a brightly colored beach ball.

Both babies sat up in the stroller and began to clap and jump with delight as they watched the bouncing ball.

I was swept with waves of gratitude for such a blessing, a simple beach ball "out of season" delivered right to us exactly when God knew the babies would enjoy it.

Father, thank You for Your grace, faithfulness and goodness. They are truly my foundation, and I am so thankful for Your everlasting arms. Papa, thank You for hearing every prayer my heart prays even before it leaves my lips.

Susan Sanoski, Praise Fellowship Church, serves the body of Christ through Family Foundations International, Littleton, Colorado.

APRIL 16

Home, Sweet Home

"The wise woman builds her house. But the foolish tears it down with her hands." *Proverbs 14:1 (New American Standard Version)*

Life was at an all-time low. Things were not going well at all in my relationships with my children. Disagreements and criticism continued on both sides.

I had always said that the Lord gave me eight children to teach me. Evidently I was not learning very well. One thing became clear— I was a good example of "how NOT to do it."

Finally I asked for help from a trusted friend. His response was to draw a graph with "goals" on one side and "relationships" on the other side. He explained that Jesus had these two concepts perfectly balanced. The goals Jesus' Father gave Him were in focus. Yet He was able to relate to imperfect people in life-giving and meaningful relationships.

My friend explained that I had been focusing too much on my strict goals and ignoring or neglecting to nurture meaningful relationships with my children.

I took this advice seriously. I prayed that the Lord would restore "the years that the locusts had eaten." I'm sure my friend prayed that I would finally "get it."

By God's grace, I'm slowly learning to listen more, to care with compassion, to respond gently, to accept and love unconditionally. Things are going a lot better!

Lord, keep the door of my lips, keep the reigns of my heart. Be exalted in my life.

Mary Ruth Lehman is grateful and blessed to be mother of eight children, grandmother of fifteen and great-grandmother of fourteen and another on the way. Ruth is part of the intercessors team at ACTS Covenant Fellowship.

Tale of Two Schools

"Two are better than one, because they have a good return for their labor." *Ecclesiastes 4:9 (Today's New International Version)*

God is about bringing people to Himself, as well as to each other. Unity was so important to the Lord that it was included in one of His last prayers recorded in John 17:20: "I pray also for those who will believe . . . that all of them may be one."

In returning to Lancaster Christian School about five years ago, I sensed the Lord lay on my heart a vision for a greater degree of oneness among Christian schools in the county. Many benefits could be reaped just from the practical side, but even more importantly it would testify to the community of how brethren can dwell together in unity.

The vision is now a reality. Lancaster Christian School and Living Word Academy gave birth to the Lancaster County Christian School in the fall of 2010.

This unity venture began three years ago. In some ways it was a most unlikely match. One school, parent owned and the other church owned. One school was located north of Route 30 and the other was south of Route 30. The combination of prayer and gracious perseverance made a dream a reality.

Truly the Lord created this marriage of two Christian school ministries. And similar to marriage, a spirit of love and humility covered the relationship from its very inception.

Sad to say this is the road less traveled by too many, because we tend to cling to the nonessentials of our belief systems.

Father, May we learn, as believers, to look for the core convictions of our faith rather than be blinded by the bias of our preferences.

Sandy Outlar and his wife attend Wheatland Presbyterian Church.

Revelation of Jesus

". . . for I did not receive it from any man, nor was I taught it, but I received it through a revelation of Jesus Christ." *Galatians 1:12 (English Standard Version)*

As I was sitting in church listening to a teaching on the book of Galatians, our Pastor read the above scripture. All of a sudden, that beautiful voice from within asked me, "Do you know what the revelation of Jesus is?"

I began to think through this question and realized I understood the basics and knew it to be true, that Jesus died for my sins, rose from the dead and lives forevermore. But that wasn't the answer that was satisfying the questioner.

I questioned. What is it God? What is the revelation that made Paul determined enough to go away for three years?

I listened. I heard.

Paul understood the death and the agony of the cross. Paul "got" the wounds of Jesus, with each nail of the cross. All of a sudden, I began to feel the revelation that is received through the Holy Spirit. The revelation of my Jesus in Isaiah 52 and 53, being marred beyond human form, taking all my dark and seeing me lovely. The revelation of Jesus, the agony of the cost, that He gave freely, knowing who I am, knowing all my shame, even as a believer, still He gave freely, but the cost was extreme.

The revelation of Jesus Christ: I am dark (He was beaten, bruised) but he calls me lovely (He gave so I could live).

Jesus, thank You for what You gave, how much You poured yourself out to see me lovely, even in all my darkness. The cost You paid in agony and love so that I can live for You. Let the revelation of Jesus be real to me as never before.

Kim Zimmerman and her husband Brian are the founders and directors of City Gate Lancaster and prayer room in Lancaster City. They attend The Lord's House of Prayer.

The Steering Wheel

"Direct my footsteps according to your word; let no sin rule over me." *Psalm 119:133*

I love mowing the yard on the garden tractor. I find it so relaxing. One time, as I was mowing through our row of pine trees, the steering wheel suddenly fell off. The mower kept right on going through the trees with me on it. The branches were slapping me in the face and my arms and it was totally out of control. All of a sudden, the mower came to an abrupt halt as it hit a tree trunk. The only thing hurt was my pride. After making sure I was OK, my family had a good laugh.

Later, as I was thinking how comical the whole scene must have been, I thought about how that steering wheel controlled where that tractor was going. When it fell off, the tractor went out of control. That is so much like life. When we take things into our own hands and try to steer our own lives, we fail. We mess up and careen out of control just like that tractor did. If we allow God to steer us, He will show us the right direction at the right speed. We will stay on course. Our lives will be blessed and will glorify and honor Him. We will experience order and peace. Next time you feel out of control, think of the garden tractor and allow God to be the steering wheel of your life.

Father, so often I go my own way and try to do things my way. God, bring me back to You. I cannot do it without You. Help me to look to You for wisdom and guidance so all I think, say and do will be because of You. Thank You, God. Amen.

Cynthia Zimmerman is a board member of Life Connection Mission, which operates a sponsorship school for poor Haitian children in Montrouis, Haiti. Cynthia and her husband Rick have two sons and one grandson and attend New Life Fellowship Church in Ephrata.

Father Time and Mother Earth

"For we know that the whole creation groans and suffers the pain of childbirth together until now." *Romans 8:22 (New American Standard Bible)*

Earth is a small planet in a vast universe. Yet, the Bible makes it clear that God has chosen the earth to fulfill His purposes. As Creator, He is also Possessor. The earth is the Lord's and the fullness thereof including they that dwell on it. (Psalm 24:1) As earth dwellers, we are stewards of the earth on His behalf.

In creation, the One who is beyond time, established time. In creation, the One who is the source of all life designed a planet that nurtures human life. Some have personified these expressions of God's nature, Father Time and Mother Earth, respectively.

On Earth Day, we do not worship the creation, but we do remember the Creator who gave Adam and his descendants the responsibility to cultivate and protect it. With water and land, plants and animals, we may labor to profit. We must also labor to preserve their usefulness.

Into this time-space world God came as a human being, Jesus, to restore the broken relationship between earth dwellers and their Creator. "Now the created world can hardly wait for what's coming next." Romans 8:19 (The Message) Like a pregnant woman with pains of childbirth, the earth, in hope, awaits a glorious transformation. Even as those who follow Christ are being transformed into His likeness, so also the created world will be transformed—freed from decay.

The Creator is generous: a fresh supply of time flows to us continually; an abundance of resources, if managed well, nurtures all of humanity.

Creator of heaven and earth, empower us to be productive with our time and resources. Your will be done! Your Kingdom come on earth as it is in heaven! Show us how to care for the well-being of the planet.

Keith Yoder, founder and president of Teaching The Word Ministries, is a member of The Worship Center and serves in leadership with the Regional Church of Lancaster County.

It All Started with a Plastic Bottle

"The earth dries up and withers, the world languishes and withers . . . . Therefore a curse consumes the earth; its people must bear their guilt." *Isaiah 24:4, 6*

Words from a student serving an African mission stuck with me for a decade: "How much water I use and how long I shower is a matter of my faith." I too began to realize that my consumption directly takes away from what is available to others as I taught environmental lessons to a church scouting group.

It started with a plastic bottle, teaching the kids all that's involved from creation to disposal. I've learned how plastic waste lodged in soil harms agriculture, waterways and leaks toxic elements in landfills. I consider the floating islands of trash on the Pacific, the acres of coral reefs dying when its holes are plugged by waste such as diapers, and animal skeletons revealing stomachs bloated with plastic caps. Littered plastic leaches estrogen-mimicking chemicals that cause reproductive problems in animals, and human studies reveal the same effects on our children, increasingly consuming more of their food from plastic containers.

I now consider how my choice to consume goods made from oil, a dwindling natural resource, changes the world and hurts people. I've seen results of the hierarchy of placing humanity's needs above the environment and see the truth God pointed to in commanding us to be earth's stewards—we must *if we want to care for people.* The two are inextricably linked—everything we pollute the earth with holds a consequence for us.

Now I ask myself if the convenience of a plastic-bottled drink or plastic picnic ware is worth what it costs the rest of the world (people and all else). I'm trying to practice myself out of "needing" throwaway items. Previous generations lived quite well without throw-aways.

Lord, help me to see the amount of nonbiodegradable trash I use as a matter of faith—because I want to care about the people and world harmed by it.

Renee Lannan, New Cumberland Church of the Nazarene, serves as a stay-at-home mother to two small ones.

Good Friday

"For Christ died for sins once for all, the righteous for the unrighteous, to bring you to God. He was put to death in the body but made alive by the Spirit." *I Peter 3:18*

Good Friday, the Friday before Easter Sunday, commemorates the anniversary of Christ's crucifixion and sacrificial death. For Christians, it is traditionally a time of fasting, prayer, repentance and meditation on the passion of Christ. Many churches celebrate Good Friday with a service of remembrance.

One Good Friday about ten years ago, I honored the memory of two of my children with a special ceremony. My children were not killed by accident, illness or disease. My children lost their lives because of my "choice."

Although Jesus' blood paid for this horrible sin and redeemed the life of my children and my life from the years I suffered in silence, I continued to carry the shame and the guilt of my sin and never mourned my loss.

The memorial service allowed grieving for what should have and could have been had these babies lived. My daughter and I cried, lit candles, had special flowers and named these children as we recognized we will never have them here with us. Thankfully one day we will go to them.

Healing from abortion and the grieving over the loss of my children has been quite a process. I carry them always in my heart. I am so thankful to have had that Good Friday service where I received release because of Jesus' suffering and death. After Good Friday is resurrection Sunday and from every evil happening, God can resurrect something good that will bring peace and hope for our future.

Heavenly Father, whether or not we choose to "celebrate" Good Friday, help us to be ever mindful of the suffering and death of Christ on the cross and His resurrection.

Sharon Blantz at the Worship Center serves in ministry to post-abortive individuals in remembrance of Peter Seth and Grace Kelly.

This I Know

"... but those who hope in the Lord will renew their strength. They will soar on wings like eagles. ..." *Isaiah 40:31*

On September 23, I suddenly remembered my husband Clete had promised that he or I would write a devotional for our church's advent booklet due September 25.

I asked my friend Linda, "How can I write something inspirational after a year that has been nothing but the pits?"

Linda looked at me and said, "Nan, just tell it like it is."

So I did. That was many years ago, but I find that devotional as relevant now as I did then. Here is what I wrote:

"It has been months of major decisions regarding our business. It has been deep concern over a friend's serious illness. It has been trying to deal with a problem with my eighty-five-year-old father. It sometimes feels like water dripping on a stone—never ending.

Some of the problems are going to be long term and on-going. It leaves me feeling battered, bruised and beaten.

At times I feel very separated from God. But there have been days when our daily devotional readings have been so right on it was like a lifeline telling us to hang in, hang on. Some days an understanding friend or small child or each other have kept us going.

But the greatest truth is this – while nothing may seem right in our current world, I know with an absolute certainty that everything is right in God's world.

I cling to the words in Lamentations 3:21–24: "Yet hope returns when I remember this one thing: The Lord's unfailing love and mercy still continue, fresh as the morning, as sure as the sunrise. The Lord is all I have, and so in Him I put my hope."

Dear Lord, thank You that your unfailing love and mercy continue even when nothing seems right in this world.

Nancy S. Gibble, St. Paul's United Church of Christ, Manheim, is a writer and an avid reader. She enjoys biking and gardening and works parttime.

Easter Scars

"But he was pierced for our transgressions, he was crushed for our iniquities . . . and by His wounds we are healed." *Isaiah 53:5*

On my right arm is a large scar that reminds me of a dreadful day when I put my arm through a glass window. The cut was extremely deep requiring many stitches. After a few weeks, the wound began to heal, my stitches were removed and usage of my arm returned to normal. Yet the evidence of that frightful day, a visible scar, still remains.

Scars can be a reminder of our walk with Jesus. We all have received many wounds in life. However, through God's endless mercy and grace, the Lord brings healing to the wounds caused by broken relationships, harsh words of criticism, death of loved ones and faith challenging circumstances. Why is it that God will heal the wound but leave a scar? Could it be that our scars stay branded upon our hearts as a reminder of a loving Father who does heal the pain but leaves a scar of evidence behind?

When Jesus was placed upon the cross, nails were driven into His hands and feet, a crown of thorns pressed into His skull, and a spear pierced His side. God healed those wounds and by those wounds we too have experienced healing and forgiveness. Jesus' wounds have also left Him with scars, which are reminders of the greatest gift God has ever given us, the gift of His one and only Son. A day is coming soon when you will see Jesus' scars as evidence of God's grace.

What scars do you have? What wounds need His healing touch? May your scars remind you that Jesus loves you, has healed you, and has put a testimony in your heart for Him. For by His stripes we are healed!

Lord Jesus, we thank You for conquering sin and death and having scars to prove it. We give You thanks for the many ways in which You heal our wounds yet leave a scar, as evidence of Your amazing grace. We love You, Lord! Amen.

Wesley D. Siegrist pastors Erb Mennonite Church, Lititz.

Flowers from God

"May our Lord Jesus Christ himself and God our Father, who loved us and by his grace gave us eternal encouragement and good hope, encourage your hearts and strengthen you in every good deed and word." *2 Thessalonians 2:16–17*

The bouquet stopped me in my tracks as I entered my dorm room. The gorgeous flowers sat on my desk. *Must be a mistake*, I thought. My roommate was the one with the boyfriend, the one who had just presented her first art exhibition, the one who always got flowers. So I moved them over to her side of the room.

As I set them down I noticed the card, partially concealed by a sunflower. My name was on it. A short inspirational message ending with "God bless" filled the remainder of the space. Wow! God sent me flowers!

God truly sent me flowers that day by way of a couple whom I barely knew from my church at the university. I discovered later that the "beyond college" church members picked students' names out of a hat to choose those whom they were to bless. The couple who picked my name prayed about how to bless me. God's answer? Flowers, which not only brought beauty into my life, but encouraged, inspired, refreshed and reminded me how much He loves me.

Years have passed, but God continues to send me "flowers" of his love, encouragement and hope through the words and actions of my brothers and sisters in Christ—including the couple from my college days who have become my spiritual mentors. I am grateful for those who deliver God's flowers in obedience and love, and I am blessed when God calls me (and I listen) to deliver His flowers to others.

Father, thank You for sending me Your beautiful flowers through my brothers and sisters in Christ. May I, in turn, be used by You to build up others.

Brinton Culp, Lives Changed By Christ Church, receives and delivers God's flowers through serving in mothers of preschoolers, teaching Spanish to homeschoolers and being a wife and mommy.

Day Dreaming

"After I have poured out my rains again, I will pour out my Spirit upon all of you! Your sons and daughters will prophesy; your old men will dream dreams, and your young men see visions." *Joel 2:28 (The Living Bible)*

Do you remember being told in school to stop daydreaming? You were supposed to be focused on something at hand and your mind was elsewhere. (For those who live in the practical, sometimes they feel that dreaming is a waste of time. It is unrealistic and in most cases won't come true). It was fun to dream about things and see them happen. I like the quote by Bloody Mary, a character in South Pacific, "If you ain't got a dream, how you gonna have a dream come true."

There are many things that I desire to see happen in my lifetime that are my desires and dreams. How about you? Are there things that are tucked away in your heart that you think about experiencing? I'm not just talking about a specific car or a certain square footage of house. I'm talking more from a perspective of dreams pertaining to God—things that are in your heart concerning your relationship with Him and things pertaining to the kingdom.

I have a dream that the church becomes the powerhouse that God designed her to be. A place of power where those who do not know Jesus can experience His power in their lives. My dream sees people being healed and set free from bondages of the devil. I have seen some of that dream come true but there is so much more to be realized.

I believe God dreams. He dreams of seeing the earth covered with His glory as the waters cover the sea. I believe that all of God's dreams will become reality. So my best bet is to dream with Him. Spend time with Him dreaming about things in the future and then take those things to prayer. When you have God working your dream, I assure you it will become a reality.

Dear Lord, help our dreams become realities in order to further Your kingdom.

Ron Myer serves as assistant international director of DOVE Christian Fellowship International.

Battle with Depression

"I will lift my eyes to the hills—where does my help come from?
My help comes from the Lord, the Maker of heaven and earth."
Psalm 121:1-2

When I was thirty-four years old, I could scarcely make it through each day. I felt worthless and overwhelmed. Normal household chores seemed enormous and I was experiencing frequent panic attacks. With seven children, thirteen years and under, there was a lot on my "plate."

My husband LaMarr and I sought the help of a doctor. However, when he quickly prescribed a mild medicine to help me cope, we decided not to get the prescription filled. As we prayed about it, we sensed God wanted to do something in my heart and mind through this experience, rather than dull my senses and slow down that process.

What I went through that next year was a painful journey of growth in God. There were days when I doubted that I would make it through the fog.

With encouragement from LaMarr and a few people who understood the battle I was fighting, I started to express myself, open up and say how I felt rather than bury my true feelings. I began to soak up Scriptures as that became life and breath to me.

A turning point came after months of depression. The Lord taught me to literally give thanks for everything, keeping my thoughts filled with truth instead of giving my mind room for any negativity. It was the discipline I needed.

I would take "mini-vacations" in my mind by simply stepping outdoors and gazing at the trees. I meditated on the scripture: "I will lift up my eyes to the hills—where does my help come from? My help comes from the Lord, the Maker of heaven and earth."

The Lord was strengthening me as I continued to look up. I worked on building a love for life, an unwavering dependency on the Lord and His Word, and a stronger, more vibrant spirit to become a better vessel for Him.

Thank You, Father. We continue to lift our eyes and hearts to You, our Maker, for help, in Jesus' name.

Naomi Sensenig and her husband LaMarr serve at Lancaster Evangelical Free Church.

Blues Turned into Joy

"You have turned my wailing into dancing; you have removed my sackcloth and clothed me with joy. . . ." *Psalm 30:11*

We have all heard or spoken the phrase, "turn that frown upside down," which is much easier said than done. Although many people have the ability to make this change by refocusing their attention to a positive rather than negative train of thought, others are not so fortunate and a case of the blues can send them spiraling into depression. No one, however, can affect the one hundred and eighty-degree turn that is illustrated in the verse above.

Grief can become an all-encompassing force in our lives. The effect of loss can consume our minds and hearts. The reality that we are powerless to change things can leave us feeling hopeless. We are not to "grieve like the rest of men who have no hope," according to 1 Thessalonians 4:13. Instead our Lord possesses the power to transform and He does it through joy. Though sometimes viewed as synonymous, there is a distinct difference between joy and happiness. Happiness is dependent on circumstances; joy reflects our emotional well-being.

Happiness comes from without and joy comes from within. Believers experience the transforming power of the indwelling Holy Spirit as we face every circumstance in life, no matter how difficult. It is this Spirit who enables us to echo the words of Habakkuk. "Though the fig tree does not blossom and there be no fruit on the vine, the produce of the olive fail and the field yields no fruit, though the flock be cut off from the stall and there be no herd in the stalls, yet will I rejoice in the Lord. I will joy in the God of my salvation."

God, thank You for Your indwelling Spirit who transforms our mourning into dancing.

Peachy Colleluori and her husband Domenic have served on the staff of the National Christian Conference Center for more than twenty-five years.

Vision for Columbia

Jesus said, "And I, if I am lifted up from the earth, will draw all peoples to myself." *John 12:32 (New King James Version)*

Clair and Beth felt a call to move to Columbia. They sold their house miraculously and found a perfect house to buy there. It's on the corner of a busy thoroughfare; many people including schoolchildren pass that way. Clair testifies that the Lord has given him a peace about moving to the city and a love for the people of Columbia. He has developed relationships with many people. Beth, a nurse, has a heart for Hope Within Community Health Center, which provides pro bono medical care for those without insurance and hopes to build a satellite center in Columbia.

I, too, have a heart for Columbia and have felt the Lord asking, "Are you going to get out of the boat and walk on the water for me?"

A few months ago, our pastor asked, "Are you willing?"

As we sang the song "Here I Am, Lord," I knew I needed to be part of the Vision for Columbia. Although I don't know what my next step is except to pray and glorify Jesus.

We, along with other prayer intercessors, gather every Friday evening and pray, "Lord, show us the way." Beth asks how relationships can be moved into discipleship.

We ask the Lord, "What is the next step You have for this ministry?"

One person prayed this verse: "And I, if I am lifted up from the earth, will draw all people to myself."

Lord, that is our desire: to exalt You, praise You and glorify You so that the people of Columbia will see You through those of us who love You. We know as we do that people will be drawn to Him.

How is this ministry going to look? That hasn't been firmed up, but we continue to pray.

Lord, we lift up Your Name. We know You're shining the Light at our feet so we know the next step. Thank You, Lord, for showing us the Way. Thank You, Lord, for the precious people of Columbia.

Yvonne Zeiset is a financial counselor for Tabor Community Services, Consumer Credit Counseling. She is a prayer intercessor.

Never Alone

"Be strong and courageous. Do not be afraid or terrified because of them, for the Lord your God goes with you; he will never leave you nor forsake you." *Deuteronomy 31:6*

Sometimes solitude can be hard to find. Other times it seeks us out when least wanted.

To me there seemed no more lonely place than waiting on a gurney in a hospital corridor for my turn in the operating room. Lying unclothed under a sheet, I felt vulnerable, helpless, scared—and alone. The hallway was eerily devoid of anyone except me.

The thought crossed my mind that I should just get up and flee. There was no one to stop me. But instead, I started to pray. I was no longer alone. As I asked God for courage and guidance, a calm descended on me. As I let go of my fears, they were replaced with a quiet confidence. God was in control—not me or the doctors—so there was no need to worry. Whether the outcome was the healing I desired or a call home to heaven, my friend Jesus was by my side and the Holy Spirit was filling me with peace.

Our kind and gracious heavenly Father, we thank You for Your promise to be by our side always. In You we have a friend and protector who will never fail to be there for us. We praise You for being only a prayer away. Amen

Sue Bowman attends Annville United Methodist Church. She is deputy executive director for Lebanon County Housing Authority and a columnist for *Lancaster Farming.*

May

With Thanksgiving

"… in everything by prayer and supplication with thanksgiving let your requests be made known unto God." *Philippians 4:6 (King James Version)*

In the youth-oriented ministry where God has called my wife Brenda and me, we find ourselves as part of the "connected generation." My two hundred Facebook friends are puny compared to many youth.My texting speed is a source of ridicule by a generation who can text under the table and hold a conversation at the same time. Despite my generational limitations, Facebook has become my way to communicate with kids from Indonesia to California, my inbox is bulging with texts and my ring tone is set to Twila Paris' "God Is in Control" for any of "my" kids. Honestly, there are days I want to drop my phone in a bucket of water and join a monastery.

It was on one of those days that I did something I had never done before. My phone rang, I looked at who was calling and ignored the call. The girl who was calling would be calling me for one of only two reasons: to ask for something or to complain about something or somebody, and I was just not in the mood. The last strains of "God Is in Control" were still hanging in the air when I was struck by a sense of guilt. Does God feel the same way when I pray? How many of my prayers begin with a whine and end with a "gimme"? Doesn't my Father, who freely supplies all of my needs, deserve at least as much from me, as I would like to have out of my kids?

Father, I come today asking for nothing. I praise You for Your hand in my life, and thank You for being in control of my life even though I cannot always see where You are taking me.

Steve and Brenda Hershey have opened their home to young adult girls. He is a teacher at White Oak Church of the Brethren.

Do You Believe Who You Are?

"After his baptism, Jesus came up out of the water . . . . And a voice from heaven said, 'This is My dearly loved Son, who brings me great joy.'" *Matthew 3:16–17 (New Living Translation)*

"During that time the devil came and said to him, 'If You are the Son of God . . . .'" *Matthew 4:3 (New Living Translation)*

Recently God got my attention as I heard a speaker share on Satan tempting Jesus to meet His physical, emotional and psychological needs. As I went back and read Matthew 3:16 to 4:11 the words "If you are the Son of God" stopped me. It struck me that Jesus' first temptation came in this question from the devil: "Do You believe who God says You are?"

Satan knew that if Jesus wavered in His belief of who He really was then the rest would be easy. But Jesus was confident, unwavering, secure and bold in who He was.

I immediately heard God ask me if I believed who He says I am. I wish I could say with confidence, "Yes!" but I could not. I then saw how my lack of confidence, wavering, insecurity and fear led me to become my own god in several places in my life.

I shared this with a few friends and each of us were moved to choose a scripture to pray each day asking God that we would see and experience it as truth in our daily lives.

I chose Colossians 2:10, "So you are also complete through your union with Christ." This really spoke to my struggle of feeling inadequate. I have found that no matter what the day holds I am growing more confident in whom I am and Whose I am. I won't say it always comes easy, but I am more intentional in choosing to believe what God says over what I am feeling.

Papa, thank You for the simplicity of Your Holy Word. I pray that each day I will grow more confident, unwavering, secure and bold in who You say I am.

Carrie Libonati is the instructor for the Learning and Career Center at the Lydia Center.

Sowing and Reaping

"He who supplies seed to the sower and bread for food will supply and multiply your seed for sowing and increase the harvest of your righteousness." *2 Corinthians 9:10 (English Standard Version)*

Over the years, I believe I have heard from Father in the form of dreams. In one such dream, I was hosting a large gathering of people who were celebrating the introduction of a revolutionary harvesting machine. The air was charged with anticipation and high hopes that the world would be a better place because of the potential that this machine was sure to deliver.

The crowd quieted in anticipation of the machine being driven out into the sunlight, then cheered wildly at its sleek styling and the quiet purr of the concept engine. A few hundred yards up a winding tree-lined roadway, there was a field of wheat waiting to be harvested. I walked and talked with others in the crowd, as they made their way slowly toward the field, anticipating the machine's demonstration. As the machine approached the edge of the field, it stopped. Instead of engaging the waving acres of mature wheat, it shut down and sat silently.

Those closest to the field stood still and appeared uneasy, almost embarrassed, as the rest of us made our way to where the field was now completely in view. I stopped and stared in utter disbelief. Before us were acres of rolling, productive soil, but no sign of any vegetation. The marks in the soil were evidence that the wheat planter had been used. A harvest was anticipated—even assumed. But no seed had been planted. For all of the hype and fanfare, I was terribly chagrined. The reaping was impossible because the sowing was insufficient. I came to new understanding and intentionality concerning God's expectations of me as a sower in His plan and purpose for a bountiful harvest.

Father, help me to discern wisely your instruction for sowing seed in the hearts of others with kingdom perspective.

Don Hoover and family are involved in sowing and reaping that to which the Lord gives the increase.

Saying Good-bye

"Let not your hearts be troubled . .... In My Father's house there are many mansions; if it were not so, I would have told you; for. I go to prepare a place for you." *John 14:1-2 (American Standard Version)*

I remember when our oldest daughter Holly got married. She had lived at home until the day of her marriage, and she and her sister Shelly (who is mentally challenged) were very close. We went to counseling as a family to help Shelly understand that Holly was not leaving forever. Holly would not live with us any longer, but Shelly was getting a brother-in-law and later would get three nieces! Even though Shelly missed her sister, she was able to grasp the beauty of the good-bye.

We have had to say good-bye to more than two hundred young women who have lived with us. For a time we helped them, and then they continued with their own lives. Sadly, some have passed away, but others come back to say thank you. Some are in our lives again because we serve together in ministry work. In time, the good-bye has brought great rewards.

Jesus understood that He had to let go of the disciples and return to the Father. He left to prepare a place for them, and for us. He knew by letting go of His earthly connection to the disciples, they could go and preach the Gospel. Holding on to things too long can stop our growth and take us out of God's will.

Saying good-bye to someone or something you love is hard. We cannot forget the memories, the laughter and the tears. Yet when we say good-bye it does not have to mean the end. It can mark a new beginning.

Jesus, help me to be able to say good-bye to those people or things You have chosen. Help me to allow people to move on beyond my sphere of knowing them. Help me to release and then receive the new things You have for me. Amen.

Anne Pierson is a wife, mother and grandmother who is called to the care of the fatherless.

Sowing Tears

"Jesus wept." John 11:35

"They that sow in tears shall reap in joy. He that goeth forth and weepeth, bearing precious seed, shall doubtless come again with rejoicing, bringing his sheaves *with him." Psalm 126:5-6 (King James Version)*

Although there are tears of sorrow, tears of joy and tears caused by physical or emotional pain, in today's world, we are often taught by our elders not to shed tears. "Timmy, you're a big boy now. Don't cry."

Several years ago a wonderful woman from the city of Coatesville, Pennsylvania, called me a Jeremiah, the weeping prophet. That was one of the best compliments that I have ever received. Even though she just met me, she knew my heart.

When I first initiated the prayer walk across America, I did not think that I would ever see any fruit of my labor during my lifetime. I was wrong. I have seen people's lives changed and my own father come to know Jesus.

One of the fruits of the walk is that I have seen the shedding of tears. When people see this gray-haired man walking with a backpack, people have a tendency to approach me and ask me where I am going.

Soon I am asking them for the prayer needs in their community and then I ask for their own prayer needs. Their eyes start to water; then the tears flow. The needs in America are many.

Do we shed tears over these words: divorce, abortion, suicide, war, substance abuse, homeless, foreclosure and violence?

We should. If Jesus wept, why can't we?

Every year, the first Thursday in May is the National Day of Prayer. Will you please pray and shed tears for America?

Father, we lift our nation up in prayer. Please forgive us and show us mercy when we as a nation do not always acknowledge You in word and deed. Forgive us . . . forgive us. You are and shall remain the chief cornerstone of our nation.

Jim Shaner attends Praise Fellowship Church and is the founder of One Nation Under God Walk Across America.

Even a Second Bike?

"And my God will supply every need of yours according to his riches in glory in Christ Jesus." *Philippians 4:19 (English Standard Version)*

It seems ludicrous that my greatest concern would be the loss of my recumbent exercise bike. Of all the things that I was giving up in order to move, this item troubled me most.

I have a history of dislike for exercise. I wore orthopedic shoes as a child, was clumsy and always had a fear of falling, so I avoided sports and many other challenging activities. Finally, rather late in life, I found something I could do without aggravating my back and developed a reasonably disciplined program to improve my physical condition: an exercise bike.

I was in a quandary about the bike when I received a strong call from the Lord to relocate to a rural location to be part of a ministry where we would spend about seventy-five percent of our time. We were not breaking up our current household or selling our home since we planned to return to it regularly. The bike was much too cumbersome to haul back and forth, and I wanted it in both places. I noticed an ad for a seldom-used new bike in our church classified posting, and I assumed it would cost far more than the good used one I had purchased second-hand. When the ad appeared for the second month in a row, I called the owner. It turned out that he knew of the ministry we were undertaking, had a heart to bless others and decided to give us his almost new bike to take with us!

I spend weeks away from my spacious suburban home, but my small mountain retreat boasts a superb recumbent bike parked right next to my bed. The Lord truly is able to bless abundantly more than we can ask or think.

Thank You, Lord, that You choose to bless Your children in unusual ways, giving out of Your abundance even when we are slow to ask or believe we are asking for too much. There is nothing too simple or too hard for You.

Joan Boydell has left behind most of her pregnancy center work to serve alongside her husband Bruce at the Haft, Inc., in New Albany. The Haft provides a place to "Refresh, retool and rebuild leaders and organizations."

Mother Is Away from Home

"He replied to him, 'Who is my mother, and who are my brothers?'
Pointing to his disciples, he said, 'Here are my mother and my
brothers. For whoever does the will of my Father in heaven is my
brother and sister and mother.'" *Matthew 12:48–50*

On Mother's Day my heart aches. I wish I could spend that day
with my mother or at least hug her. But I can't. She lives thousands of
miles away. So I content myself with a phone call and a gift I cannot
hand deliver. Yet every year, the Lord reminds me of all the women
who have in one way or another filled, even temporary, that mother's
place in my life.

I think of all the women the Lord has given me in this country. I
remember the ones who babysat my daughter when I needed to study,
work, attend conferences or when I was ill. Some picked up groceries
or medicines for me. Others would call just to check on me. I recall the
times some of them had to take time off work so they could be of assistance to me. I reminisce the times they let me pour out my heart, the
times they cried and laughed with me, the times they provided good
Christian counsel and encouragement.

Now on Mother's Day I rejoice and thank those ladies for being
mothers to me, many of whom have no children of their own. I have
learned that motherhood is not just nine months of pregnancy and painful hours of labor. It's accepting a stranger as your own. It's being there
when it matters the most. Without these women I wouldn't have been
able to accomplish many of the things I did accomplish here, away
from my biological mother, and for that I'll forever be thankful.

*Dear Lord Jesus, thanks for my mothers away from home, thanks for
godly women who so selflessly do Your will by being sisters and
mothers to others.*

Chou Gabikiny serves in the Global Impact Team at West Shore Brethren in
Christ Church.

Companion of Solo Mothers

"A father to the fatherless, a defender of widows, is God in his holy dwelling. God sets the lonely in families . . . ." Psalm 68:5–6

When I decided to be a mother, it was because I wanted to start a family. To me family meant mom, dad, and the children living together. But things turned out differently. I got married overseas and had to return to the United States to maintain my immigration status. I came back pregnant. What I thought would take a few months ended up taking years. I've faced the pregnancy and our daughter's four years of life with a solo parent. We get to visit her father, but we have yet to be successful at bringing him here.

I never imagined I would be a "married-single mother." But through it all, the Lord reveals Himself as a father to my daughter and a husband to me. He provides what we need, comforts us when we are lonely, wipes our tears and tells us He's always there. He also puts amazing people around us and has given me a new definition of family.

It breaks my heart to watch children play with their dads and see husbands hold their wives' hands. It's even more depressing when I'm sick and can't care for my daughter. I wish my husband was right beside me during those times. Then I hear a voice calling, "Mama."

Oh, the joy of being a mother! I have someone to care for, a character to forge and a future to prepare. It is hard to be a single mother, but I'd rather be a single mother than simply a wife far from her husband because motherhood is the most important role I'll ever have.

Dear Lord, thanks for being my husband and father to my child. Thanks for filling the voids in our hearts and lives with your overflowing love. Thanks for making me a mother, and please help me to always enjoy this role despite the hardships.

Chou Gabikiny serves in the Global Impact Team at West Shore Brethren in Christ Church.

To My Mother

"I am reminded of your sincere faith, a faith that dwelt first in your grandmother Lois and your mother Eunice and now, I am sure, dwells in you as well." 2 Timothy 1:5 (English Standard Version)

I remember fondly, when my daughter and your granddaughter, Lisa, was about two years old. She spent the weekend with you and Grandpa. You always had a way of making her feel special. I can remember the pretty blue spring coat and hat you bought her because she was your first granddaughter (and you had had only sons).

Lisa was blonde-haired, blue-eyed and the apple of your eye. We had three sons after her, but I always knew Lisa held a special place in your heart, as she does in mine.

For years, you kept a container of dusting powder on your dresser in your beautiful farmhouse bedroom. After you dressed and headed downstairs, Lisa quietly got up and helped herself to your dusting powder (just like she saw Grandma do, and wanting to copy her actions). Her little footprints on your carpet were outlined with this dusting powder. You told me you couldn't vacuum this for several days, it was too dear.

At the time, I was too young and inexperienced to appreciate that moment like I do now. Last Sunday, our family was together for our annual summer picnic. Grace, our two-year-old granddaughter, enjoyed her peanut butter ice cream, eating from a plastic cup, sitting on our kitchen linoleum floor. Of course, there were the normal drips, and she was barefooted. She left a footprint that has since dried on this grayish kitchen floor. I cannot make myself wipe this off. A lesson passed from one generation to another.

I pray that our footprints (our lives) lead these little ones to bigger and better things, lives that help develop their character into strong Christian women.

Lord, thank You for a wonderful Christian heritage in a godly mother and father and god-fearing grandparents.

Ruth Robenolt lives in Watsontown with her husband. She recently retired after giving twenty-five years of service to Bucknell University in Lewisburg. She and her husband attend Community Mennonite Fellowship in Milton.

Hold the Sauce

"Put on, then, as God's chosen ones, holy and beloved, heartfelt compassion, kindness, humility, gentleness and patience."
Colossians 3:12–13

Adapted from a recent church bulletin of St. Peter the Apostle R.C. Church: "Welcome to McParish. May I have your order, please?"

"Can I have two baptisms, one confirmation and one marriage?"

"Would you like any extra sauce with that?"

We have grown up in a McWorld and have gotten used to fast food and instant everything. It is not so surprising, then, that church members—non-registered and registered parishioners alike—want sacraments for themselves and their children instantly.

It doesn't work like that. We don't do drive-through sacraments. Sacramental preparation is a process that takes some time.The time allows the candidates, or in the case of a child's baptism, the parents and godparents, to be formed in the faith. What we need is some patience on the part of those inquiring about sacraments.

Actually, what we really need is to have patience with God. God will not be rushed. He takes his time. The way God's church conducts his business of dispensing grace reflects this slow but sure way God often works.

Thanks for Your understanding. Thanks for Your patience. And hold the extra sauce.

Lord, sometimes I want something done my way and done now.
Remind me that You are God and I am not and that You have my best interests in mind. The best things do come for those who wait on You.
Amen.

Rev. Thomas J. Orsulak is pastor of St. Peter the Apostle Parish, Reading.

Welcome to the Family

"Consequently, you are no longer foreigners and aliens, but fellow citizens with God's people and members of God's household."
Ephesians 2:19

May 21, 2010, was a very significant day for my eldest daughter Keyla and me. On this day we both became U.S. citizens after being permanent residents for eight years.

That morning when we went into the Lancaster County Courthouse, the judge came into the room. He brought a picture of his family with him and shared his own experience of how he was adopted by his family that he grew up with. He said to us, "Today we have here forty-one people from twenty-two different countries from around the world that have been adopted by the United States as a nation and I want to say to you, 'welcome to our family, and God bless you.'"

While the judge was sharing his own story, I recalled my own experience. I was being adopted into the United States family and it was a great blessing for me. There was at the same time a deep sense of gratitude in my heart; because of the work that one day, Jesus did on the cross, I was adopted into God's family. It happened when I recognized that I was a sinner and I invited Jesus to be my Lord and Savior. At that moment, I also received a new citizenship, but it was for heaven. As it says in the Bible: "Consequently, you are no longer foreigners and aliens, but fellow citizens with God's people and members of God's household."

Heavenly Father, I want to give You thanks for the work of Jesus Christ on the cross/ This act made it possible for me to be forgiven of my sins and to receive citizenship in heaven. In the name of Jesus Christ my Lord and Savior, I pray. Amen, amen and amen.

Mario E. Araya is pastor of "Iglesia Menonita de New Holland JESUCRISTO ES EL SENOR, where he together with his wife Jeanette and children, Mario Jr., Katie, Keyla and her husband Juan Carlos, have served the Lord since 2001. Mario and Jeanette have also served as pastors in Costa Rica and Mexico.

Downsizing for a Purpose

"Set your affection on things above, not on things on the earth."
Colossians 3:2 (King James Version)

The Lord had made clear to my husband and I that we were supposed to buy a house that we could pay in cash in order to be completely debt free. But like Jonah, we decided we just couldn't do what God was asking. After all, we could afford better. So we moved into our dream home!

Immediately it became the house of our nightmares! We experienced plagues, just like in the Bible! In fact, we had blood-red water for eight months! And that was just the beginning. One year later we finally obeyed the Lord and sold the house.

In its place, we found a little house in town with a postage stamp of a yard. The day of closing my husband lost his job due to a buyout. Of course, this was all part of God's plan, for He had already provided a carriage house, formerly used as a business, in the back of the house we just bought. This was where our new business was birthed.

Two years earlier we had asked the Lord to help us do more for orphans. We had adopted and I spoke for the cause of adoption, but we both felt a nagging feeling that it just wasn't enough. It was now beginning to make sense. John had to lose his job so that we would be willing to risk starting our business. We needed to be debt free so we could give lavishly from our earnings from our new business to help orphans in China! We needed this unassuming house because it had a fully furnished office in the back.

That was three years ago. Today a song's lyrics fill my mind: ". . . and the things of earth will grow strangely dim in the light of His glory and grace."

Father, we have so much material wealth in this country. Help us not to ever get so consumed in the "stuff" of this world that we forget the things that really matter. Help us align our hearts with Yours and build up treasures for eternity. Amen"

Deborah Roche attends Calvary Church with her husband and three (soon to be four) beautiful blessings from China. Deb is an adoption/pro-life speaker and homeschooling mom.

Love Is Priority

"If I give all I possess to the poor and surrender my body to the flames, but have not love, I gain nothing." *1 Corinthians 13:3*

This verse shakes me to the bones. It brings me back to the reality of God's view on life and mission. It is a stark reminder that how we do something is far more important than what we do.

Giving everything I own to the poor would be a very generous gift. It would be a great sacrifice and come at a big cost . . . but without love, it would mean nothing to the Lord.

Early Christians were burned at the stake for their faith. It was the supreme sacrifice . . . but without love, it meant nothing.

I have been involved with Good Works, a Christian nonprofit organization, for twenty-two years. We assist low-income families living in substandard housing in Chester County. Our mission is repairing homes and restoring hope. Through the Lord's provision, we have assisted more than five hundred and fifty homeowner families. Houses are transformed into homes that are warmer, safer and drier.

Through all this, hope, joy and dignity are restored. Improved living conditions, enthusiastic volunteers, meaningful relationships, generous donors . . . but without love, we have gained nothing.

I have noticed that when my guard is down and when the task-oriented part of me takes over, I focus on the work: What I am doing, not how I am doing it. I am a human being who has been trained to get things done. Through my involvement in Good Works, I am learning the importance of love, both giving it and receiving it.

Lord, thank You for loving us. Teach us to incorporate Your love in all that we do every day.

Jim Ford serves as the director of Good Works, Inc.

You Always Have the Advantage

"If it had not been the Lord who was on our side, when men rose up against us, then they would have swallowed us alive."
Psalm 124:2–3 (New King James Version)

You need to know that you always have the advantage no matter what the challenge is in front of you. No matter how difficult it may seem, you have the upper hand. Even if it requires you making a major change in your life, you have the trump card to make it happen. You have the Lord on your side!

David mentioned in Psalm 124:2–3 that his enemies would have destroyed him without the Lord. Can you capture what is happening here? David is emphatic: If it was not for the Lord being on my side, I would be toast. Then David reminds us that we need to understand that if the Lord is not on our side, we all would be overwhelmed by the circumstances and situations we find ourselves in.

I illustrated it this way in a sermon I presented one day: I had a young man come up front who was strong and told the congregation that we were going to wrestle each other. There was about a thirty-year difference in our ages and by the looks of his biceps, I wouldn't stand a chance. Right before we engaged, I said, "Oh, let me read Psalm 124." After reading the first verse, I called three other big men to the front representing the Father, Son and Holy Spirit. I said, "Oh, I forgot, I have the Lord on my side. Now we can engage."

The dynamics had totally changed. Suddenly things looked totally different. In what looked to be a sure thing for the young man, suddenly, with the reality of three other huge men on my side, the challenge changed to an extremely weighted advantage in my favor. That's the way it is in the spirit when you realize that the Lord is on your side. "If God is for us, who can ever be against us?" (Romans 8:31)

So, no matter what you are facing, know that the Lord is on your side, and if He is on your side, you have the advantage.

Lord, with You on our side, we can triumph in all things.

Ron Myer is assistant international director of DOVE Christian Fellowship International.

Drinks Only, Snacks Are on the Way

"Now we see but a poor reflection as in a mirror; then we shall see face to face. Now I know in part; then I shall know fully, even as I am fully known." *1 Corinthians 13:12*

On a recent flight to Israel, the well-dressed flight attendant captured my attention with just a simple sentence, "Drinks only, snacks are on the way."

As that sentence bounced around in my mind, my thoughts drifted to the familiar place of spiritual application. It's an occupational hazard for those of us who are pastors. My mind settled onto the person of the Holy Spirit who was given as a down payment or foretaste of what is coming when we fully inherit the kingdom of God. You see, the drink offered by the flight attendant was only one part of the refreshment offered by the airline. The snack or chewable part of the refreshment was the completion of the scheduled pick-me-up.

My soul was strengthened and my heart lifted as I meditated on the truth of Scripture—the power and comfort available to us by the Holy Spirit is just a small part of what awaits us when we see our amazing Lord face-to-face. Now, we partially know the fullness dwelling within the Godhead. Then, we will know in entirety. Now, we see just a small portion. Then, we will see everything.

In other words, we will know God and all of His ways just as fully as He knows us now. The truth of this future hope brought great encouragement to my very discouraged heart. Remember, we now have our "drink," but "snacks" are on the way

Father, thank You for what You have revealed thus far and thank You for what You will reveal to us when we see You face-to-face.

Pastor Ellen Dooley, itinerate pastor and MDiv candidate at Evangelical Theological Seminary.

The Family of Christ

"And all the believers met together constantly and shared everything with each other . . . ." *Acts 2:44 (The Living Bible)*

The appeal was announced on Easter morning. "There is a lady who belongs to one of our sister churches in Ephrata, Pennsylvania. Her husband is very ill and will be in Johns Hopkins Hospital for an unknown amount of time. She needs a place just to sleep so she can be near her husband."

Perry Hall Family Worship Center was only a small church right outside of Baltimore, but they were eager to serve. Two people enthusiastically raised their hands in response to Pastor Dominick's request.

"No problem here," Janice announced. "I have an empty apartment in my basement, and I'm only twenty minutes from the hospital. She is welcome to stay with me."

I didn't even know these people, but after a friend of mine put in a call to the church telling them of my need—how could I refuse? Paying one-hundred dollars a night even to be near my ailing husband was not an option.

Jan and I hit it off. I was given a key to come and go to her home as I pleased and then relax in her completely furnished apartment complete with a 42-inch TV. The Lord showed her this was to be her ministry and there was no charge to me. I eventually met the whole church family and was invited to a Bible study where they all bathed me with prayer, friendship and fellowship.

It was a huge blessing at a very difficult time in my life, but I was not surprised. We serve a living God and this was the family of Christ in action. No matter where we live, or what our need, the family of God will come through.

Lord, I pray I can touch someone's life with the love and servanthood which I received. Thank You for the body of Christ!

Jan Dorward is a Messianic Jew who resides in Ephrata. She attends DOVE Westgate Church. Jan loves to write and she presents Messianic Passovers.

His Strength in My Weakness

"My grace is sufficient for you, for my power is made perfect in weakness." *2 Corinthians 12:9*

My life has undergone a transformation over the past couple of years—but not the kind I would have initially chosen. Despite much prayer for healing, both personally and receiving ministry from others, I still find myself struggling with a thyroid condition and working with a doctor to try to find the right balance of thyroid hormone replacement. Some of the symptoms that have been most difficult are tiredness, low energy and "brain fog."

My brain had always been quite reliable in directing my daily activities, but suddenly I found myself forgetting things and being unable to think clearly sometimes. Before thyroid problems, I would have said that I relied on God for his strength and direction. But now I have had to learn to trust Him in a whole new way. Every morning I fall on my knees and ask for God's strength to get me through another day. Throughout the day I often pause and ask, "God, is there anything important that I'm forgetting, or anything you want me to know or do?" And He is always faithful to show me what I need to do next, one step at a time. Sometimes, though, I may need to rest to gather strength for the next task. It hasn't been an easy journey or transformation.

I can say that I'm thankful, because by necessity I have come to a deeper level of trust, leaning on the Lord. His strength is made perfect in my weakness, and I have found that His grace is sufficient.

Lord, I pray for my brothers and sisters in You who are experiencing weakness or trials. Meet their needs as they lean on Your grace and find it sufficient.

Jane Nicholas is a proofreader, writer and editor. She lives in Elizabethtown and serves as an intercessor and volunteer with two ministries in western Lancaster County.

Being Sensitive to the Open Door

"See, I have placed before you an open door that no one can shut. I know that you have little strength, yet you have kept my word and have not denied my name." *Revelation 3:8*

Even in my life, it was an unusual request. It was 11:00 at night, I was milking when an acquaintance asked me to run to Virginia to pick up her friend for his brother's memorial service.

We left at 1:00 a.m. Josh looked exactly like the type of person my mother had always warned me not to pick up. I listened for three and one-half hours on the trip back as they talked. They discussed the drug overdose his brother died of and the drugs they both grew up with. They talked about the anger and the violence that were part of their lives. Josh talked about how the police in that small community were afraid of him.

When I dropped her off at work, I talked to Josh for the first time. He told me that he enjoyed writing music and growing flowers. When we got to my farm, he followed me with wide eyes. He was afraid of the cows and asked, "Do they bite?" He was in awe as I delivered a calf and practically in tears when it was stillborn. "Can't you do something?" He was fascinated as I bred a cow.

I have kept in touch with Josh since that day, and he has been back to my house several times. He asked me to set up a Bible study for him, which I did. I don't know what God has planned for Josh, but I know that if I had chosen sleep over a seven-hour trip that night, it would be a door that would remain forever closed.

Father, make me sensitive to the open door. Give me the courage to step through and the wisdom to deal with what You have placed on the other side.

Steve Hershey is a teacher and speaker at White Oak Church of the Brethren. Steve and his wife Brenda have opened their home to young adults.

Never Alone Again

"I will be glad and rejoice in your love, for you saw my affliction and knew the anguish of my soul." *Psalm 31:7*

It was about two months since I was saved and I still wasn't allowing God into my life.

I thought that He was distancing Himself from me. I had felt God's presence that day two months ago, but where was He now? I thought God was angry and that He was bringing pain into my life. I felt so lost in a sea of emotional turmoil and shame. I was completely hopeless.

Not long ago, I hit yet another low in my recovery. I thought my world was over and wanted to die. I thought there was no escape from the pain. I thought God had surely forsaken me.

But God never ceases to amaze me. He met me in the midst of that pain. It was as if God reached His arms down and swallowed me in the most comforting hug I've ever received. At the same instant it was as if God whispered in my ear, "I am by your side, and I will always be with you."

Until then, I felt completely alone. It was I who was pushing Him away. I haven't felt alone since that day. I have more of an internal peace than ever before. I have happiness in my life. I don't need to numb my emotions anymore; the emotional pain is manageable with God's help. My heart understands peace. I know I will never be alone again. Greatest of all is that I have an insatiable desire to get closer to Him. I know God is my one true healer, and I refuse to push Him away for one more day. He is the hope that fills the emptiness.

Dear Lord, thank You for loving me. You are such an amazing God, and I pray Your will for my life.

Stephanie is a resident at Lydia Center, a division of Water Street Ministries.

Thought Provoking

"'My thoughts are nothing like your thoughts,' says the LORD. 'And my ways are far beyond anything you could imagine. For just as the heavens are higher than the earth, so my ways are higher than your ways and my thoughts higher than your thoughts.'" *Isaiah 55:8–9 (New Living Translation)*

One day as I was picking up my four-year-old daughter Sonja from the nursery, the mother of four-year-old Bobby pulled me aside and asked what psychology I had been teaching my daughter.

I asked her why. She explained that Bobby had come home from church the previous week and said he was going to be kind from now on because Sonja told him that she was going to be his friend no matter what he did.

My psychology, I told Bobby's mother, was nothing more than what I was learning from the Bible. I explained, "I tell my daughter the things I learn as I learn them and teach them to her as well. Apparently, she of her own initiative applied what I had taught her to her own life.

I had told Sonja what Jesus had said in Matthew 5:44, that we are to love our enemies.

Bobby had been a troublemaker in the nursery. No one liked him because he was always hurting them or taking things from them. Sonja, with childlike faith, obeyed Jesus and chose to love Bobby (her enemy) even though he was being a bully. Her obedience to Jesus, by expressing friendship to Bobby, the bully, gave him desire to change his life.

This example of childlike faith and obedience is an encouragement to me every time I remember it. Obey Jesus, even if it doesn't seem like the sensible thing to do. He knows what He is doing.

Dear Lord Jesus, please help me to always obey You knowing that You, the creator of all, know what is best.

Sue Breckbill and her husband John are life group leaders and coaches at Lives Changed By Christ, Manheim.

Jesus Loves Me, This I Know

"God is love. Whoever lives in love lives in God, and God in Him."
1 John 4:16

I put myself in a position to lose my daughter for good. My mother threatened she'd take her because of my alcohol abuse, pot smoking, running off with men for days and especially because I didn't have a home or job. One day my mother told me she was picking my daughter up and filing for full custody. I loved my daughter very much but there was something missing. So I told myself, "I can't do this anymore. I need to start over."

Going to a homeless shelter was my only choice. As soon as I arrived, I started learning about God. I knew I couldn't turn to alcohol, drugs or sex like I used to, so I turned to God. I started reading the Bible and praying every day. I learned so much about faith, forgiveness and especially love. That's when I realized what was missing in my life that I needed so badly . . . love. I felt love like never before when I accepted Christ in my life. Only then could I look back on how I used to live and realize that I was looking for love in the wrong places. One day I heard a woman quote a Bible verse that stuck with me. "I can do all things through Christ who strengthens me." (Philippians 4:13)

That is so true! Once God transformed my life, He showed me things I couldn't see while I was living in ignorance.

In less than two months I enrolled in college, got accepted to a housing program, got an apartment and quit smoking cigarettes! I took parenting classes and drug and alcohol counseling to show the court I was working hard to keep my daughter.

I believe God called me to the mission. He knew if I lost my daughter for good, I'd lose myself for good. So by His grace . . . He saved me.

Thank You, Father God, for always providing for me and loving me unconditionally.

Allyson Arlington (name changed to protect her identity) has moved out of the mission and is reconciled with her daughter.

Be Prepared

"Blessed are those who hunger and thirst for righteousness."
Matthew 5:6

As young mothers with small children, my neighbor and I were spending much time together as our children played. At twenty-eight years old, I had not accepted Jesus as my Savior. I went to church my whole life but did not know what a personal relationship with Jesus was.

My neighbor was a Christian. She was kindhearted, compassionate and had a gentle spirit. There was a peace about her that radiated whenever we were together and I knew she had something that I wanted. She would gently ask me, without judgment, about my spiritual life. It made me more curious about this peace that seemed to flow from her. One time she invited me to church. My family visited. What I saw and heard caused me to desire more and more until I finally understood what a personal relationship with Jesus meant. I confessed I was a sinner and I asked Jesus into my heart.

I learned a valuable lesson from this precious neighbor and it stays with me to this day. As Christians we need to realize that people are watching us. That it is important to be on our guard and set an example for others to see God in us. My neighbor's example touched me in a way that made me hunger and thirst for God. I saw something in her that I knew was missing in me. I am grateful for her example and her gentle spirit. I learned from her example to allow God's love to shine through me so that others may see God and desire a relationship too.

Dear God, help me to be the person You want me to be. May others see You in me so that they too may desire a relationship with You. God help me to be prepared to share with them the peace and joy You have provided me. Thank You Lord. Amen.

Cynthia Zimmerman attends New Life Fellowship Church, Ephrata. She and her husband Rick have two sons and one grandson.

Value Relationships

"The Lord God said, 'It is not good for the man to be alone . . . .'"
Genesis 2:18

My drive to work takes me past a development where I noticed something one day. In my short glimpse of the houses I could see sitting off the main road I was traveling, I counted at least six playsets. Many of them were less than twenty feet from each other due to the way their respective backyards adjoined. Sadly, most of the yards were surrounded by fences. I wondered if and how the children played together amongst the fences.

As I pondered what I'd just seen, I realized that the culture seems aimed at alienation. If I need a cup of sugar while in the middle of baking, I'll run to the store before asking a neighbor. The culture tells me I need to be self-sufficient. Facebook logs millions of interactions, but quenches the need for personal conversation. Based on its success, it seems the culture values the efficiency more. Even my schedule, filled with the things I am told I should be doing, leaves little time for investing in others.

God, however, designed us for relationship. He created Eve for Adam. The early church grew dramatically as people observed the beauty of Christian fellowship (see Acts 2:42-47). Even the plan of salvation is rooted in an individual's *relationship* with Jesus Christ. When we are alone, we become weak. Our influence is diminished, our convictions become vulnerable and our sense of purpose erodes. Isn't this the purpose of solitary confinement in prisons?

When these things happen, the light God placed in us when we became his follower grows dim and has little effect on the world. If I am going to influence the world for Jesus, I need to identify and tear down my culturally acceptable fences and focus on building relationships.

Jesus, help me to value people and relationships instead of the values of the culture. Help me to be salt and light in a lonely world.

Rebecca Nissly, Community Bible Church (Marietta), serves at Susquehanna Valley Pregnancy Services.

Landfill Lesson

". . . casting all your care upon Him, for He cares for you."
1 Peter 5:7 (New King James Version)

Buried treasure led me to the landfill. Not the prospect of unearthing treasure there, but the unexpected treasure uncovered beneath layer after layer of worn vinyl and linoleum on my kitchen floor. For under these layers of decades-old flooring laid a coveted hardwood floor. Once removed, the exposed wood was sanded and refinished. The result was a shining jewel.

My car was packed with garbage bags, heavy with asbestos-contaminated flooring. I headed to the landfill. Once there, my nose led the way toward the stench of rotting garbage. The sights, sounds and odors overwhelmed me. Trucks dumped their contents onto the growing pile, while a roaring bulldozer constantly shoveled the refuse onto the heap, relentlessly building a mountain. Once parked, I strained to drag my heavy garbage bags to the pile.

A metaphor came to mind. Why not throw away all the mental and emotional debris I've been struggling with—unexpected home repairs, people annoying me and on and on? I could throw all that toxic junk away just like I'm throwing away this flooring. So each bag was named for a difficult relationship or situation and cast onto the rubbish heap. The labor was backbreaking.

This purging of regret, anger and bitterness had been a spiritual experience. Doesn't God remove our sin and cast it away from us forever? His grace frees us and now I've dumped twice the expected garbage. The main difference is that God's grace is free, but I'll have to pay the landfill. Undaunted by this discrepancy, I rejoiced in my freedom.

At the weigh station, I was surprised when the attendant told me that I would not be charged. As my heavenly Father had forgiven my sins, likewise I felt released from these personal struggles. I savored my triumph as I headed home. This indeed had been a mountaintop experience!

Lord, thank You for inviting us to cast our care upon You.

Sally K. Owens lives with her husband Don in Lancaster, where they participate in two church fellowship groups.

The Rest of the Story

"For it is by grace you have been saved, through faith—and this not from yourselves, it is the gift of God—not by works, so that no one can boast." *Ephesians 2:8–9*

While sharing my landfill experience (yesterday's devotional) with a trusted friend, it occurred to me that I may have omitted an important part of the story. After mulling it over, I realized how crucial this missing piece really was to the landfill lesson.

As I struggled with two or three heavy bags at the landfield, a man appeared from nowhere with an offer of help. (Actually, he may have been a contractor unloading his pickup truck). I immediately protested his offer, for I was involved in serious emotional work. I've got to do this myself! But my groaning back and shoulders rebelled against the labor and when the stranger offered a second time, I reluctantly accepted. He effortlessly disposed of two bags at once, tossing them like twigs onto a bonfire. His strength amazed me. I felt robbed of my emotional work, but grateful for the needed assistance. I thanked him and he was gone.

Accepting God's free gift of grace, His unmerited favor, has been difficult for me. I feel compelled to do the work myself, to purge sin single-handedly, to gain credit for my efforts. In the original account I was too focused on my work and only partially perceived the full measure of God's grace. The authentic message at the landfill was the perfect illustration of my ignorance.

Now this event is shared with a different attitude—one of humility and gratitude. No longer, "look what I accomplished at the landfill," but "look what God graciously revealed to me at the landfill."

Father, thank You for Your salvation for which I can do nothing to gain. May I forever cherish Your gift of grace.

Sally K. Owens lives with her husband Don in Lancaster, where they participate in two church fellowship groups.

Perseverance

"You need to persevere so that when you have done the will of God, you will receive what he has promised." *Hebrews 10:36*

For the last couple of years I've been praying and agreeing with a very dear friend of mine for change to come in her life. She longed to not have to continue working the night-shift job she was currently working a couple nights a week. She looked forward to being able to be home with her children and pursue some of her dreams, being very talented with music, photography and design. And, she knew God also had more for her and her husband. The waiting was hard and change felt impossible at times.

Recently, I felt the Lord put it on my heart to get her a gift, but wasn't sure what. In one of our conversations, she told me about a bedspread she really liked at Target and she wanted a king-size set in hopes that they would get a new bed soon. I knew that's what I needed to get for her. By the time I actually went shopping, the set was marked down! Needless to say, I came home with the bedspread, plus a throw pillow that matched. *(All you ladies out there can relate to the excitement of getting that extra throw pillow for your bed, right?)* I dropped it off a few days later, but I had no idea of the bigger story and how God was working.

She told me a couple weeks later that the day I dropped off the bedspread was their anniversary! Then, she went on to tell me that she got an almost new king-sized bed on eBay for $1.25. And *then*, she went to Target to get some sheets and found the exact color and size she needed on a clearance sale! The story keeps getting better: her husband so graciously took her shift at work so she could be home!

Wow, what a faith-builder! God is good. All the time.

Father, help us to persevere through the hard times! May we never give up hope and learn to rest, knowing that You are for us and You have our best in mind.

Cindy Zeyak and her husband Ken reside in Manheim Township along with their two young sons.

Have You Been Zapped by God's Love?

"... may have the power, together with all the saints, to grasp how wide and long and high and deep is the love of Christ." *Ephesians 3:17*

My daughter is fascinated by the world of horses. This is due in part to my own love affair with them for as long as I can remember. The frustrating reality is that purchasing a horse and immersing ourselves into this hobby is financially out of our league.

We have been blessed to know some in the privileged crowd of horse owners. Because of their kindness, we have been able to indulge in this pleasure. Because we are frequent visitors at a friend's stable, my daughter has become enamored with a certain horse named Zap.

Recently, this friend approached me with her idea to give Zap to my daughter as a birthday present. I immediately began wrestling with whether it was appropriate to accept such an extravagant gift. How could I ever pay back this friend? Why would she even consider doing this for us? Strong feelings of pride and unworthiness competed with my heart's desire to shout, "Yes! Yes! Yes!" After an intense wrestling match, my heart did win over my head and my daughter was "zapped" with the most amazing birthday gift ever!

Watching my daughter receive her gift with happy tears in her eyes, I was struck by the contrast of our responses. I heard God speak to my heart, "Receive my gifts of love for you in the same way as your daughter receives her gift." There is no need for me to resist His extravagant grace in Christ Jesus. Even though I am not worthy, He does choose to ZAP me with His love in ways perfectly designed for my enjoyment.

Lord, You are the giver of all good things and we thank You. May we wrap our arms around Your many gifts of love in the same joyful, uninhibited way that my daughter demonstrated for us.

Teresa Siegrist serves alongside her husband Wes, who is the pastor at Erb Mennonite Church in Lititz.

What's for Dinner?

"But the fruit of the Spirit is love, joy, peace, patience, kindness, goodness, faithfulness, gentleness and self-control."
Galatians 5:22–23

It was a hectic day that sometimes a hostess can find herself in when she invites someone to dinner and decides to cook something new. I found I needed some ingredients that I don't keep on hand so off I went to the market.

I had to search more than usual for what I wanted and was now running late. Finally, as I was checking out I glanced at the groceries of the person next in line and then I remembered I had missed buying the mushrooms I needed!

Without thinking I said loudly, "Oh no, I forgot the mushrooms!"

And then it happened. One of those examples of the fruit of the Spirit in action. This dear woman turns to me and says, "Here, take mine as I don't want to see you have to get in line again."

I was so stunned by her act of kindness that I stammered something like, "Oh, thank you, but I couldn't." But she insisted in such a kind and sincere manner that she disarmed my resistance and I gratefully accepted her mushrooms.

This seems like such a simple story, but for me it was profound. The profound part was that I honestly don't think I would have ever thought to do such a random act of kindness. On that day, my fellow grocery shopper put a smile on my face and a warm feeling in my heart.

I have related this story to several people and told them I felt the Lord's gentle reminder that living the fruit of the Spirit each day blesses Him, blesses others and blesses us. I pray that after receiving such kindness that I will now have a whole new awareness and will not miss future opportunities to be kinder.

By the way, the new recipe I prepared was extra delicious if I do say so myself!

Lord, thank You for the amazing truths You teach us in such simple ways.

Patti Wilcox serves with Good Works, Inc.

Finding the Way

"Jesus said to him, 'I am the way, the truth, and the life. No one comes to the Father except through Me.'" *John 14:6 (New King James Version)*

I love maps. People keep telling me that I need to get a GPS, but I really do not want to give up my maps. Because of the ministry we serve, Jimmy and I have traveled in all fifty states and most of Canada. In the past thirty-nine years of these ventures, we have always had our trusty atlas with us.

God has given us His Word to be a map for our lives. His Word is Truth, and as we follow His map, our lives are filled with true life!

My family did not travel much when I was a little girl, but I hoped life might give me a few vacations where I could travel. I never dreamed that this desire God had placed in me would send me all over the country and around the world to bring Him glory!

As I grew up, God put His Truth in my heart concerning the incredible value of human life. He placed me in pro-life ministry and gave me the grace to share and experience the beauty of life with thousands of people around the country. We have been on interstates, back roads and dirt roads. We have traveled by train, plane, ship and car. The Lord has provided the way, I spoke His Truth and as a result there has been much life!

Jesus truly is the way, the truth and the life. I cannot imagine life without Him, and I am thankful for the Word of God which guides my heart, and my maps which guide my way. Put God's truth and calling in your heart and have fun on the journey He takes you!

Thank You, God, for this wonderful world You have created for us. Thank You for the Truth that Your Word brings. Give us grace to serve You and our world as we work to bring the Kingdom of God to earth. Amen.

Anne Pierson is the executive director of Loving and Caring, Inc., a ministry that works to resolve fatherless issues around the world.

Releasing Our Fruit

"Through Jesus, therefore, let us continually offer to God a sacrifice of praise—the fruit of lips that confess his name. And do not forget to do good and to share with others, for with such sacrifices God is pleased." *Hebrews 13:15, 16*

Our church was in the midst of searching for our mission and transitioning into our calling to be a ministry to the community. Our deacon had contacted a local choir for the evening service. After the second song I was to have some words of welcome and prayer.

To start the program, the leader came in alone. Then the choir came in waving flags and praising the Lord. It was a new experience for our congregation. As a young pastor, I prayed for wisdom. The Lord opened my eyes to see that the choir members were young people many of whom were teenagers. They came to praise the Lord when many of their age group would not have been in church.

That evening as we responded to the Spirit of God in worship, we could feel a new joy and awe filling our hearts. So many times we have closed our hearts and bodies to what God wants to do by saying, "We didn't do it this way before." As leaders we need to open the door for the Spirit. We had a feeling of the presence of God as we worshipped. Worship in Spirit and Truth will cut right through our emotions when we release our bodies to worship.

Praise God for an evening of worship that changed my heart and my attitude.

Thank You, Lord, for the times you have helped me to open my heart to walk closer to You. It is Your joy that fills my heart as I come into Your presence. Help me to open my heart to worship You in spirit and in truth. Amen.

Glenn Hoover and his wife Ginny serve on the leadership team at Carpenter Community Church.

Oceans of Love

"For this reason I bow my knees to the Father of our Lord Jesus Christ ... that you, being rooted and grounded in love, may be able to comprehend with all the saints what *is* the width and length and depth and height ... to know the love of Christ which passes knowledge; that you may be filled with all the fullness of God." *Ephesians 3:14,19 (New King Jsmes Version)*

In 2008, my husband and I were part of a group from our denomination that was enjoying a Bermuda cruise. The group Bible studies in the book of Jonah and the fellowship was great, but one of my best memories came about from the first morning at sea. The evening before, we stood on deck and watched the New York skyline slip past as we left. We had an outside stateroom, and when I woke up the next morning, all I could see was wave after wave of the ocean. We were totally surrounded by water.

I couldn't help but think that we, as Christians, are often like someone who chooses to stay on land and just look out at the bit of water he can see from there. We experience some of God and all that He is, and it seems good. But until we leave the safety of shore to become totally surrounded by Him, we will never know the full blessing of giving ourselves to Him 100 percent. Even when we go through some storms and rough seas, we are assured of His presence with us, His protection, power and guidance.

Are you willing to leave the safety of shore to commit to God totally, to experience His presence completely surrounding you?

Dear Father, thank You for Your presence with us. I pray that we will each begin to know You more and more as we take steps away from shore and into the vast ocean of Your love.

Diane Kirkpatrick and her husband Kevin serve Berean Bible Fellowship Church in Terre Hill as pastor and pastor's wife.

June

You Call Yours a Popsicle?

"I am telling you this so no one will deceive you with well-crafted arguments." *Colossians 2:4 (New Living Translation)*

Sometimes kids say and do the cutest things, and my youngest granddaughter is no exception! She loves Popsicles, and one day she asked her mom for one. The only box left in the freezer was some fat-free, sugar-free version that my daughter and I bought on a whim one time. I had told my daughter they tasted terrible and not to waste her taste buds on them. She warned my granddaughter about them, but the packaged picture of a Popsicle was too enticing. She wanted it anyway.

She took one lick, held the Popsicle up in front of her and said, "You call yourself a Popsicle?" She promptly marched over to the trash can and threw it away. She knew the "real deal" and was not about to be deceived into eating a counterfeit one!

I couldn't help but think that we need to be more like that spiritually. We should not settle for less than the best, not choosing well-crafted packaging or well-crafted arguments that try to deceive us.

Jesus said, "I am the Way, the Truth and the Life and no man can come to the Father except through me." (John 14:6) Jesus is the visible image of the invisible God. He is the Real Deal! Making Jesus Lord of all and keeping our eyes and minds in His Word will help us from being deceived or disappointed. This world has so many distractions, counterfeits, deceptions, especially in what we believe and do. That is not God's best. "Be not conformed to this world, but be transformed by the renewing of your mind in Christ Jesus so you will know God's good, pleasing and perfect will." (Romans 12:2)

Lord, help us renew our minds daily in Your Word and fill us with Your spirit, so we will not be deceived!

Jeanette Weaver is a wife, mother of two, grandma of six and serves along with her husband Don at DOVE Westgate Church as deacon and small group leaders.

God's Surprise!

"O taste and see that the Lord is good." *Psalm 34:8*

It was a sad time for my daughter, son-in-law and me. At that time, their daughter was crazy about black-and-white cows and the Christian books that featured them. This set of books was costly, and neither her parents nor I could afford to purchase them for her as a birthday present.

That weekend while we waited for other family members to reconnect with us, I was talking to the Lord. I was lamenting that I was frustrated that I couldn't purchase the books for her, knowing that she would glean much from them. Sensing my despondency, my granddaughter wandered back to the entrance of the bookstore.

Suddenly, she rushed back to me, telling me that there was a contest being held in the middle of the mall in a few minutes, and the winner would receive the entire set of "cow" books. Rushing to that area, while reconnecting with the rest of the family on the way, she barely had time to enter the contest before the winner was chosen. Providentially, she was the winner! We began to cry for joy, as we were reminded that the Lord delights to give good gifts to His children.

We shared with my granddaughter that although we had all wanted to bless her with the books, the Lord, her heavenly Father, wanted to give them to her in a very special way to show her how much He loved her. It became a very special weekend as we were all reminded of His love, faithfulness and perfect timing. Most importantly, my granddaughter's relationship with the Lord has grown in the years since she received that blessing. Her faith in Him has increased, and His faithfulness has blessed her with a substantial college scholarship for the next four years.

Thank You, Lord, for reminding us that sometimes You prevent us from meeting someone's need, because You want to meet it—and increase their faith in You.

Denise Colvin and her husband Rich, who is a pastor at The Villa Chapel in West Reading, are blessed with four daughters and ten grandchildren.

Oh No, Lord, Not Again, Please!

"For our light and momentary troubles are achieving for us an eternal glory that far outweighs them all." *2 Corinthians 4:17*

"Not again, Lord. Please not again!" I pleaded. I couldn't believe my dear husband was being admitted to the hospital again. Four different times in the past four months he spent a week in the hospital, not to mention doctor visits and chemo treatments several times a week.

It began with a routine twice-a-year blood work with his cardiac doctors. He always had midline blood results and other than "our years are slowing us down days," we both seemed to be okay. About a half an hour after the blood work, we got a call, "Take Lew to the emergency room immediately. He is very anemic. We'll meet you there."

The cardiologists called in a hematologist/oncologist who later explained Lew had non-Hodgkins Lymphoma. He would be admitted to start treatment.

Added to that concern was the fact that we owned several businesses we needed to take care of!

The questions came in bunches, but not the answers. Confusions and despair fogged our minds. I would stay with him, even many times overnight, to encourage and comfort him. Days turned into nights and then more tests and treatments. But we turned it all over to the Lord.

Our dear pastors, neighbors, hospital chaplains and friends ministered to us. Such an outpouring of blessed love! How could we not believe in a cure?

Then a heart attack … then an intestinal bleed … then a trip to Johns Hopkins Hospital in Baltimore for another procedure. It was so overwhelming. In answer to prayer, God supplied family to get the work done at home in this very busy time of spring work. God is faithful!

Now another admission from another side effect of the chemo. I prayed again, but inside I knew we would get through all of this in His timing. We would definitely learn lessons He has for us in all of this!

Dear Lord, we must trust Your every word and simply put ourselves in Your care, custody and control. We know Your great grace and love will sustain us.

Jackie Bowser is a member of DOVE Westgate Church, Ephrata.

Hope and Forgiveness

"Is not this the kind of fasting I have chosen: to loose the chains of injustice and untie the cords of the yoke, to set the oppressed free and break every yoke? Is it not to share your food with the hungry and to provide the poor wanderer with shelter—when you see the naked, to clothe him, and not to turn away from your own flesh and blood? Then your light will break forth like the dawn, and your healing will quickly appear; then your righteousness will go before you, and the glory of the Lord will be your rear guard. Then you will call, and the Lord will answer; you will cry for help, and he will say: Here am I." *Isaiah 58:6–9*

On a recent medical mission trip to Iraq, I was drawn to the scripture in Isaiah encouraging true fasting to include service to the poor, the hungry, the homeless and to those suffering from injustice.

While we ministered to many with medical care and prayer, I was particularly amazed to learn of the plight of the Kurdish people in northern Iraq. We heard stories of many injustices done to them especially during the past twenty years under the regime of Saddam Hussein. We heard of thousands buried alive and stories of thousands killed by chemical weapons. Yet, these people demonstrated hearts full of hopefulness and forgiveness.

Our team felt real freedom to build relationships, to pray and to serve these dear people in northern Iraq who have been oppressed through the years for being Kurds. Some have even been martyred for their faith in Jesus.

Join me in praying for the people of Iraq including the Kurdish people in the north. Pray for peace, prosperity and continued freedom to preach the good news of Jesus.

Father, help us to loose the chains of injustice, to serve the poor and hungry. Give us Your heart of compassion as we serve the world around us.

Dr. Scott Jackson serves as the coordinator of DMI Medical Missions. He works as a family physician at Crossroads Medical Center and also serves as an elder at Oasis Fellowship in Akron.

JUNE 5

Cake in Heaven

"... I looked and there before me was a great multitude that no one could count, from every nation, tribe, people and language, standing before the throne and in front of the Lamb." *Revelation 7:9*

"Mommy, will there be cake in heaven?" my curious three-year-old daughter asked.

"Of course, sweetie, there will be a big wedding feast and where there's a wedding, there's cake!" I explained.

A few months after our conversation, a new couple from Indonesia started attending our church. They were fresh out of college and very much in love. Their joyful spirits and genuine smiles were evidence that their love for each other was eclipsed only by their love for the Lord. My daughter took to them right away, even naming two of her dolls after them.

Then I got the call from a friend asking for prayer. Yusnan, whom everyone liked so much, was killed in a car crash. It just didn't make any sense. How could this intelligent, talented young man with a promising future ahead of him be gone? I grieved the loss of my friend, and I dreaded telling my innocent little girl.

Finally, I put my hands on her tiny shoulders, looked into her huge brown eyes and told her that her friend had gone to heaven. She clenched her fists, stomped her foot and exclaimed, "That's not right! He has to come back to marry Mega!" I shook my head and with tears in my eyes, I explained that a person couldn't come back from heaven.

Then she looked at me and matter-of-factly stated, "Don't worry, Mommy, you said that we'll all be up in heaven for that big wedding."

Lord Jesus, help me to remember that this world is not my home. Thank You that You have a plan, and I will someday see my loved ones again.

Leah McKelvey is married to Ed and is mom to two amazing preschoolers. Leah is a volunteer counselor at the Columbia Pregnancy Center and a youth leader for New Christian Fellowship in Marietta.

Basic Survival

"As the deer pants for streams of water, so my soul pants for you, O God. My soul thirsts for God, for the living God. When can I go and meet with God?" *Psalm 42:1–2*

I hesitated, thinking I should change my mind about plunging into this dark hole full of cold, gurgling water. Bob and I were in Israel, touring the region of Jerusalem called the City of David, and before me Hezekiah's Tunnel dared me to enter.

About 700 B.C., this winding 1,750-foot tunnel was hewn through the bedrock to provide a water source for the people inside Jerusalem's walls and to deny water to the Assyrian army during an impending siege. King Hezekiah devised a plan to divert the water from the Gihon Spring, which was outside the city walls, to the Pool of Siloam inside the walls using a six percent gradient. Two teams started excavating at each end to "meet in the middle." If each team had dug in a straight line, the tunnel would have been forty percent shorter.

During our wade through the tunnel, we were amazed at the time and manpower it cost the Israelites to complete such an undertaking through solid rock. The importance and value of ancient "means of survival" began to penetrate our Western "have it your way, now" microwave mentality.

We visited more archaeological sites, all having tunnels or cisterns to ensure a "safe from enemies" water supply for that city.

Later, a visit to the oasis and springs of En Gedi in the Judean Desert highlighted the contrast between its flora and fauna, and the nearby wasteland of the Dead Sea. No wonder David chose to hide there while fleeing from King Saul. What a refreshing refuge!

The Psalmist, a son of Korah, likens the deer's need for water to sustain its life to the human soul's need of the living God, our source of spiritual life. He, like David, experienced many hostile deserts and realized his needy thirst was quenched only by the One True Oasis—Jehovah God.

Father, help us to realize just how much we really need You, and that the oasis of Your presence far exceeds the cost of our time.

Tamalyn Jo Heim enjoys traveling with her husband Bob and "traveling after" their two-year-old grandson Isaac.

Choosing to Trust

"Surely, He has took our infirmities and carried our sorrows . . . ."
Isaiah 53:4

This past year has probably been the worst year of my family's life. Our dear son "Abie" died in a car accident in South Dakota.

Our son was only twenty-three years old and starting his career, having hopes to get a PhD in zoology or ornithology. The night before the accident, he called us and talked for an hour. We had no idea that it would be our last conversation.

Suddenly, we were overwhelmed with having to make decisions about the funeral service, grave plot and coffin. How could a good God allow this to happen to us? We were faithful in serving the Lord and our son loved God as well. Why did He take him? Is God cruel and capricious? After many nights of anguished prayer, all we heard was silence.

We have never known such grief before. It overwhelms us unexpectedly at the strangest times and places. Months later, we still feel as if our hearts are horribly broken and will never be the same. Yes, we are thankful Abie is with the Lord—but that does not take away the pain. Our lives have been shattered, and we will carry this grief until our own dying day.

Yet, we trust God. Though our lives have been torn asunder, we need to hold on to Him—even through the darkest days. We need to be like Job, who after his ten children were slain, said, "The Lord giveth and the Lord taketh away—blessed be the name of the Lord. Though he slay me, yet will I trust Him."

These words are easier said than believed. Nevertheless, these words are true and we choose to hold on to them.

The Lord never promised to make our lives easy—but He will walk with us every step of the way.

Lord, someday, we will know the answer. But now, we choose to trust and obey.

Jim Schneck is a freelance interpreter for the deaf, the husband of Rosalee and a doctorate student.

Owning Up and Turning toward God

"... her sins—and they are many—have been forgiven, so she has shown me much love." *Luke 7:47 (New Living Translation)*

I was thinking about Mary who'd been forgiven much and had been able to love lavishly. I always thought it just depended on how bad you were that made the difference. But then it hit me, the important point in the matter is to make certain that whatever sin I have, whether it's eigthy-five or five percent my fault, I must own up to it and turn from it. Then I'd know forgiveness as God's love meets my need. Through His example, I'll be able to love others as He loved me.

Some time ago when I was young and trying to make my mark as a Christian, I tried to look good, be right and act like I had it all together even when bad times hit. I tried everything I could to get myself out of a bad situation, but to no avail. It was only when I got a glimpse of God's unconditional love that I was humbled and motivated to take a step of faith. I sought out a person who had never really talked to me and who I had drawn away from throughout my life ... my own father. I owned up to my part of the problem and took the time to just ask questions and listen to him.

That simple act of owning up to my part of the problem and turning towards God changed me from someone trying to impress people to someone who just wanted to love them. I was able to meet others with open arms, the way God came to me. As in the case of Mary, without saying a word but loving much, that act transformed my entire life and has continued to multiply, changing the lives of people surrounding me.

Father, help me own up to my sins, no matter how small, so I can know the depths of Your love which endures forever.

Jere Mellinger serves as a greeter at LCMI.

How Is Your Garden?

"But some fell on good soil and produced a crop that was thirty, sixty, and even a hundred times as much as he had planted." *Matthew 13:8 (The Living Bible)*

I think two phrases pretty well sum up what the Lord has called us to do: to grow people and expand the kingdom of God.

Let me drill down on the "growing people" piece. I was a farmer for many years and focused on was growing plants. My success as a farmer was dependent on my ability to grow crops that produced as much as they could. Let me emphasize, I always believed for a harvest for every seed that I sowed, no exceptions. There are some real spiritual connotations there. Every time I sowed something, I was expecting a return. Why do we accept anything less in the kingdom?

For a seed to grow, I needed to place it in the right environment. That environment needed to cause the seed to germinate and take root. For things to grow it takes variations and combinations of a number of things, like dirt, nutrients, rain, sunshine, light and darkness; a combination of things that at times can be uncomfortable. Soaking wet, baking hot sun, cool nights and dirty surroundings make for growing healthy plants that produce well. In fact, if we had a summer that in our natural eye was a "perfect summer," yielding tall corn, but there was no substantial root system, a storm might come in the fall and before we could get the corn off, we would lose a lot in the field.

For us to grow spiritually, we need a variation of things, or the right environment to cause growth. We need to teach people that growth is not always comfortable, but it is the most beneficial in the long run.

Our goal in "growing people" is to place them in an environment that causes them to grow spiritually, not the one that preserves them where they are at. As I asked in the beginning, "How is your garden?" What I am really asking is how are your people growing? Are you keeping things constant to preserve them, or are you adding variation to cause growth? Grow the people the Lord has given you and the garden will increase. Then the kingdom of God will expand.

Lord, help us to develop strong roots so we may grow and expand the kingdom of God.

Ron Myer is assistant international director of DOVE Christian Fellowship International.

Peekaboo!

". . . which is Christ in you, the hope of glory." *Colossians 1:27*

Can one look, one glimpse of the face of Christ on earth as in heaven, heal and transform?

Here we were in the malnourished-baby ward of a hospital in Swaziland. This was our team's idea of a safari to find the one God had sent us to love.

We walked throughout the hospital giving oranges and toys, playing little lullaby songs on the harmonica and praying for mothers, grandmothers and children. Suddenly, we saw two little babies more the size of sick kittens than of human beings. We were told one child was eight months old and one was ten months. They were born malnourished and had never left the confines of that room. Neither of them could have weighed more than two or three pounds. They were lying on their backs connected to breathing tubes as their concerned and fearful young mothers sat at their feet.

Suddenly, Hannah, the dynamic fifteen-year-old on our team let out a spontaneous "peekaboo" as she shook her blonde curls over the babies' faces. The response was clearly miraculous—a baby giggle coming out of this little one who could barely breathe! Over and over with every peekaboo came this resounding contagious giggle. The mother was so delighted! We were so amazed! That laughter is etched into my heart forever.

As I ponder those moments, I wonder if God has surely programmed us to delight. Perhaps we recognize that no matter what our size or circumstance, we can see the face of God in another. How can we not respond with sheer exuberance?

The cordial invitation to laughter came that day through one youth so alive with God's love that a lifeless child could not help but respond.

Dear Lord, today may we reflect Your joy all the more and want to be Your peekaboo face to a dying world.

Nancy Clegg is a worshipper and mobilizer in the body of Christ throughout the nations.

Stir Up the Gift

"I remind you to fan into flame the gift of God, which is in you through the laying on of my hands. For God did not give us a spirit of timidity, but a spirit of power, of love and of self-discipline."
2 Timothy 1:6–7

Various translations use different wording for "stir up, fan into flames, keep your gift ablaze, made full use of the gift, rekindle the gift, stir up the inner fire and keep alive the gift." Timothy was timid. So many Christians are timid especially when it comes to obeying the great commission. Remember the great commission is the not the great suggestion. It is a commandment for every Christian.

Paul writes: "Exercise daily in God—no spiritual flabbiness, please! Workouts in the gymnasium are useful, but a disciplined life in God is far more so, making you fit both today and forever." According to 1 Timothy 4:7, Paul commands, "Train yourself to be godly."

In the New Testament, believers are described as being bold or encouraged to be bold twice as often as they are told to be humble. The disciples were timid, and lacked courage before the resurrection. Compare that to Peter's boldness on the day of Pentecost. Look at how the early church turned the world upside down. As the Christians were scattered they went everywhere preaching the word.

The devil has de-passioned us. He has robbed us of our power. We must stir up the gift of the Holy Spirit in us. Pray for God to give you eyes to see opportunities and then to take the risk to follow through. It may not feel comfortable at first but learn to go with the flow of the Holy Spirit. That's when life becomes exciting as you bear fruit for our Lord.

Lord Jesus, I will fan into flame the gifts You have given me. I will move out in faith as the Holy Spirit leads me. Amen.

J. David Eshleman is pastor, professor, church planter and author of *Living with Godly Passion*.

Truth

"Then you will know the truth, and the truth will set you free."
John 8:32

Just as I was about to leave for a dental appointment my unit manager called stating that my registered nurse license would expire in three days. I had renewed it online three months prior and said I would bring her the hard copy. I went to get my hard copy but the only one I could find was the expiring one.

When I returned from the dentist, I went online and no renewal was on record since 2008. I sent an e-mail to the Pennsylvania State Board of Nursing explaining my situation. I received a response that said my renewal was on hold. I received a second email message stating that I had answered "yes" to the question "Do you have a criminal conviction?" If this was answered incorrectly, I needed to fax a document indicating the error. I faxed a letter quickly. Within two days my license was renewed and I was free to continue practicing my profession of thirty-nine years!

This incident reminds me of two spiritual truths. First, God allows us to make things right when we do wrong. Secondly, when we know the truth, we are set free to serve and worship God.

Thank You, Lord, for Your redemption and truth and for the freedom we have to serve You. Amen.

Ginny Hoover is the wife of Pastor Glenn Hoover of Carpenter Community Church and works in the Recovery Room at The Heart of Lancaster Regional Medical Center.

Why Not?

"Jesus looked at them and said, 'With man this is impossible, but with God all things are possible.'" *Matthew 19:26*

As my husband and I anxiously await the arrival of our second child, I can't help but think back to the birth of our first one. Although it was two and a half years ago, it still seems like yesterday. And there are two incidences that stick out in my mind.

The first one was when the doctor came in to check on me when I was in labor. He mentioned that the baby would probably be around seven pounds. Being short in stature, I couldn't imagine that my baby would weigh quite that much. I asked, "Are you serious?" The doctor's immediate response was, "Yeah, why not?"

I didn't know how to respond, so I said nothing.

The second incident happened a day or two after my son was born, and I was still in the hospital. The very first doctor I met after I found out I was pregnant came in to see how I was doing and take a look at Caleb. The last thing he said to me before he left was, "You better enjoy him while you can, because it probably will be hard for you or take you awhile to get pregnant again."

But here we are, over two years later, expecting a little baby girl. And I am left with the same question, but only this time I am saying it to myself, "Why not? Why wouldn't you, Lord, in Your loving- kindness, bless us with another child? If it's in Your plan, nothing the doctor can say will stop You."

May the same be true in your life as well. May you be faced with the same question as why not? And may you realize that our God is a big God and nothing is impossible with Him.

Heavenly Father, thank You for those times that you remind us of just how great and powerful You are. Amen.

Jenn Paules works part-time for WJTL but more importantly is a full-time wife and mother.

The God of Jacob

"Happy is he who has the God of Jacob for his help, whose hope is in the Lord his God." *Psalm 146:5 (New King James Version)*

Jacob came out of the womb grasping the heel of his elder brother Esau. Into his adult years his reputation as a schemer and deceiver grew. He knew how to make a deal to his advantage. He traded for his elder brother's birthright and "took his place" to obtain his father's blessing.

Jacob's deceptive ways were part of a generational pattern that was evident in Abraham, Isaac and his Uncle Laban. He made the most of the inherited tendency as a breeder and manager of Laban's flocks.

On the way to his homeland, and facing the prospect of meeting his estranged brother Esau, Jacob met God. In an extended wrestling match with a godly messenger, Jacob finally came to the end of his strength, self-effort, manipulation, and control. More than gaining an advantage, Jacob chose to yield to God and persist in receiving the blessing of God.

In meeting God in this way, Jacob's character was transformed. God changed his name to call forth in him a new identity and character. He was now Israel (prince with God) one who rules his life through the power, strength, and grace of God.

Even so, God chose to identify Himself as the God of Jacob in the Scriptures centuries later. He did so as a picture of acceptance and hope in His capacity to transform an individual as He brings that person to a point of exchange of their own life for His.

What truth or characteristic of God may be revealed through your life story if God were to show Himself as the God of (fill in your name)?

God of Jacob, we put our hope in Your help to transform us unto the identity and purpose You have for us. Amen.

Keith Yoder, founder and president of Teaching The Word Ministries and member of The Worship Center, serves in leadership with the Regional Church of Lancaster County.

Accepted by the Father

"For the kingdom of God is not eating and drinking, but righteousness and peace and joy in the Holy Spirit. For he who serves Christ in these things is acceptable to God and approved by men." *Romans 14:17–18 (New King James Version)*

Growing up in a large farm family, my siblings and I could never measure up to our abusive father's expectations. We never worked hard enough or smart enough to please Pop. As a result, I strived to do everything perfectly, becoming a perfectionist. It was many years after I left home and married that the Lord lovingly showed me that perfectionism was not a positive trait to cultivate but rather a trap of the enemy to bring discouragement into my life, and it needed to be eradicated.

As I set out to break this stronghold in my life, with the Lord's strength and wisdom, it dawned on me that the reason I struggled to complete jobs and procrastinated on projects was that I spent too much time trying to figure out how to do them perfectly. God showed me that His standard is excellence, not perfection. Our Lord Jesus was the only perfect one to ever live on this earth. No matter how hard I tried to do my best, it is still far short of the mark of perfection. When I turned my life fully over to the Lord, before Him I was innocent and faultless. As a result of His gift of righteousness, I could live a life of peace and joy, enjoying the freedom that comes from being a child of the heavenly Father. What a productive way to live!

Gracious heavenly Father, I thank You for the freedom You purchased for me by Your shed blood on the cross and Your resurrection from the grave. I rejoice in Your acceptance of me, imperfect as I am. Help me always to be aware of Your gift of love.

Grace Arnold is a retired homemaker and a member of DOVE Westgate Church, volunteering in the nursery and other areas of ministry.

Broken Shells

". . . looking up to heaven, he gave thanks and broke the loaves."
Matthew 14:19

At the beach, my husband and I walked along the shore gathering broken shells. Why? The shells were useful to us. We wanted to use broken clam shells as mulch for the paths between our garden beds. The shells break down even more as feet walk on them, providing useful and attractive white mulch.

The broken shells reminded me of how God uses broken things. Jesus broke five little loaves of bread that a young boy had given, and more than five thousandcpeople were fed. Mary broke a bottle of expensive perfume to anoint Jesus, and the fragrance filled the room. Jesus said that her story would be told wherever the gospel reached.

Toward the end of Jesus' earthly life, He said, "This [broken bread] is my body, which is broken for you. . . ." and our redemption was sealed.

David said in Psalm 51:17, "The sacrifices of God are a broken spirit . . . and a contrite heart."

Does your heart feel like a broken shell? Maybe you've even felt the crush of feet walking over you. If so, be encouraged that God can use you. He heals the brokenhearted (Psalm 147:3). He can take the broken pieces that are yielded to Him and use them to miraculously feed others. The fragrance of Jesus will be shed abroad as you share your testimony and allow God to use your life for His glory.

Lord, as difficult as it is, I give You thanks today for the broken areas of my heart. I yield them to You. Use my life for Your glory.

Jane Nicholas lives in Elizabethtown with her husband Bill. They are part of the Evangelical Free Church of Hershey.

Father's Day Keeper

"And my God will meet all your needs according to his glorious riches in Christ Jesus." *Philippians 4:19*

"I want to send a Father's Day card," said Bob.

"But we don't have the money," I answered.

In fact we didn't have much money for anything.

The news about the card, however, hit Bob pretty hard. So he sat on the couch and ran fingers through his hair.

After a few minutes, I made a suggestion. "We have paper and envelopes, why don't you write a letter to your dad and tell him how much you love and appreciate him." Bob brightened at the idea and went to his typewriter.

Our boys and I were working on a homemade card for Bob. During the day when he was at work, we had a lot of fun creating pages with pictures, poems and cutout captions. It actually was turning into more than a card, more like a collage booklet.

Bob busily typed away in the other room. Later in the evening, he produced a letter for me to read. He'd even typed it with few mistakes.

The letter was warm and witty—truly reflecting Bob's affection and sense of humor—a gift he inherited from his Dad. They joked more than they hugged.

"Your dad will treasure this letter above any card you could buy for him," I said, choking back tears.

Nine years later after the memorial service, as we went through Dad's things, there was the letter. One hand written word was scrawled at the top of the page: "Keep"!

Lord, help us to remember that sometimes our lack of finances is really a blessing in disguise.

Kathy Scott is a freelance writer and editor, a member of Calvary Church and a Stonecroft Ministries coordinator and Bible study guide.

Love, Dad

"For God did not give us a spirit of timidity, but a spirit of power, of love and of self-discipline." *2 Timothy 1:7*

I had only met Mary twice. She was a friend of my daughter. They had met as members of the New Life Drama Company. Mary's mother had died when Mary was in her teens, and her father died while she was on tour with the drama company. She was now living in Indiana with extended family. Her dream of life was to get married and have a family, and that seemed to be within her grasp. When the engagement was broken, the dream fell apart.

When I sat down for lunch that day, I saw a letter on the table addressed to my daughter from Mary. As I glanced at it, a question jumped out at me. "I need your advice. Should I demand of God that He give me a husband or should I resign myself to being miserable the rest of my life?"

I asked Andi for Mary's email address, sent Mary some advice and signed it "Love, Dad." As I hit the Send button, I immediately thought, *that is the dumbest thing I have ever done in my life. I barely know the girl, and I had signed the letter "Love, Dad."*

Within a day I got a response. It began "Dear Papa Hershey. You have opened up in my life something I thought I had buried a long time ago: the need for a father." That began five years of weekly emails. Mary lives in my house now as a constant reminder that God did not call us to be timid, but to take the risk of failure and rejection so that He can work.

Father give me the courage to stand up and speak Your truth when everything in me calls out for me to take the safe route and to remain silent.

Steve Hershey is a teacher and speaker at White Oak Church of the Brethren. Steve and his wife Brenda have opened their home to young adults.

The Net that Catches Us

"How great is the love the Father has lavished on us, that we should be called children of God!" *1 John 3:1*

Father's Day is a day to honor our dads and our heavenly Father. It can be a day of good or bad memories depending on our relationships.

A few years back I was sitting in church listening to the pastor go through a list of positive attributes of a father. I started to unfairly compare my dad to the list that was being presented.

The Holy Spirit arrested my spirit and gave me a picture of trapeze artists. One began to swing while the other waited to catch the first by either the feet or hands. Instead of catching the person, they were dropped and into the net they fell. The Holy Spirit then said to me, "I want to be that net Diana; where other relationship let you down, I want to be the net that catches you. I am Your all in all."

Within seconds I got a different perspective. I was set free in my expectations of holding others to a degree of perfectionism that is unobtainable. I was set free to love and accept others, including myself for imperfection; understanding where we lack, the Lord makes up the difference.

We are all capable of letting each other down at times, knowing and unknowingly, due to our human nature. Our Father God is more than able to catch us in those times, to dust us off and encourage us to forgive and to try again. He is our heavenly Father that fulfills all the positive attributes on all our perfect "Human Day" lists. As we look to Him may we walk in grace and forgiveness in all our relationships.

Happy Father's Day, Dad, and to all fathers out there!

Father God, we love and appreciate You. Thank You for being our net that breaks the fall when we let each other down. Help us to forgive, knowing that You are our all in all!

Diana Sheehan is a wife, mom of three and attends DOVE Westgate.

Abba Never Fails

"When you are in distress and all these things have come upon you, in the latter days you will return to the LORD your God and listen to His voice. For the Lord your God is a compassionate God; He will not fail you. . . ." *Deuteronomy 4:30–31 (New American Standard Version)*

In church on Father's Day, the pastor called all the children forward for a special Father's Day story. The sanctuary was silent as he spoke.

"Did you know," he began, "that daddies aren't perfect?"

"MY daddy is perfect!" my son's voice piped out.

The people in the pews roared with laughter as my husband emphatically shook his head, "no."

"No, not even *your* daddy is perfect," the pastor said with a smile.

Father's Day is a wonderful time to remember our daddies, to thank them for what they do for us and to spend one specific day a year focused on Dad. But not everyone has good feelings and memories about their father. Some people feel a great deal of resentment on that day. For others, it's simply another day on the calendar.

However, there *is* a daddy who's perfect. Deuteronomy 32:4 says, "The Rock! His work is perfect, for all His ways are just; a God of faithfulness and without injustice, righteous and upright is He."

Our Father in heaven is perfect. We may not always understand His ways, life doesn't always make sense and we may feel like blaming God for life's imperfections. But God is always with us, that perfect Daddy whose hands constantly reach for us, whose arms long to enfold us, that tender voice that calls out to us.

Abba Father, may we look to You when our earthly fathers don't meet our expectations. May we trust in Your everlasting faithfulness and turn to Your loving embrace when we're hurting. Thank You for blessing us with daddies who want to be like You. Amen.

Jennifer Hamilton is a wife and mommy with a passion for writing. The Hamilton family is raising support to serve as missionaries in Peru.

Unique Father's Day Present

"I am the good shepherd: I know my sheep and my sheep know me—just as the Father knows me and I know the Father."
John 10:14–15

A group of alumni men who had graduated from Water Street Mission's Residential Recovery Program were having a cookout on Father's Day 2010 at Long's Park, Lancaster County. It was a gorgeous June evening with a gentle breeze and plenty of sunshine. I felt alive surrounded by people that my wife and I enjoy. Former counselees and other men that I knew well were hosting this celebration picnic for recent graduates of the Mission's year long program.

All in attendance were asked to join in a circle. My wife was at my left side. A young man with whom I had walked through many life issues together, stood next to me in the circle while some announcements were made. I was a dad, but this was not my biological family, yet this was Father's Day. Why were my wife and I invited to this meal? Shepherding thoughts swirled in my head about the Lord and His sheep.

I was struck by the simplicity of what a group of believers in Christ were doing standing in a circle and giving praise to God in a public park. These strangers evolved somewhat into a close-knit group of men through the bonds of a faith in Christ. They had a desire to move forward in a new approach to living life to honor Him. Amazingly—this was not the local church where I would have expected bonds to form and where sheep flock together.

The true Father at this Father's Day picnic was our shepherding heavenly Father. He alone was the One who herded this group of folks together in life's circumstances first at Water Street Mission. The picnic was a celebration of new life in the Father's kingdom.

Lord, help Your sheeplike children to honor You at all times, wherever the family of believers is gathered.

Jim Stanton is a program counselor at Water Street Mission.

Lost and Found

"We have this hope as an anchor for the soul, firm and secure."
Hebrews 6:19

Losing an anchor in a storm-tossed sea does not a good day make. Just ask the Apostle Paul. In Acts 27 we find him and his shipmates driven off course by harsh winds. They had taken such a battering that they began throwing cargo overboard. Their losses were great. One piece of precious cargo, however, was never meant to be sacrificed to those storms: hope, the anchor for their souls. Sadly, in verse 20, with the storm raging on, Paul confesses, "we finally gave up *all* hope." It, too, succumbed to the sea.

Battered, tossed, beaten and exhausted from the relentless storm, "we finally gave up hope."

Been there, done that.

When my body experienced a quickly progressing illness, many things were thrown overboard to lighten the load: church responsibilities, jobs and household chores to name a few. A busy schedule suddenly cleared to focus on the present storm. As the battering continued, more was lost to merciless winds. Hope, peace and joy were ripped from my tired grasp to sink beneath the waves.

Many things in life will be painfully lost to us. But some things are meant to remain within our grip. That's why, when Paul's hope sank out of reach, God sent an angel to retrieve it. Visiting Paul at night, he told him not to be afraid, God would see them through. Paul emerged from this encounter with his soul once again firm and secure, anchored by retrieved hope. God will do the same for us.

Father, come in the dark night to this battered child of Yours, open my empty, tired hands and restore my hope. Forgive me for throwing it overboard with my other losses. Retrieve for me what I can't reach on my own. Help me to "take hold of the hope offered."

Jenny Gehman, founder of LiveWell!Ministries is anchored in Millersville. Through writing, speaking and mentoring, Jenny helps others take hold of retrieved hope.

God Pleaser or People Pleaser?

"Be holy because I am holy." *1 Peter 1:16*

I want to be a God pleaser, an authentic follower of Jesus Christ. Christianity is a supernatural walk with a living, dynamic, speaking and personal God. Authentic means real or genuine, reliable, trustworthy. To have a vital relationship with Jesus Christ takes time—not leftover time but quality time. Time for sitting in His presence, for solitude, for meditation and reflection.

The first time we had an eight-hour Prayer and Praise Day at Susquehanna Valley Pregnancy Services, I thought, "Eight hours. That is a long time. What are we going to do all day?"

But the hours were sweet and the time went fast. I no longer work with that agency so those times are not built into my schedule. My desire is still to spend time with my Lord. I ask Him to help me be disciplined to spend quality time with Him. When I put aside distractions and focus, the time is so sweet.

It's a challenge to focus on the Lord—to be totally in His presence. My thoughts dart here and there. The phone rings. The children come home. My husband wants to tell me something.

My actions say, "You know, I really don't have time for You, Lord. We'll get together tomorrow."

Does tomorrow ever come? We need to declare war on whatever is keeping us from quality time with God. Second Corinthians 10:4-5 says, "For the weapons of our warfare are not carnal, but mighty in God for pulling down strongholds, casting down arguments and every high thing that exalts itself against the knowledge of God, bringing every thought into captivity to the obedience of Christ."

The enemy doesn't want us to spend quality time with God. Spending time with God gives us a different focus. We want to please Him instead of people. We will display the fruits of the Spirit: love, joy, peace, patience, gentleness, goodness, kindness, faithfulness and self-control. We display His wisdom and courage. When we are authentic, we are exciting to be with because we exemplify Christ's vitality.

Lord, help me be a God pleaser!

Yvonne Zeiset is a financial counselor for Tabor Community Services, Consumer Credit Counseling, in Lancaster. She loves to pray.

Taming the Waves

"The disciples went and woke Him, saying, 'Master, Master, we're going to drown!' He got up and rebuked the wind and the raging waters; the storm subsided, and all was calm." *Luke 8:24*

Standing ankle deep in the Atlantic Ocean, the waves were churning around me, kicking up sand and creating a dark foamy spray. The undercurrent of the high tide pulled forcefully at my legs as I walked farther out into the ocean and pushed a mini foam surfboard in front of me in an effort to achieve my goal of riding a few waves.

Finally I was waist deep in seawater, the surf crashing around me in quick succession. As I turned back toward the shore to check on my daughters, a wave several feet taller than me slammed into my back and knocked me off my feet. Trying to regain my balance I grabbed at the board, but it offered little assistance. I swallowed a mouthful of seawater and saw through my goggles the caramel-colored liquid swirl around me as the force of the current pushed my knees into the grainy sand below. It took a few seconds before I stood up gasping for breath and coughing up the salty water.

Many years ago my life was like those churning waves. Depression had wrapped itself around me, and every day had felt like I was fighting the high-tide undercurrents. Depression was the seawater that was knocking me down and choking the life out of me. Crying out to God, "I know you can heal me. I don't want to feel like this any longer!" was my daily petition. Eight months later while praying with a friend, God chose to permanently remove depression from my life.

As the Atlantic breakers rushed past me, I stood there dripping wet, remembering when my heavenly Father rebuked the waves that once threatened to conquer me.

Heavenly Father, I am forever thankful that You are the tamer of waves.

Jill Printzenhoff is an earth sciences teacher at Lititz Christian School.

Weeds

"Search me, O God and know my heart; test me and know my anxious thoughts. See if there is any offensive way in me, and lead me in the way everlasting." *Psalm 139:23–24*

In spring, I found a new little plant beginning to grow in my flower bed. I didn't remember planting it, but it was so pretty and green and was hidden under all the other plants. I knew it wouldn't thrive there so I decided to transplant it so it would have a better chance to thrive. I planted it, watered it and nurtured it until it began to grow. After a while I realized it was just a big, old weed. I couldn't believe I had spent all that time caring for it and now it was growing and even multiplying. So, I pulled it out by the root and got rid of it.

It made me think of the sin in my life. How much time do I spend watering, nurturing and tending the weeds of sin? When sin is nurtured it grows bigger and bigger until it is out of control. We need to realize our sin is like a weed, that it is useless and ugly. We need to pluck it out before it is able to take hold, grow and multiply into more.

When God shows us our sin, we are able to repent and receive forgiveness. Thank God for His amazing grace.

Dear God, search me and help me to realize when sin is present in my life. Give me the wisdom and strength to just stop and pull it out by the root so that it may not take hold. Lord, I want to honor You with my life. I give You my all. In Jesus' name, I pray. Amen.

Cynthia Zimmerman is a board member of Life Connection Mission, a sponsor ship school in Montrouis, Haiti, for poor Haitian children. She and her husband have sons and one grandson.

A Prayer Journal

"Therefore I tell you, whatever you ask for in prayer, believe that you have received it, and it will be yours." *Mark 11:24*

Growing up in a Christian home, I knew the importance of prayer and how powerful prayer can be. Every once in a while, I would write down prayer requests in my diary, but it was sporadic. It wasn't until after I was married that I really became more serious about it.

I am sure that if you have grown up around the church, you might have heard Sunday school teachers or pastors mention about writing out your prayers and concerns in a book and seeing how God answers them. But maybe you're like me and didn't pay too much attention to it. May I encourage you to start a prayer journal today?

After having done a prayer journal for a couple years now, I can see what a blessing it is to have one. It is such an encouragement to look back at past prayer requests and see how many the Lord answered. I would even write the date and a "thank you" to God when they were answered.

Now a prayer journal is not a magical book. Not all of my requests were answered the way I wanted. There were times that God said, "No". But looking back and seeing how many the Lord did say, "Yes" to is amazing, especially during those times when it seemed like God wasn't listening. So take the prayer journal challenge today and prepare to receive the Lord's blessing on your life too.

Heavenly Father, thank You for the power of prayer; it is the tool You have given us to communicate with You. May we never take it for granted. In Jesus' name. Amen.

Jenn Paules is a part-time radio announcer for WJTL and full-time wife and mom.

Faith, Not Fear

"For God did not give us a spirit of cowardice, but rather a spirit of power and of love and of self-discipline." *2 Timothy 1:7 (New Revised Standard Version)*

Recently, I was returning from a family visit in New Mexico, walking through the airport with a woman I met traveling on the same flight nine days earlier. We had also crossed paths again at our grandchildren's school, chatting about the joys of visiting the week of Grandparent's Day. I noticed this woman because of her tunic Lugade dress and turban head covering and later learned that she was a member of a Hindu community.

As we talked about our visit, we approached a long escalator. The woman said she needed to use the elevator because she can't go down escalators. My thoughts spiraled back to thirty years before when I had the same fear … the fear of death if I stepped on that escalator. As unrealistic as this may seem, I was afraid, and for many years never stepped on an escalator.

After having walked with the Lord for almost as many years as my fear, I came across today's verse. Accepting the presence and touch of the Holy Spirit, I no longer felt this fear. I realized that I was no longer alone, that even when facing difficult transitions I can count on Jesus Christ walking with me. God gives us the power to overcome fear, to boldly step out in faith and to persevere through whatever the obstacle that is causing us to stumble. I had the courage to step out, to get on that escalator.

As the woman and I parted with our farewell greetings, I knew I will hold her close in my heart, hoping that in our brief time together, I may have touched her with God's love.

Yahweh, thank You for showing me, and may this woman come to know that You are the God of power, love and self-discipline.

Joan M. Zercher, Evangelical Free Church of Hershey, ministers to women and children from disadvantaged circumstances.

No Greater Love

"Greater love has no one than this, that he lay down his life for his friends." *John 15:13*

Karen and I first met when she and her family moved into the area and our children were in the same classes at a local Christian school. We became instant friends, many people calling us "partners in crime." Eventually we ended up in the same church, and did skits together as two elderly ladies . . . she as "Fannie" and me as "Sadie." We didn't need a script. We knew the details we had to get across, and the rest was ad lib. And ad lib we did! Our minds thought alike, our hearts beat the same. I'm so thankful that the skits are all video taped. When I view them I still can't believe, after all these years, how funny we were!

For many months we met as couples on Sunday mornings before church to pray for our adult children. I vividly remember her saying one Sunday morning that she would gladly give her life if that meant her children would come back to the Lord and serve Him.

In the fall of 2002, Karen was diagnosed with a brain tumor. I walked the halls in the hospital while she was in surgery. I felt in my spirit that it was cancer, and that she would not be healed this side of heaven. Even so, we prayed for a miracle. Winter passed and then spring. It was difficult seeing her beautiful dark hair disappear and to witness her declining health. I took her to doctor appointments and sat with her in her home, helping her wherever I could. I felt so inadequate. "Lord, are you there? Do you see this? Do you care?"

The day before she passed away I sat at her bedside reading scripture to her. She barely responded, but I knew she heard me. For weeks before her passing "I Can Only Imagine" could be heard blaring loudly in her home. She knew. She was ready.

Sunday morning, June 29, 2003, Karen quietly and peacefully walked into the arms of her Lord. The final chapter has yet to be written, but God is faithful even when we are faithless!

Jesus, I don't understand Your ways, but I trust in Your sovereignty. Thank You for being faithful, even when I am faithless. One day I know I will see clearly!

Linda White serves on the worship team and the leadership board of Manheim Brethren in Christ Church.

The Lesson of the Butterfly

"For we are God's workmanship, created in Christ Jesus to do good works, which God prepared in advance for us to do." *Ephesians 2:10*

Have you ever noticed how God brings comfort to your heart when a trusted friend tramples it into the dirt? Have you ever been so thoroughly rejected and abandoned by a spiritual leader that you want to forget you ever heard the word *church?* That is precisely what happened to me. I discovered that a trusted spiritual leader had been completely dishonest with me and I was left with a myriad of painful questions. "What in the world just happened? Where do I fit in? Did God really call me into this position at this particular place or was it a ploy from the enemy of my soul? Where do I go from here? What am I supposed to do now? Do I really have the spiritual gifts that I thought I had?"

I was sinking farther and farther into the thick muck of depression as I struggled to make sense of what happened. But then, our heavenly Father, who loves with an incalculable, uncontainable love, gave me an upfront and personal object lesson.

I love butterflies because they are symbolic of transformation and new hope. I kept seeing butterflies dancing through the air as I went for my daily walk and the Holy Spirit brought this thought into my mind—"the butterflies are doing precisely what God has genetically coded them to do without fear of consequences." God had wired them to flit about without regard for their circumstances, and that is exactly what they were doing!

Ah-ha! God has wired each one of us with certain spiritual gifts to be used for His glory, and we are to continue exercising those gifts in spite of untrustworthy people or circumstances.

Lord God Almighty, thank You for being trustworthy, even when others are not.

Pastor Ellen Dooley, Itinerate pastor and MDiv candidate at Evangelical Theological Seminary.

Power in the Name

"By faith in the name of Jesus, this man whom you see and know was made strong. It is Jesus' name and the faith that comes through him that has given this complete healing to him, as you can all see."
Acts 3:16

Have you ever spoken out loud "in Jesus' name" and witnessed His power in action?

As a young single adult, I was living in Florida and acquired a fair skill at surfing. One summer a friend from Ohio came to visit, and I invited him to try his hand at surfing. Unbeknown to me, my friend had never seen an ocean before nor could he swim. We jumped on our boards and paddled past the breakers.

After giving my friend some pointers, we both took the first good wave. Somehow, I, the expert, lost my board and ended on the beach along with my board. To my surprise, my friend's board appeared but with no friend. Looking out past the breakers, I saw my friend bobbing like a fishing bobber. Realizing he was in trouble, I jumped on my board and paddled as hard as I ever had reason to paddle in my life. As I saw my friend's head bob under the surf for longer and longer periods of time, I suddenly screamed above the roar of the waves, "In Jesus' name, help us."

I witnessed instant renewed strength in my arms that day and reached my friend just in time to thrust him my board to hang onto as I paddled both of us to shore.

As we laid on the sandy beach at the edge of the water regaining our breath, we thanked Jesus for His wonderful name. Then my friend told me that until that day, he could not swim and had never seen an ocean.

Father, thank You for the power that is in Your name, Jesus.

Joe Nolt serves as assistant to the director of DOVE Mission International, Lititz.

July

Daddy Can You Get Home?

"Thou wilt keep him in perfect peace, whose mind is stayed on thee: because he trusteth in thee." *Isaiah 26:3 (King James Version)*

As a child, I remember going out for Sunday evening drives. My dad had a 1941 Ford Coupe with two little jump seats in the back and a piece of lumber across the two to make more room for two little girls and a baby brother.

Especially when I would get sleepy and after we had passed all the landmarks familiar to me, like the park and church and stores, I would become anxious that Dad would never be able to find the way home if he just kept driving.

He would assure me and then I would be right back to the question, "Daddy can you get us home from here?" He and Mom would giggle a bit at my anxious tone and let me know I could rest my little head. I would still wonder and be fearful as I watched the streetlamps stream by.

Then suddenly we would pull into the Neapolitan ice cream store and Dad would pick me up and put me on his shoulders. My fear would fade in an instant. One lime sherbet cone and then the sleepy girls and brother would be back in the car. My whine (persistent questions of insecurity) would stop at that point and I would drift off to dreamland as we drove toward home.

The next morning I would wake in my bed and never know how I got home.

My earthly father has gone on now and I find I am still asking Papa God, "Can you get me home from here? I don't know where I am in this new place, but must trust that You do."

If I close my eyes and rest, I find I wake up where I am supposed to be with a loving remembrance of riding around on His shoulders.

Father, thank You that You are the Way that always leads to home and rest. Your perfect love casts out fear and uncertainty.

Nancy Clegg is a child of Father God who loves His children.

Lord, Please Protect His Bible

"Call upon Me in the day of trouble; I will deliver you, and you shall glorify Me." *Psalm 50:15 (New King James Version)*

"Lee, there it is. Hurry, stop the car." My mind quickly reflected back to a prayer I had frantically prayed earlier that morning.

Our family was vacationing in Ocean City, Maryland, and it was Sunday, July fourth. We had decided to get up early and attend services at Ocean City Worship Center.

On our way to church, Lee, my son-in-law, gasped and excitedly exclaimed that he had put his Bible on top of the van before we left and forgot to get it off before we drove away. Because of the heavy traffic, we had traveled the back way to Route 50 and crossed over the Route 90 bridge. It was too late to turn around and retrace our steps, so after church we planned to return to our condo the same way we came.

While sitting quietly in church waiting for the service to begin, I silently prayed that the Lord somehow would conceal the Bible from other people's eyes and protect it from being run over and being damaged. I also prayed that the seagulls would not (you know what) on it. And, I prayed that as we drove back to our condo that the Lord would open our eyes and we would be able to see it.

All eyes were fastened on the road before us on our return trip. When crossing the Route 90 Bridge, my daughter Michele spotted the Bible sitting on the middle line right between the east and west lane traffic. Although the Fourth of July traffic was heavy, at that moment, there was no one behind our vehicle. Lee jumped out of the van to retrieve the Bible. It's cover had come off and was lying on the side of the road, just a few feet from our van. Michele opened the door, ran out and grabbed it before the traffic increased.

The Bible and the cover had been there for three and a half hours. Neither item had been run over or hurt in any way! How big is our God!

My little granddaughter most adequately put it all together when she exclaimed, "Daddy, that was a God thing."

Thank You, Lord, for understanding our anguish, hearing our prayers and answering in such an amazing way.

Joyce Thomas is an adult Sunday school teacher and facilitator of Cleansing Stream Ministries at Central Worship Center in Laurel, Delaware.

Overcoming Fears

"Even though I walk through the valley of the shadow of death I will fear no evil, for you are with me; your rod and your staff, they comfort me." *Psalms 23:4*

I memorized the above scripture as a young child, but it was not until recently that I experienced what it really meant to fear no evil and experience the comfort of God's rod and staff.

As far back as I can remember I have feared many things. In my childhood I was afraid of the dark and as I grew so did my fears. I became fearful of wars, of persecution in the end times; I feared things that had not happened to me.

A few years ago my children's middle school started to scan fingers for identification instead of using photo cards. This sent me into an anxiety attack because of the fears that consumed my life. In my mind I perceived a pattern of terrible things that were beginning to happen and I allowed my thoughts to control me instead of the Word of God.

Throughout my life I have had little victories in overcoming specific fears but it seemed like fear would poke its head up in many different areas of my life. I hated having these feelings especially as a strong Christian. I did not understand why the thoughts of fear did not just go away when I prayed. Two years ago when my son was diagnosed with cancer I had to face a lot of my fears. Through that time the only thing that kept me going was to trust that God was there with me.

As I began to trust God and give up control of every area of my life, He started to take my fear away and replace it with His perfect love. I have learned to face my fears with the love of Christ knowing He loves me so much that He will give me the strength to face anything that happens in my life.

I do not need to walk in worry and fear but in the trust of the Lord, trusting that He is faithful!

Dear Jesus, I pray for Your perfect love to comfort all who fear and that they will feel Your hand holding onto theirs as they walk through life.

Marie Good, her husband Todd and four children are members of DOVE Newport Christian Fellowship where they serve as youth group leaders.

Cost of Freedom

"So if the Son sets you free, you will be free indeed." *John 8:36*

Today is the day that we in America celebrate our independence from Great Britain and gained a great ability to choose for ourselves our religious beliefs.

It is interesting to me that so many of us in America—even good Christian people—do not appreciate their freedom from sin and death. We celebrate the fourth of July but forget the real independence is the ability to be free from sin and fully dependent on God for everything. I suggest that we celebrate our dependence on the Lord every day we are given by Him to breath.

It is a great privilege to know God and be known by Him. We could desire no greater life.

On this fourth of July begin to write a list of the things that the Lord has freed you from and spend some time thanking Him for all those freedoms. Please do not forget what your freedom costs God's Son.

Lord, cause me to have a grateful heart for all the freedoms I enjoy presently and the new ones that are coming as I walk in You. Your Word says that I walk about in freedom because I sought Your Precepts. Help me to seek more after You and Your Word. Amen.

Patrick Wilson is pastor of Living Truth Fellowship.

God Means "All Things"

"We know that in all things work together God works for the good of those who love him, who have been called according to his purpose."
Romans 8:28

My wife and I attend a church with a large congregation. Last year the pastor said, "I need a mature couple to lead the counseling ministry for the church. Every time I go to prayer I see your faces."

We listened to his proposal, the timing of the transition, and then said we would go home and pray about it. We looked at each other and asked the Lord, "Why us?" We had been married for thirty-four years. Seventeen of those years without the Lord had ended in failure and for three years we were not living together, but for fourteen years we were fully sold out to the Lord and lived in the joy and peace of the Lord. He had done a mighty work in both of us—He had broken us, He had shown us His love, He had saved us and He had reunited us in a brand new marriage after the failure.

We got back to the pastor with a "yes". One day he said we should write a marriage manual for the church and start teaching a marriage class. He said, "I want a manual that gives total dependence on the love and power of Christ to be the answer for every issue of marriage. I don't want anyone to come out of your teaching and think they can do anything to fix their marriage. I want them to know that as we go to Him for every need in our marriages, He will change us and give us a loving, joy-filled, Christ-centered marriage, one that is even more than we could ever hope for or imagine."

We suddenly saw that all of the hurt and pain, all of the struggles without God could now be used by God. We saw that all of the mistakes we made depending upon our own strength were not wasted and all the joy of the new marriage of total dependence on God could be shouted from the highest rooftop. We saw that the scripture that says, "All things work together . . . ." truly meant "all things.

Lord, thank You for Your love and power to live God-filled, joyous marriages as we depend totally on You for all of our needs. Thank You for allowing our weaknesses and failures to become a blessing in Your Kingdom.

Dr. Robert and Nora Rew counsel at Times Square Church in New York City.

God Stories 6

Unfolding Plan

"By wisdom a house is built, and by understanding it is established; through knowledge its rooms are filled with rare and beautiful treasures." *Proverbs 24:3, 4*

Oh, no! The carpet was soaked! My son had shown me his little wet sock after a long stormy weekend. I felt around the floor and discovered a large half circle of the carpet was thoroughly soaked at the double doors leading to our deck. I groaned inside.

The carpet was only a small problem. It was quite old and needed to be replaced anyway. The biggest problem was the whole room that extended into the kitchen needed an updating. Changing the carpet meant we should do other changes as well. A few years ago, my husband and I had talked about how we would rework the area. I dreaded it and we put it off into the future that was now here!

Much to my surprise, our project began to unfold as beautifully as a rose. Someone mentioned that there was still a good selection in the furniture clearance at the store down the road. Then friends emailed about a refugee family needing furniture. Our couch was perfect to help someone get started. They picked it up in perfect timing.

The flooring store across the street had a sale we were able to get in on. We picked carpet and tile at a really good price. We found a bent and dent stove that was perfect for what I wanted. My husband and I even agreed on a paint color for the kitchen!

The project I dreaded worked out better than I ever imaged that it would. It kept me busy a few weeks – cleaning and reorganizing the living space. We were happy with the results. One bonus was I cleaned things I no longer needed and freed up some valuable space.

God does care about all parts of our lives! Our original plan for the spring was taking outdoor pictures of our son, but I didn't get time. God took care of that detail when our neighbor, exploring a photography career, offered to take some photos of Ben and did a beautiful job!

I have often prayed the verse above, for our home. I did see God answer my prayers!

Thank You, Lord, for helping us in every area of life.

Sarah Sauder enjoys being a mom, works as a graphic designer and attends DOVE Westgate Church with her family.

A Night on the River

"In His hand is the life of every creature and the breath of all mankind." *Job 12:10*

On a Saturday evening in the middle of July, I joined my friend Ted at the Susquehanna River. We waded into the river about five p.m. and navigated through the slippery rocks until we were about waist deep in the water. We started casting, hoping to catch a fish or two. After an hour and with hardly a nibble, a couple big rocks protruding out of the water near us seemed to invite us to have a seat. We watched as the sun kept sinking lower in the sky. Ted reassured me they would come right at dark. He was referring to the white fly hatch, which usually happens on the river in July. The flies are in a larva form on the bottom of the river. They come to the surface and hatch into large white flies, not houseflies, but flies with large butterfly-like wings and a long tail.

The sun sank below the trees and we saw a few fish jumping far away but didn't see a single white fly. We had our rods ready and white fly imitations on, ready to go after any fish that came up to to feed. The water started to smooth out and looked like a mirror. When it was almost dark, we saw lots of fish feeding near the island and we saw our first white fly. Within minutes of seeing our first white fly, there were hundreds, then thousands. One square foot of water contained twenty to thirty flies, and the ones that already had hatched were flying all around us. It was like it was snowing. The flies were so plentiful that the fish were feeding and churning up the water while gobbling up the flies.

Later that night it struck me how amazing the careful orchestration and design the Creator had showed me – how larva remain in the river until just the right time and then hatch at the same time and how the fish, birds, bats, frogs and other wildlife depend on them for food. All creation testifies to the existence of God and all we need to do is look at the intricacies of nature to confirm an Intelligent Designer.

Prayer: Lord, thank You for Your creation and Your supreme design and attention to details. We are in awe of You. You are amazing and the one and only Creator.

Randy Wingenroth is vice president for E.F. Martzall, Inc. and is servant administrator of property at Mohns Hill Evangelical Congregational Church.

I'll Be With You

"When you pass through the waters, I will be with you . . . ."
Isaiah 43:2

My year of losses began when we had to euthanize our beloved elderly dog. Shortly thereafter, our son and his family moved to a far-away, dangerous part of the world to serve God. My father-in-law was diagnosed with a terminal illness and went home to be with the Lord. My husband faced a cancer scare but, to our great relief, his biopsy was negative. Just hours after receiving that welcome news, however, my elderly mother passed from this life to eternity. To round out my year of turmoil, a family member underwent surgery for a life-threatening tumor.

Just like ocean waves continually crashing against the shore, one devastating loss after another battered my weary spirit. I struggled to hold my head above the raging currents of grief that threatened to over-whelm me. I mentally recounted my losses and reminded the Lord that I could not handle any more problems. During sleepless nights, I some-times questioned whether God knew, or cared, about my situation.

Despite my questionings, however, I sensed God's presence as the waves of adversity churned about me. Often, God revealed Himself through people. The day before my mother's death, a volunteer musi-cian from "Songs for the Journey" sang to her and our family. Soft harp music and songs about heaven quieted our troubled spirits and soothed our aching hearts. Another time, a friend just "happened" to see me in the hospital and prayed with me as I waited for a family member under-going surgery. Notes, calls and encouraging words helped me to realize that God, and others, cared about me. Although menacing waves still swirl around me, God's past faithfulness reassures me that he will not abandon me today, or in the future. To that hope, I cling.

Lord, thank You for walking with us during the difficult and good times of our lives.

Nancy Witmer is a wife, mother, grandmother, writer and speaker. She attends Hernley Mennonite Church.

Can You Hear Me Now?

"Jesus replied, 'Blessed are those who hear the word of God and obey it.'" *Luke 11:28*

Most of us have been on city streets or in public places where we hear these words from someone with a cell phone at their ear: "Can you hear me now?"

As we go through our fast-paced lives, clear and connected communication is valuable. We work hard to get and stay connected with other people.

I wonder how this relates to connections to the heavenly Father. There are many biblical references about hearing from and listening to our God. In the Luke setting of the scripture used today, many were following Jesus to see miracles, to hear teachings and to observe the Master's power over demonic forces. Then a woman in the crowd shouted out how blessed his mother must feel. Jesus response challenges us all to hear and obey God and His Word.

I remember the time I was meeting with our chaplain staff inside the Lancaster County Prison. Several chaplains were concerned that so many inmates continue with negative, dysfunctional lifestyles. The consensus of the chaplains was, "If only more would listen and know how much God loves them."

Later that day I met a man who recently came to faith. He said, "I found a living God, my true Father. My life will never be the same."

He was listening to the voice of God. Are you and I hearing from God? Can you hear him now?

Lord, thanks for sending Jesus to show us truth and to dwell in our hearts. May we always hear Your word and do it.

Nelson W. Martin is director of support for Prison Ministries, a Lancaster County-based prison ministry and chaplain program. He and his wife Anna Mae live near Lititz and are active at Millport Mennonite Church.

Peace in Our Hearts

"The Lord will give strength to His people; the Lord will bless his people with peace." *Psalm 29:11 (New King James Version)*

Every night for three long weeks, I walked the long corridors of the hospital to the parking garage. I was thoroughly discouraged and frustrated that the medical profession could not figure out what was causing the blood clots that resulted in my husband having had three heart attacks within two weeks.

I prayed for peace to accept whatever the outcome might be in my husband's life. As I left the hospital one night, I caught the words broadcast over the intercom: "Sleep in heavenly peace." Those words were like a sign from God to me.

Two months later, my husband met his Lord and Savior. I was blessed by so many people who continued to pray for peace within my own heart to face the journey ahead without my soul mate. Most amazing to me was that God used people I didn't even know to encourage me along the way.

One example of that happened about a month after my husband's death from mesothelioma cancer. A package arrived in the mail with a note from the secretary of the billing office of the heart doctor. She wrote that she did not get to meet too many nice people in her job, but when she did, it was memorable.

After my husband had died, she said she could hear the sorrow in my heart and she wanted to let me know that I was in her prayers and that God loved me.

The package included a glass etching of the words found in Numbers 6:24-26: "The Lord bless you and keep you. The Lord make His face to shine upon you and be gracious to you. The Lord turn His face toward you and give you peace."

I placed that etching in a spot where I can see it every day. It's a daily reminder that God grants us peace not only through our own prayers and those we love, but also through people we do not know personally.

Thank You, Jesus, for the power of peace. Help us to think of others and how we can comfort them with peace in their hearts.

Louetta Hurst is a member of Forest Hills Mennonite Church, the mother of three and grandmother of eleven.

Am I an Ambassador?

"Pray also for me, that whenever I open my mouth, words may be given me so that I will fearlessly make known the mystery of the gospel, for which I am an ambassador in chains. Pray that I may declare it fearlessly, as I should." *Ephesians 6:19–20*

In the hustle and bustle of our daily lives we often miss so much. I think of the quote from Alice in Wonderland, "People come and go so quickly around here!" In the midst of our coming and going, do we take time to note the divine opportunities around us? The moments God places us right in the midst of? Are we so busy looking ahead to our next meeting, appointment or destination that the 'here and now' becomes history before we do what God has called us to do?

We are called to be ambassadors for Christ; in fact we represent him 24/7 to everyone we meet and everywhere we go. I am an avid Black Friday shopper. I like to find amazing deals for the loved ones on my Christmas list. However, that's not the number one reason I like to head out to the crowds very early in the morning. I LOVE to represent Christ to the workers, the shoppers and all the little children that face long, busy, often grumpy days, all for the sake of the perfect deal for the people on their Christmas list. A kind comment, a word of encouragement and a smile can often change someone's mood instantly. As I walk away from a divine moment, I often find myself praying for the person I just met. Yes, we are all called to be ambassadors. I wonder what divine moment God has planned for you today

Thank You, Lord, that You did not create us to be lone rangers, but instead to stand together as we serve You. Help us to be humble enough to stand alongside our brothers and sisters as we reach the lost in Your name.

Karen Pennell is the chief executive officer of Chester County Women's Services Medical, a life-affirming pregnancy care medical ministry in Chester County.

Custom-Designed Application

"But when He, the Spirit of truth, comes, He will guide you into all the truth. . . ." John 16:13 (New American Standard Bible)

I was speaking on the life of Hannah to a group of pastors' wives during a ministry trip to India, recounting how it took a long time for her prayer for a child to be answered. During the "wait," Hannah experienced the *external pressure* of living alongside a woman who was basking in Hannah's dream to have children, as well as the *internal pressure* of an unmet longing, and feeling alone. I likened it to the process of a diamond being developed—the common factors being the *duration of time, intense pressure, and hiddenness* in the depths of the earth. During those times, as difficult as they may be, God's outcome is to create a beautiful diamond of our lives, fashioned to be clear of impurities and prepared to display His light through the many facets of our lives.

I'd speak a few sentences and my interpreter would follow. However, as we got to the diamond illustration, she continued speaking for several minutes. Finally, she turned to me and told me that they held to a myth that diamonds are formed by being spewed out of snakes' mouths! She had to address the wrong belief and then replace it with the truth before relating it to the "waiting times" of their lives.

I was grateful for her awareness of their belief system and commitment to apply the truth to their lives. It was a wonderful reminder of the work of the Holy Spirit. It is ultimately His responsibility (not mine) to take the Word and rightly apply it, confronting wrong beliefs and guiding us into all truth.

Thank You for the unchangeable truth of Your Word, Lord, and the privilege and freedom to speak it, knowing Your Spirit uniquely applies it to each one who hears it.

Cindy Riker is involved with Teaching the Word Ministries with her husband Don and enjoys being a wife, mother, homeschooler and leader at Change of Pace Bible study.

Changed Forever

"Therefore, if anyone is in Christ, he is a new creation . . . ."
2 Corinthians 5:17

It was a summer that changed my life forever. That summer I was in a battle for my soul. I had been living my life my own way. It was drugs, sex and rock n' roll for me. But that summer it became intense. I was using more and more to numb the conflict going on inside me. But unbeknownst to me, a church was praying for me as part of their fall revival. A friend's mother put me on their prayer list.

The conflict culminated when I finally surrendered my life to Christ. It was a Sunday morning I will never forget. I didn't tell anyone what happened. Two days later I was traveling on the Pennsylvania Turnpike and thought, if this decision for Jesus is real, I don't need this, and proceeded to throw all my drug paraphernalia out the window. Immediately a peace filled me. It was a peace that passed all understanding.

It was time to share with someone. I called my friend. Her mother answered the phone—the same person who was praying for me. She was the first person I told of my salvation.

Someone prayed for me and I am eternally thankful that she did. Let us never grow weary of praying for the lost. Our prayers put things in motion whether we see it or not.

Father, we know we are praying Your will when we pray for the lost. Your will is that none should perish. May we never give up believing You are at work in the lives of those we love.

Gary Nolt lives in Lititz with his wife Kathy and is a business owner. He also helps facilitate a Twelve-step recovery group at The Worship Center.

Moving Mountains

". . . and anointed many sick people with oil and healed them."
Mark 6:13

My best friend lives 1,700 miles away in Colorado. Our children have known each other all their lives. Her son was the first to make my infant baby laugh. Our daughters consider themselves among their best friends.

Recently she and her husband asked our family to join them in leading a high school youth camp high in the Rockies. Our children were to be together as campers, my husband and I as counselors. With much prayer and preparation, we accepted. We went deep with the teens around campfire communion. There were relationship challenges, sunrise mountain climbs and baptisms.

During the final morning of camp, our speaker felt led to lay hands and anoint my friend's fifteen-year-old daughter. She had been suffering from near constant headache pain for more than seven months. Surgical procedures had been done. Pokes, pricks and numerous tests had been run. She was on a battery of medications. Two nights previously she was hospitalized overnight in the local emergency room when the pain had reached an unbearable level. Quietly beside a group of teens singing in worship, my friend and her husband gathered around their daughter as she was anointed. There were tears and murmurs of prayer. The teens continued singing. Calmly the leader stepped toward my friend and whispered, "I felt a lot of heat leave your daughter's head. I believe she's been healed!"

My friend rushed to hold her only daughter. "I feel so relaxed, Mommy, and I'm not doing anything," the fifteen-year-old said.

By now my own daughters were at her side. Streams of joyful tears poured down their faces. Though we believe in a God that can do the impossible, we stood amazed at what we had witnessed! We had prayed for a week of heart change and before us stood a young girl transformed!

Saviour, You can move the mountains! My God, You are mighty to save!

Debbi Miller is the assistant to the president at Water Street Ministries. Her friend's daughter praises God for her healing.

Building a Kingdom

"Take my yoke upon you and learn from me, for I am gentle and humble in heart, and you will find rest for your souls." *Matthew 11:29*

Herod the Great, known as the greatest builder of the ancient world, left his footprint all over Israel. The size and grandeur of his structures were second to none.

He remodeled the great Jerusalem temple, and along with ten thousand men, built the retaining walls around the Temple Mount, which remained under construction for ten years. One solid stone on the second course of the wall's foundation was sixty-four feet long, eight feet high and twelve feet deep. Our tour group sadly joked that "many hernias" of "free" labor got that stone into place! Capable of holding twenty-four football fields, the Temple Mount still remains the largest manmade platform in the world.

Herod built Herodion, an ambitious architectural project, serving as his summer palace, fortress, monument, burial ground and district capital. Upper Herodion contains water cisterns, tunnels and hidden apertures for sneak attacks. Lower Herodion had a large pool in the center of a garden surrounded by columns.

Herod built Masada, a sprawling palace with many fortifications on a high plateau overlooking the Dead Sea.

Herod built a large deepwater harbor city, Caesarea, a "planned city" of crisscrossing roads, a Roman temple, amphitheater, hippodrome, markets, residential quarters, aqueducts, piers and giant warehouses.

But cruel and paranoid Herod the Great murdered members of his own family and numerous rabbis to secure his leadership role in his kingdom. It was all about him!

In contrast, Jesus left His footprint over the entire world. He didn't own a home to rest his head. With peace and contentment, He chose to do His Father's will. With all power at His fingertips, He willingly gave up His own life. God stooped down to become a servant. For us.

Lord, help us not to follow the world's visible and ostentatious ways of building a kingdom. Instead, remind us the kingdom of God is inside us, as we choose to obey Christ's example of a meek heart.

Tamalyn Jo Heim leaves her footprint in Willow Street and at Calvary Church in marriage and parenting ministry with her husband Bob.

Rise Above It All

"The thief comes only to steal and kill and destroy; I have come that they may have life, and have it to the full." *John 10:10*

It's inevitable—life is promised to have its ups and downs amid storms and quiet times. Knowing that is half the battle. It's how you perceive it and then deal with it that sets you apart from the rest of the world.

The enemy would love it if you stayed in the place of doubt, frustration, having the mind-set of retaliation, giving up or giving in. Keeping you stuck in your circumstance is exactly where he wants you. In that place, he can keep you focused on the negative and your heart from seeing God's best for your life and fully understanding truth. Seriously, who wants to live there?

Here's the truth: in whatever situation, good or bad—whether you understand it or not or have a solution to the problem or an explanation for the predicament, when you stand firm in who you are and even more securely in who Christ is in you, you cannot fail.

When God is in control of your life, let Him drive and trust the journey He's taking you on. Each situation has been handcrafted by the Craftsman so that you can live the abundant life, one "to the full." Full is the ability to not allow your circumstance to determine your attitude, but your trust in God defines not just your attitude but your entire life. Embrace it, rise above it and be that person that He has created you to be.

Lord, living a mediocre life is not enough for me. I need more of You so that I don't allow my circumstances to determine my outlook and more of Your power to rise above it all to live that abundant life. I trust You to take the wheel of my life and steer me in the direction that is best for me.

Joy Ortega is an associate pastor of Living Word Fellowship, an urban church plant whose purpose is to "reach people and change lives!"

Precious Gift from Abba

"Children are a gift from the Lord. They are His reward."
Psalm 127:3

Timidly the young woman approached me and asked, "Will you please pray that I can carry this child to term? I'm scared because I have had a couple miscarriages. Please keep this in confidence, I haven't told anyone yet."

I prayed with her and assured her I would continue to remember her before our Father in the days ahead. I wrote encouraging emails reminding her the Lord's hand was upon her and all would be well.

Sometime later I heard talk of concerns about her baby's well-being and with problems in the womb.

I again reassured her that God is with her and prayed God's peace and presence to be with her.

She continued believing in faith and quiet assurance for a safe delivery and healthy baby.

Many others in our church were also praying and encouraging her.

Later, it was a joy to hear the good news of a healthy newborn born into her household.

Her parents and two brothers welcomed the little girl with much thanksgiving.

Recently we were invited to join in her first-year birthday party!

What a joyous celebration of our Father's goodness and faithfulness.

Lord, I pray all Your good purposes and plans for this child will come to pass for Your glory. Amen!

Ruth Lehman is grateful and blessed to be mother of eight children, grandmother of fifteen and great-grandmother of fourteen with another on the way. Ruth is a member of the intercessors team at ACTS Covenant Fellowship.

Decision Making

"Trust in the Lord with all your heart. And lean not on your own understanding. In all your ways acknowledge Him. And he shall direct your paths." *Proverbs 3:5, 6 (New King James Version)*

"This child will bring complete devastation to your family." Despite this and other warnings from some of the most reputable pediatric cardiologists in the United States, my husband and I felt an inner peace about going ahead with the adoption of this little boy from China who was born with an incomplete heart.

Just days later, we were told that the damage to his lungs would be irreparable and he might not live long enough for us to bring him home from China. Our social worker said we could have 48 hours to decide whether or not we wanted to submit acceptance paperwork to China, which would "lock us" into this particular child.

After hours of much praying and many tears, we asked the Lord to make the decision for us. At precisely forty-eight hours, the phone rang. What would we say? The Lord hadn't shown us yet. Reluctantly, I answered the phone. Sure enough, it was our social worker. She explained that our signed acceptance paperwork was sitting on the corner of her desk as we spoke. However, The China Center for Adoption Affairs had contacted her and informed her that they had our signed paperwork and that we were officially "locked" into this child. He was ours now and there was no way to change that! She kept saying how sorry she was and how impossible it was all at the same time.

With tears flowing down my face, I told her that this was not bad news at all. The Lord had made HIS decision as we requested and this precious boy with half a heart would soon fill this mother's heart with love that only I would ever really comprehend. That was twenty months and two open heart surgeries ago and our little Josiah (meaning healed by God) is surprising physicians all the time. Of course, the Great Physician isn't surprised at all.

Gracious, most merciful Father, thank You that we don't have to face life's decisions alone. Thank You that we can come to our Father and He will direct us according to His good purposes.

Deborah Roche attends Calvary Church with her husband and children. Deb is an adoption/pro-life speaker and homeschooling mom.

Trusting God

"For by grace are ye saved through faith; and that not of yourselves: it is the gift of God." *Ephesians 2:8 (King James Version)*

I volunteer at a pregnancy center Thursday evenings. On Valentine's Day, February 14, 2008, a client I have worked with for several years decided to trust Jesus as her personal savior. I was so excited that she wanted to be saved. We talked about the importance of reading and studying God's Word. We also discussed how beneficial it would be for her to attend church with other believers so she could have fellowship and Christian friends. Although she stated she would read the Word and attend church she never began to attend church anywhere.

I questioned why this new believer was not doing what I thought she should be doing as a new Christian. Did I do or say something wrong? Should I keep after her about attending church?

Now I can only tell you that I do not know her heart, only God does. I believe she meant it when she asked the Lord to save her. This client still has many struggles she deals with each day, and I don't walk in her shoes!

What did I learn? TRUST! God was changing me! I learned that God is in control. I have to trust that He knows more then I do about this situation and He knows what is best. It is my responsibility to share the Good News and the Holy Spirit's responsibility to encourage this new believer to grow in grace. I need to continue to love and encourage her, but trust her growth and any changes she needs to make to the Lord. If I am willing to allow God to use me to share His word, He will bless me for being obedient.

Father I thank You that in Your time You will make all things new. Allow me to trust You completely. Amen.

Christine Harsh, Susquehanna Valley Pregnancy Service volunteer, is a wife, mother and proud grandmother. She and her husband attend Community Bible Church, where he serves in the nursery.

Water Leak

"... casting all your care upon Him, for He cares for you."
1 Peter 5:7 (New King James Version)

I was recuperating at home following a nine-day hospitalization. Then, the infection flared up again. I had nausea, headache and fever. My energy level dropped. My morale hit bottom! I was in despair!

The next morning, as I was hooking up my intravenous antibiotic, I was startled by a loud sound, like water gushing. I rushed to the basement to shut off the main water valve. By the time I struggled back upstairs, the floor was covered with water! Obviously a water line had burst inside a wall ... but where?

Reyn, the friend I always turned to in such emergencies, was in Louisiana. Another burden added on my already-too-heavy load. I sighed. "Lord, I could sure use Your help!"

Minutes later I glanced out the window and spotted Reyn's van parked near our neighboring apartment building. Turns out he had returned a week early from his trip and was working on a project right next door. We called him and he hurried over.

He surveyed the situation briefly. Taking a couple of measurements, he put a pencil mark on the wall. Then, with his utility knife, he cut a nine-inch square and popped out the drywall. We stared in disbelief ... the burst pipe was centered in the cut-out! What could have taken hours or days was found and fixed within forty-five minutes!

There have been other discouraging times in my life when I felt as though God wasn't responding to my cry for help. And then .... He did something small that conveyed a huge message. "John, perhaps I've not answered your big request as you've wished, but I am still watching over you." And that has given me the strength to go on!

Lord, thank You for little reassurances of Your care! Help me remember today that You ARE watching over me, no matter what difficulties I may be facing!

John Charles is director of Abundant Living, a family counseling ministry in Lititz.

Life in the Bones

"He asked me, 'Son of man, can these bones live?' I said, 'O Sovereign Lord, you alone know.'" Ezekiel 37:3

I watched in awe as a dim light began to flicker in the eyes of the emaciated form lying on the raised platform, which served as his sick bed.

On a trip to Thailand, my work as a catalyst for Eastern Mennonite Mission's response to HIV and AIDS, I was blessed to meet Christians who had laid aside stigma and judgment to minister to those who had been infected or affected by HIV/AIDS. These faithful Christians traveled to many homes throughout the week to visit patients, checking on their health and medications.

These volunteers also shared their faith with those they visited and this day the transformation was astonishing. At first I was unsure of what we would find lying beneath the single wool blanket; it looked as if it might only be covering bones. Then the young man adjusted his position to see his visitors a bit better. That is when the transformation began.

Both his body and his spirit began to react in wonder to these visitors who offered caring and support. Inch by inch he was able to support his weight to a sitting position and his face began to regain expression from the earlier mask it had worn. Where he had lain just moments before with an expressionless and immobile form of a body, I now saw the unmistakable light of life begin to enter. It almost seemed like the embodiment of Ezekiel's vision. Bones, sinew, flesh—transformed into humanity longing for the connection and comfort of others. "Can these bones live?"

Lord, speak to us today and show us life where we may see no life. Show us hope, where we may see no hope. We ask that You bless us with the opportunity to share that hope and life with someone in need.

Beth Good works as a volunteer with Eastern Mennonite Missions HIV/AIDS program. She and her husband Clair are church planters, living in Columbia.

Faithfulness Is Rewarded

"But a Samaritan, as he traveled, came where the man was; and when he saw him, he took pity on him." *Luke 10:33*

Lately, I've been excited to start playing tennis with my family. I picked up a few rackets at yard sales, but I only have one ball so far and with our budget being tight, I've been too cheap to buy more.

With that said, I was taking my walk one morning and chatting with God about how He wants us to help others by letting Him use us how He wants to. I am sometimes discouraged by the thought that there is so much need, and I'm just one person. As I was thinking that, I saw a soda cup along the side of the road. My initial reaction was to pick it up, but I passed it by, remembering that I was fifteen minutes from home and there was no trash can nearby. I told myself that someone else would get it, but it really bothered me.

About thirty feet later God whispered to my heart and I realized that I have looked at people that way. I would see a need and feel God's nudge, but wouldn't help because it was inconvenient, I didn't have time or someone else was better equipped for the job and similar excuses.

So, I turned around and went back and picked up the cup and carried it with me up the road and turned off my usual path, in search of a trash can. It just so happened that the trash can was right beside some tennis courts. When I lifted the lid of the trash can, there was a huge pile of brand new tennis balls inside.

I just had to help myself to a few. The first thing that popped into my head was "faithfulness is rewarded." I also saw some other trash along the road as I walked home, and I think God wanted me to remember that we don't have to do everything, just what He asks us to do.

Dear Lord, open my eyes to see how I can help this world be a better place and to be obedient to what You show me.

Kelly Good attends Lives Changed by Christ, where she sings and plays keyboards on the worship team. She has two wonderful kids, ages eight and five.

Honor Where Honor Is Due

"Whatever is true, noble, just, pure, lovely, of good report...meditate on these things." *Philippians 4:8 (New King James Version)*

I was wallowing in my disappointing experiences with spiritual leaders. As I mulled over the memories, it seemed that most of them had let me down. All I could see were their mistakes and failures as men of God. Up close and personal was my father, a church leader. I lived with Papa on a daily basis. So I observed things that bothered and puzzled me. But I was too timid to ask or talk to him about them.

My negative attitude came to a head one Sunday in worship. Prompted by the Holy Spirit, I knelt at the altar. As I confessed the sin of my negative focus, the Lord cleansed me and brought healing to my soul. Then He gave me a picture of my father giving the benediction blessing, as he often did at the end of a service: "Now may the God of peace who brought up our Lord Jesus from the dead, that great Shepherd of the sheep, through the blood of the everlasting covenant, make you complete in every good work to do His will, working in you what is well pleasing in His sight through Jesus Christ, to whom be glory forever and ever. Amen." (Hebrews 13:20–21)

I could clearly picture this in my mind. The memory of the countless times I had seen and heard my father give this blessing gave me something to focus on. This memory and blessing continue to sustain and encourage me. As a further step, I was able to forgive and bless my father's memory. I was able to focus on all the ways he had been good and helpful and caring and encouraging to me. I was able to be grateful for the father the Lord had given me.

Heavenly Father, thank You for the earthly father You provided for me. Thank You for leading him in the path of righteousness for Your Name's sake. Thank You for providing the very special father that I needed. I am blessed and grateful and I love You. Amen.

Ruth Lehman is grateful and blessed to be mother of eight children, grandmother of fifteen and great-grandmother of fourteen and another on the way. She is part of the intercessors team at ACTS Covenant Fellowship.

Don't Worry about Tomorrow

"Do not worry about tomorrow, for tomorrow will worry about itself. Each day has enough trouble of its own." *Matthew 6:34*

My life changed with a phone call two years ago when I learned that our precious eleven-year-old grandson was diagnosed with a malignant brain tumor. I immediately got alone with God and my Bible searching for reassurance that God would walk through this ordeal with us. God assured me that He would take care of my grandson.

The tumor was successfully removed with surgery, but he needed more than a year of radiation and chemotherapy treatments. The oncologists painted a very bleak picture of how the treatments could affect him. He could have hearing loss, stunted growth and learning disabilities in addition to other chemotherapy side effects.

Sometimes my faith in God's provision was strong, but there were days when I worried about the "what ifs." I couldn't imagine our family without our fun-loving, energetic grandson who could always make me laugh.

God gave me grace for each day, but when my mind went ahead to the future, I was moving beyond God's grace.

It was a very difficult time for my grandson and his family as they traveled back and forth from Manheim to Johns Hopkins Hospital in Baltimore, Maryland. The treatments were brutal and my grandson became very emaciated. He had nerve damage to his feet, which made walking difficult.

Today, my grandson is almost fully recovered. He's a bright well-adjusted teenager who loves God and enjoys being a kid again. He continues to be cancer free and has a good prognosis.

God is so good.

Lord, thank You for Your healing and provision for my grandson and for teaching me once more not to worry but to trust in You for my family.

Joanne Miller lives in Lititz with her husband John and is a member of Ephrata Church of the Nazarene.

Perfect Alignment

"I pray also that the eyes of your heart may be enlightened in order that you may know the hope to which he has called you, the riches of his glorious inheritance in the saints, and his incomparably great power for us who believe. . . . " Ephesians 1:18–19

I had been praying for some time that God would align me properly. In my mind that was a physical alignment with people, places and opportunities. I was asking to be in the right place at the right time for His plans and purposes to be fulfilled. At just the right time God put into my hands a book by Graham Cooke called *Coming into Alignment*. When I began to read it I knew it was an answer to prayer but I also knew God was taking me to a new level and wanted me to look at things from a higher perspective, a heavenly perspective.

God had already taken me on quite a journey to get me out of a place of negativity and self-defeat into a place of knowing who I was in Christ, so I was quite familiar with the scripture in Romans 12:2. But this was a new place of insight and understanding as the Lord encouraged me that He was calling me to a new place of power and place of the Spirit. Upon acceptance of this upgrade, I know there was a shift for me in the spirit realm. New dimensions of overcoming, however, are not obtained without a battle. And the Lord is teaching my hands to war and to stand firm on His Word.

This has truly been a point of transformation in my life. Although it may not yet be evident to those around me, I know there is a change happening on the inside of me. And isn't that where all transformation begins?

Father, thank You that You do Your work from the inside out and that You desire to transform each and every one of us into the image of Your Son.

Alice Brown serves as an intercessor for Teaching the Word Ministries and is a member of Acts Covenant Fellowship, where she also serves on the prayer team.

Loving Comfort

"The Lord is close to the brokenhearted and saves those who are crushed in spirit." Psalm 34:18

Today it is three years ago that my precious mother died of pancreatic cancer. It still seems like a dream. She was sick seven months from the time she was diagnosed until the time she went home to be with Jesus. I miss her so much.

Today there is a loneliness and emptiness within me that is overwhelming. I cannot be comforted. My heart aches.

I am sitting here, with tears streaming down my face. I am seeking God's presence, His strength and His comfort. I just want to curl up in His loving arms, sit in his presence and know that it will be OK.

As I sought the Scriptures I read Psalm 34:18, "The Lord is close to the brokenhearted and saves those who are crushed in spirit."

Even though my heart is breaking, I can rest assured that God is with me. I have sweet memories of my mother. We shared so many precious moments. Some are happy, some sad and some hilarious. She was always active and smiling. Always ready to lend a listening ear and a helping hand. These memories revive me. They comfort me. They bring me alive again.

Dear God, when I am feeling lonely, sad and scared, I can trust You to be my source of strength and courage. Lord, I need You. I cannot do it by myself. Thank You for holding me in your loving arms and comforting me. Amen.

Cynthia Zimmerman attends New Life Fellowship Church, Ephrata. She and her husband Rick and have two sons and one grandson.

Breakfast with the King

"He cuts off every branch in me that bears no fruit, while every branch that does bear fruit he prunes so that it will be even more fruitful." *John 15:2*

I had been walking on the Rails to Trails on my daily early morning time with the Lord. A discussion about John 15 had come up recently during a Bible study and again from a speaker at a meeting I had attended the previous evening.

He had recently "cut off" a business relationship that had turned ungodly. He had to cut it off. I could see that. What I couldn't see was how I was going to survive since it represented 90 percent of the income that came into the business. I knew it was necessary. Whether cutting or pruning, it is painful.

As I'm walking, praying and pondering John 15, I notice masses of red raspberries growing along the side of the trail that I hadn't noticed before. I started picking and eating them—the deep, dark red ones were the best, touched with dew and very sweet. I spent a few minutes enjoying these berries when I sensed the Lord speaking to me:

"Marti, I have a plan for you and it's a good plan. You don't need to be afraid. I love you. Now, Marti, how are the berries? Pretty good, huh? Did you go to the store to buy them? Did you need money this morning? Did you have to plant these bushes? Water them? *Prune* them? Fertilize them? Do you see how much I love you? I am taking care of you today and forever."

Peace flowed over me. Today is all I need to do. I do not need to worry about tomorrow.

Today, I had breakfast with the King.

Father, You are so awesome. Thank You for the assurance that You will meet my every need. Thank You for reminding me that You alone are my Provider. I love You.

Marti Evans serves on the board of Lebanon Valley Youth for Christ.

Blindsided

"So do not fear, for I am with you; do not be dismayed, for I am your God. I will strengthen you and help you; I will uphold you with my righteous right hand." *Isaiah 41:10*

It's distressing whenever congregational leaders resign abruptly, especially if it is a pastor. Congregants, especially board members, feel as though they have been blindsided. They question what went wrong or what "signs" were missed. Sadly, some of those who announce the change were given little advance notice of the pastor's decision and were unable to formulate a God–honoring response to present to the congregation.

There are several reasons for the abrupt resignation of a pastor. Some of them are related to the congregation, some of them are related to the pastor and some are rooted in pastoral and congregational burn-out. Regardless of the reason, the church has the opportunity to face a wonderful transformation. The Lord may want to lead the church in a new direction that requires a different type of leader, or He may want to lead the pastor in a direction that calls for a different type of congregation.

The good news is that El-elyon (God Most High) will continue to build His church and the gates of hell will in no way, shape or form prevail against it. No plan of His can be thwarted and He, alone, will have the final say. He knows exactly what He is doing or permitting and He can be trusted because He will not betray His Word or His character.

Throughout the process, it's important to focus not on other people, but on seeking God's wisdom, doing His will in the right time and in the right way and trusting that God will guard your path.

Transformation is never easy, but it is abundantly rewarding!

El-elyon, thank You for the enduring strength and wisdom You give to those who love You.

Pastor Ellen Dooley is an itinerant pastor and MDiv. candidate at Evangelical Theological Seminary.

Brown Spots

"... straining toward what is ahead, I press on toward the goal to win the prize ...." Philippians 3:13–14

At any given time, there are a number of little boys in our house. Outside the back door of our farmhouse we have ... well, we have a brown spot, a place where the grass never grows. One day one of those little boys ran up to me and said, "Hey guess what, Grandpa? I just peed in your boots!"

I said, "You better not have peed in my boots."

But he had. I had parked my barn boots too close to the brown spot, and they were just too tempting. That brown spot did not suddenly appear. At first it looked like any other part of the lawn. Soon the grass began to die, and the brown spot began to be evident to all who were in the house.

We all have "brown spots" in our spiritual lives, those places where bad habits have poisoned the spiritual ground in our lives, and nothing productive can grow. Those habits are often not all that bad in themselves, but done over and over, the soil is poisoned, and God cannot work there. Too much television. Too much Internet. Too much attention to sports. Too much secular music. Too much attention to the way we look and the way we dress.

There is just about nothing in this world that is safe from getting out of balance: food, travel, work or hobbies. None of them bad in themselves and in moderation, but when they take our time and attention away from the God of the universe, that part of our lives becomes dead and unproductive.

Father, take all of me. Open my eyes to the "brown spots" of my life, those places where the world has intruded and taken over, making me unproductive in Your kingdom.

Steve Hershey is a teacher and speaker at White Oak Church of the Brethren. Steve and his wife Brenda have opened their home to young adults.

Re-centering My Wheel of Faith

"Therefore, since we are surrounded by so great a cloud of witnesses, let us also lay aside every weight and the sin that clings so closely, and let us run with endurance the race that is set before us." *Hebrews 12:1 (English Standard Version)*

Like many Christians, I have struggled with faith questions for many years. A few years ago, my wife and I attended an older adults conference. I was excited about going to that conference, where I hoped to find some direction in my spiritual quest.

The wheel within a wheel that the prophet Ezekiel saw in his vision is a perfect metaphor for my dilemma. His description fits what we today call a gyroscope, a device used for navigation. Since the wheel in my gyroscope was off center, I kept changing directions as it wobbled. I needed somehow to re-center my faith.

As I sat among more than a thousand older adults who had been running the race for many years and who were preparing to hand off the baton to the next generation, I became acutely aware of the cloud of witnesses surrounding me at the conference. I finally understood that this God I sought was squarely within that cloud of witnesses who grace my presence from the past, as well as the present, namely the body of Christ, the church. I finally felt at home, sensing that feeling of safety that I experienced as a boy, sitting with my dad in church.

Although my quest is not over, I have rediscovered the center of my faith, and my gyroscope has settled down. Our God is so vast and so great that we can never really grasp it all while we run this race. But I have found the way back within that cloud of presence.

Great God of the journey, keep me in the presence of that great cloud of witnesses that brought my faith into new focus. As the old spiritual says, "Guide my feet while I run this race, for I don't want to run this race in vain." Amen.

Jay D. Weaver, a member of the Lancaster Church of the Brethren, is a retired mathematics professor at Millersville University.

God Heals

"He said to her, 'Daughter, your faith has healed you. Go in peace and be freed from your suffering.'" Mark 5:34

I had read this scripture many times in my Christian walk and I believed in my head that God healed people. Still I thought that God healed when He wanted and who He wanted . . . and that certainly He did not heal in an emergency situation. I could not get my brain to accept that fact.

In May 2010, I went on a mission trip to Arizona with my church. We were located forty-five minutes from the nearest town and did not have transportation most of the time from the Indian reservation where we were working. To place a cell phone call, we had to climb up a mountain.

A group of us climbed up one evening and after calling home, we began our descent down the mountain. I slipped and fell about a foot down the side of the mountain. Immediately I knew my back was hurt and I was having trouble breathing. The people that were with me immediately went to God in prayer. I cried out to the Lord in my spirit saying, "Father God, it is getting dark and we need to get out of this mountain. I need you to heal me now." Since I was the team cook, I needed to get up the next morning and cook for our team.

With some help from the guys, I was able to get up and walk down that mountain. All through the night I prayed, "Lord I believe You will do this . . . . Please allow me to get up and do what You brought me here to do"

I am pleased to say I got up the next morning to cook our team breakfast, praising the Lord the whole time. I now believe that God heals in a way that I never did before!

Father God, teach us all to believe in You always and in all ways to be dependent on you. Amen.

Kendra Kramer is a youth director at St. Jacob's Kimmerling's Church in Lebanon.

August

Be Still and Know

"Be still, and know that I am God. . . ." *Psalm 46:10*

Shocked, sad, angry . . . were a few of the emotions I felt when a dear friend was sentenced to four years for vehicular homicide and committed to a Virginia state prison. I had known him almost twenty years and loved him like a brother. When it came time for his trial, I never suspected there was anything to worry about. He was a truck driver and there were no drugs or alcohol involved. His log books were current, and he had just come off an eight-hour break. The only problem was he couldn't remember a thing about the accident!

It turned out there had been a series of accidents involving other eighteen-wheelers, and for that reason the state of Virginia said that's it!

When word got back to me that my friend was imprisoned, I was stunned to say the least! I thanked God for his strong faith, and I prayed fervently that God would be with him and keep him safe.

One week later, I received a collect call from the Virginia State Penitentiary, and I nearly jumped out of my skin. I was so excited to hear his voice and made sure he was okay. I was somewhere near hysteria when he said, "Ruthi, stop talking. Calm down!" I started to breathe again, and the first words out of his mouth were, "I just keep telling myself, be still and know that I am God. That's all I'm thinking about."

Every phone call and letter after that was filled with the amazing miracles God was doing for him on a daily basis. Even more importantly, he keeps reporting about all the lives he is touching by telling them about God's love.

Dear heavenly Father, when we are in that place of chaos and confusion and don't know where to turn, remind us to be still and know that You are God. You are in control Lord and only You! In Jesus' name. Amen.

Ruthi Schultz lives in New Holland with her husband Dave and son, Sam. She is a consultant for Mary Kay Cosmetics for almost twenty years and enjoys being the Women's Ministry director at her church, DOVE Westgate.

The Sand and the Stars

"How precious also are Your thoughts to me, O God! How great is the sum of them! If I should count them, they would be more in number than the sand . . . ." *Psalm 139:17–18 (New King James Version)*

Recently I was walking on the beach with my kids and being mesmerized by God's amazing creation. I love the ocean as it breaks across the sand — the indentations, tracks left from sea life, shells, wood, little pebbles, all the cool treasures that wash up on the sand.

As we walked my son said, "You know they say that for as many grains of sand there are, there are just as many stars in the sky." I gave some sort of awed response.

However, the next night I sat in the cool sand watching the waves cut across the beach. I stared up at the starlit sky and began counting the stars. Although there didn't seem to be that many that I could see, I tired quickly of trying to count them. As I dug my hand into the cool depths of the light grainy sand, sifting it through my fingers, a soft voice said, "Go ahead. Count all the grains of sand you can see."

I stirred some more with my hands, I drizzled the sand across my legs. "Oh, wow God! You are absolutely, incredibly, beyond imagination and clearly, beyond words amazing! For all the sand, which shall remain unnumbered, there are more stars—even though I can only see a few! That means the universe (or universes) must be massively huge— beyond huge!

I laid back in the sand and stared at the immense blackness that held this immense world of stars that I could not even begin to see and let the immensity of my God, my Lord, my heavenly Daddy wash over me in waves. I will forever love those moments alone with Him, when He reveals Himself and His immense love for me.

Thank You, Daddy, for showing me who You are and for letting me drink in just a taste of the depth and height and width of Your love for me.

Lisa Hildebrand, Valley View Alliance, works for Susquehanna Valley Pregnancy Services and ministers as a teacher and speaker in local churches.

Promised Bracelet

"In my integrity you uphold me. . . ." *Psalm 41:12*

I was in Brazil on a short-term missions team. As I stood watching a program at a town park one evening, a little girl emerged from the crowd and took my hand. We began talking. She was neither a Christian nor from a Christian family. But she asked me for one of the "gospel bracelets" she had seen our group distributing earlier.

I was sad I didn't have any more to give her, but told her I would send her one after returning to Pennsylvania.

Somehow in the busy travels of the following weeks, I lost her name and address. All I could remember was her first name—Priscilla.

I felt guilty for making a promise that I could not keep. I prayed for Priscilla, but worried that my broken promise would drive her away from Christianity.

Several years later, I again traveled to Brazil. One day our group planned to visit Priscilla's city. "Lord, this seems impossible," I prayed, "but, if You could somehow arrange for me to find out Priscilla's whereabouts, that would be awesome!" Just in case, I tucked a gospel bracelet in my pocket.

We gathered at an evangelical church before heading out to visit homes in the community. I began looking at photographs of a recent baptism, which were mounted on the wall. "Could it be?" One girl being baptized surely looked familiar!

Just then, I turned to see a group of Brazilian young people entering the building. Though she was taller and lankier now, I recognized her immediately—It was Priscilla.

I learned some important lessons that day: First, it's best to not make rash promises. Second, when I desire to walk in integrity, God will help me do that. And, third, although *we* may lose touch with people, God *never* does!

Father, help me to watch my words today, being careful not to promise what I can't deliver. And let me never underestimate Your ability to do what seems impossible to me!

Sharon Charles assists her husband John, director of Abundant Living, in this family counseling ministry near Lititz.

Most Valuable Player (MVP)

"Give ear to my prayer, O God, and do not hide yourself from my supplication. Give heed to me and answer me; I am restless in my complaint and am surely distracted." *Psalm 55:1–2 (New American Standard Bible)*

As with all sports, the competitiveness is extreme. Did you ever notice that in every crowd there seems to be one heckler who seems to get joy out of taunting the players and the umpires and often upsets the whole crowd.

One day, my wife told me that she was no longer able to tolerate a heckler's behavior. She decided to move behind the heckler and silently ask the Lord to stop the man's obnoxious comments.

"Watch and see what the Lord will do when you silently pray," she said. She stood behind the seats where the heckler was located and worshipped the Lord silently in her heart, seeking God's intervention. She stood at the same location for about fifteen minutes eagerly awaiting what the Lord would do.

The next thing I noticed the man started stuffing red licorice strips into his mouth until his face looked like a chipmunk with food stored in his cheeks. It was funny how the licorice prevented him from speaking. The man soon walked away from the game and left his chair behind.

I could not believe my eyes and was amazed that she had not said one word to the man. It was the power of prayer that literally moved the man. Praise the Lord!

We have been blessed by the Lord with two sons who have the ability to play baseball. I have coached for years and my wife serves as concession stand coordinator. Our family has fallen in love with the game of baseball. We are blessed with the opportunity this sport has given our family to minister the love of Jesus at baseball fields. The Lord loves sports and wants us to be part of the game plan! After all, God created everything.

Dear Lord, thank You for changing the atmosphere at the base–ball field. You are the MVP. It's an honor to have You on our team!

The Vincent Apicella family are members of Christ Community Church in Camp Hill.

Lifted by the Winds of Adversity

"... they will mount up with wings like eagles ...." *Isaiah 40:31 (New American Standard Bible)*

My trip to Prince George, British Columbia, required a total of four plane connections. The delay in the first flight was the beginning of "just making" every connection thereafter.

Little did I know that what began as a tension-filled cross-country trip would find its high point on Air Canada's Flight 850 from San Diego to Vancouver, Canada. The seat I was assigned was 4A, a window seat. The twenty-nine-year-old young lady sitting next to me was Trina. She had been severely crippled in an auto accident when she was fourteen. Her mother had fallen asleep while driving. The result was that her younger brother was killed and she was left with a broken neck.

Instead of being bitter, she had a spirit of blessedness. She was like a bird that had a broken wing but still made every effort to become airborne and ride on the winds of a new day. As we talked for over three hours, she lifted my soul and strengthened my belief that God does all things well. He can take the buffetings of our lives and use them to polish others with untold blessings.

What might be the trials of your life today that can be turned into blessings for others? Our choice each day is to become more blessed or more bitter, grounded in grumpiness or grateful in God's goodness.

Lord, help me to see Your presence in every person and circumstance so that I may choose to be blessed and not bitter.

Dr. Sandy Outlar and his wife attend Wheatland Presbyterian Church.

Health and Prosperity

"Beloved, I pray that you may prosper in all things and be in health, just as your soul prospers." *3 John 1:2 (New King James Version)*

What in the world does prosperity have to do with health? Being a nurse, I could not make sense of what God wanted me to "get" in this verse. In studying the word "prosper," the bond was found in scripture. God told Joshua in 1:8: "This book of the Law shall not depart from your mouth, but you shall *meditate in it day and night*, that you may observe to do to all that is written in it. For *then you will make your way prosperous* and then you will have good success." In Psalm 1:1–3, "Blessed is the man who walks not the counsel of the ungodly, nor stands in the paths of sinners, nor sits in the seat of the scornful, but his delight is in the law of the Lord, and in His law he *meditates day and night*. He shall be like a tree planted by the rivers of water, that brings forth its fruit in its season, whose leaf does not wither; and *whatever he does shall prosper*."

One day it all clicked! The connection was to meditate on God and His Word. If my soul would prosper by doing this, then so would my health and my life. That's where prosperity starts, in our soul (mind, will, and emotions) according to God. I need to keep His Word in my daily thoughts, submit my will to His and keep my emotions in check. The relationship of health and prosperity are clear. So, as my soul began to prosper, so did all areas of my life. I now have increasingly more joy and peace. Peace with God is the beginning of wholeness, health, and prosperity. Shalom.

Dear God, thank You for Your spiritual food that nourishes us and gives us wholeness.

Jo Farner, Worship Center, serves at Hope Within Community Health Center, promoting health, wellness, wholeness to the medically uninsured as a Parish nurse.

Hands Off!

"I am the vine, you are the branches . . . for apart from me you can do nothing." *John 15:5 (New American Standard)*

At age five, I was asked by my father if I was interested in taking piano lessons. At the time, the question seemed harmless enough, so I signed on. It wasn't until later I realized that lessons meant practice; practice meant a daily hour of tedium; and my father meant business!
"Did you practice the piano today?"
   "Ah, I ah, well ah, maybe ah, I think."
"Get upstairs and practice now!"
"Yes sir."
And there I'd be, sitting at the piano, trying to endure an hour that seemed much longer than sixty minutes.

Despite my displeasure, not the least of which was due to my father's insistence that I read the music (he would often supervise my lessons and practice), it turns out I had a knack for playing by ear, and by my early twenties I was playing on weekends in restaurants and hotels. In these venues I rarely worried about making mistakes, since the music was typically obscured by the sounds of hurried servers, famished diners and spirited conversationalists.

It wasn't until years later, when my wife urged me to start playing in church, that I became absolutely paranoid about hitting clinkers! So, after preparing an arrangement, I would practice it over and over and over again, right up to the moment we left for church on Sunday morning! After all, practice makes perfect, right? In reality, this routine had reached a point of diminishing returns.

Then, one Sunday as I started to practice, it was as if the Lord was saying "Hands off! Too much practice, too little trust!" I was convicted. My supposed diligence was nothing more than spiritual delinquency. From now on I would prepare responsibly and leave the outcome with Him—not just in music, but also in life!

Lord, help me never be wise in my own estimation or think more highly of myself than I ought to think.

Peter Bilotta and his wife Susan are members of Hephzibah Baptist Church in East Fallowfield.

"Gloriation" of God

"Father, the time has come. Glorify your Son, that your Son may glorify you . . . . *" John 17:2*

Most Easter mornings of my life you would have found me in a pew at a church. This memorable Easter I was positioned next to my four-year-old granddaughter on my couch. She and I were having an overnight together to avoid the flu at her house. It seemed our family Easter plans were canceled.

She had tiptoed down the stairs and found me in the midst of my devotions in the living room. She snuggled up silently next to me for morning hugs. We were both quiet, just being together. Then she had an observation. "GG," she said, "You sure have a lot of mirrors on your walls. You must really like to look at yourself."

Silent pause. "Well actually, that is not at all why I have that collection of mirrors," I said. There was a silent longer pause as the Easter sunrise came in the east window and suddenly lit up all the walls with a "light" explosion!

"I know!" she exclaimed. "It's because you want to reflect the 'gloriation' of God!"

Yes, indeed it is the "gloriation" of God that we want to reflect! Light of the world, you have visited us and shown us your risen glory and transformed our darkness into light.

Easter came to us and exploded in our hearts! We didn't miss Easter after all!

Thank You, Lord for quiet moments of splendor to feel Your "gloriation" and to see once again that You are risen and alive in our lives. Alive from generation to generation!

Nancy Clegg wants to be a mirror that reflects the risen hope of Christ.

Little Christs

". . . The disciples were called Christians first at Antioch."
Acts 11:26

On my way to Sunday celebration service recently I was blessed to have God give me a very clear picture of what He desires for His children.

A man and his son, I would guess the son to be about eight to ten years old, were jogging together on the sidewalk. The son was the "spitting image" of his dad. Their facial features were alike. They were dressed alike: red shirts, tan shorts and sneakers. They were obviously enjoying each other's company.

The Lord spoke to my heart. "This is how I want My children to be, the likeness of Jesus."

I realize that I can't make myself look like Jesus, but the Word says that we are being conformed to the likeness of His Son in Romans 8:29. The footnote in my Bible says that God foreknew us and this knowledge is couched in love and mixed with purpose.

As I thought about the real picture of the man and his son, I wanted to look like Jesus. When I said this to God, His response seemed to be, "No, you don't, he was a suffering servant."

Father by Your grace I want to be willing to be Your suffering servant.

Kathleen Hollinger loves the family God gave her, attends ACTS Covenant Fellowship, and coleads the prayer ministry there.

A Cinderella Story

"... and may you be able to feel and understand, as all God's children should, how long, how wide, how deep, and how high His love really is; and to experience this love for yourselves. . . ." *Ephesians 3:18–19*

After my father remarried, I suddenly became the oldest of fourteen children. My strict stepmother treated me like a Cinderella stepchild. As a young teen I was made to cook all the meals, care for the house and look after my younger brothers and sisters. I felt trapped, unloved and unwanted. Just to get out of the house, I married at age nineteen. I didn't love my husband, and I told him as much. Children came along, but I neglected them just as my mother had neglected me. Life to me was getting what I wanted, not what I needed, so eventually I divorced. To this day, my mind has blotted out a lot of memories of how incapable I was of loving my husband and children.

Another man came into my life and for the next twenty-five years, I moved time and again, dragging my daughter along with me until she finally left me to live with her father. Thank the Lord, for seventeen years during this time I had a Christian aunt who prayed for me, pleading with the Lord to show me what true, unconditional love is.

Reality hit hard when the relationship ended after I discovered that the man I thought loved me had been cheating on me all along. I was broken and lost. Through my tears, the Lord spoke to me, saying He wanted me to be near my daughter and grandchildren. In order to do that, I had to ask forgiveness from God and from my children for so many things.

Through this process, I received a fresh understanding of God's love and it has allowed me to begin building a relationship with my children. The Lord knew what I needed, not necessarily what I wanted. Healing of my troubled past has come through God's perfect love for me.

Thank You, Lord, for showing me how You have been there for me all along.

Kathleen Masters is an encourager who serves in the Solid Rock Café at the DOVE Westgate Church.

He Carries Our Sorrows

"He was despised and rejected by men, a man of sorrows, and familiar with suffering. Like one from whom men hide their faces he was despised, and we esteemed him not. Surely he took up our infirmities and carried our sorrows, yet we considered him stricken by God, smitten by him, and afflicted." *Isaiah 53:3–4*

Our daughter was in the Intensive Care Unit of the hospital for eighteen days hovering between life and death. Her kidneys had failed, and the doctors gave us little hope.

On Wednesday of that first week, we reached out to others. We asked the leaders of our church, as well as a circle of our friends all over the world, to pray for her. After one week in the hospital something happened to all of us with no rational explanation as to why. The fear and anxiety was lifted. Our daughter's physical condition had not improved, but our emotional and spiritual well being had greatly improved. It was as if God had whispered, "I know what you are going through. Trust me. We will make it through this together."

We knew that our daughter needed good scientific medicine in order to get well. Eventually, she needed a new kidney. However, we also knew she needed more if she were to be healed. Even the doctors agreed with us on that.

The prophet reminds us that the Messiah is one who understands our sufferings, is acquainted with our grief and was afflicted just as we are. In short, God knows what we are going through because God has gone through it. The one who created us will also work in concert with modern medicine to bring healing to our bodies and peace to our souls.

Lord, I know You know what those who suffer go through. You suffered. You were afflicted as we are. Help us, when we ask the "whys" of illness to remember Your presence in our lives as the source of healing. Amen.

Rev. Randolph T. Riggs is senior pastor of First Presbyterian Church in Lancaster.

Extending Grace

"The Lord is gracious and compassionate, slow to anger and rich in love." Psalm 145:8

A car speeds past me on the highway. I'm doing seventy, so he must be doing eighty. I used to think, "That is so irresponsible and dangerous. I hope there is an officer farther up the road that will give him a ticket." ow, though, I'll say a short prayer for the driver—that he will be safe and whatever situation is causing him to drive so fast will turn out for the best.

I pass a house whose flower beds haven't been weeded in weeks and whose grass is in dire need of a visit from a lawn mower. I used to think, "How can someone let their property look so unkempt?" The word lazy would flash across my mind. Now, though, I wonder what event has happened in the owner's life that demands so much time and attention.

We see glimpses into people's lives and draw conclusions about what type of persons they are. The speeder is reckless. The property owner is lazy. The mother whose child misbehaves in the grocery store is too tolerant. But we don't see the entire picture—all the circumstances that led to the moment we happened to witness. I have changed my thinking about all these situations because I have found myself in all three scenarios and not because I was reckless, lazy or tolerant.

It is easy to pass judgment when instead I should extend grace. When I take an *additional* moment to ponder a situation I witness, I can often imagine a number of different circumstances that resulted in what I just saw. My own life experiences have broadened my imagination. I hope, though, that I can learn to be gracious without having to go through too many of those experiences personally!

Father, keep me humble so that I am able to extend grace. Give me a mind with a vivid imagination to counter my flesh which leans toward judgment.

Rebecca Nissly, Community Bible Church in Marietta, serves at Susquehanna Valley Pregnancy Services.

Enjoying the Ride of Life

". . . whatever is right, whatever is pure, whatever is lovely, whatever is admirable—if anything is excellent or praiseworthy—think about such things." *Philippians 4:8*

My life seemed cluttered with unanswered prayer and stuff not to my liking. "Let's go biking," I suggested to my husband. Bicycling often helps me break free of stress and clears my mind to refocus on tasks ahead.

The biking trail at Mt. Gretna was stunning with green growth, fragrant honeysuckle and sturdy trees. "Everything is so glorious," I breathed in prayerful adoration. As I pedaled along, I inwardly questioned why God did not make my life as beautiful as nature.

I sensed God saying, "Open your eyes."

When I looked more closely at the green undergrowth, I noticed that it was mostly weeds—an invasive species amongst God's beauty. The vibrant growth was strewn with dead and decaying debris. I noticed an alarming amount of dead branches in the leafy canopy above my head and massive tree trunks leaning dangerously toward the trail. I couldn't believe how quickly my perspective of the perfect woodland had changed as I concentrated on all the imperfections of nature.

It did not take long for me to grasp the connection between my life and the wooded environment. When I concentrated on what was wrong with the setting, all I saw were problems, but when I focused on what was right, I was filled with awe and wonder.

Since that biking excursion, I make a conscious effort to focus on what is right in my life instead of what is wrong. It makes all the difference in enabling me to enjoy the ride of life.

Lord of the universe, open my eyes to see Your goodness, to sense Your power, to revel in the beauty of Your handiworks.

Lou Ann Good, DOVE Westgate Christian Fellowship, delights in the gift of ten grandchildren.

Discernment

"I keep asking that the God of our Lord Jesus Christ, the glorious Father, may give you the Spirit of wisdom and revelation, so that you may know him better." *Ephesians 1:17*

An interesting thing happens in prayer when communication with God becomes a lifestyle—I receive revelations directly from the heart of God. These may be through scripture, or a subtle communication that is more like an impression than a voice. But I know that something new is being uncovered for me.

Immediately I want to know what it means—I want the interpretation! Sometimes I think I already know. It seems obvious when I look at what's happening in my life. Other times it seems totally unrelated to anything.

I ask, "Lord, what do you want me to do with this revelation?" I am not naturally content with lingering over something God reveals to me. I want to know, "What is the application?" But lingering and listening may be the most important link between the revelation and its application. This illuminating process brings the light I need to correctly interpret and apply the revelation to my life.

Illumination is often the ignored step in navigating deepening levels of spiritual perception. The biblical truth regarding spiritual knowledge is that with many things we see in a mirror dimly. We need more light than what is naturally available through human reasoning to interpret what God reveals to us. We need ". . . spirit of wisdom and revelation as we come to know Him, so that the eyes of our heart may be enlightened. . . ." (Ephesians 1:17)

Enter application. With the benefit of the Spirit's illumination I have a more correct interpretation. I now see areas where the revelation is applicable—areas that I did not see at the beginning of the discernment process.

I keep asking that the God of our Lord Jesus Christ, the glorious Father, may give you the Spirit of wisdom and revelation, so that you may know him better.(Paul's Prayer)

Robert Woodcock, D.Min., is director of leadership and personal development at Global Disciples, empowering churches and their mission-sending entities to train and send their local workers into the least reached areas.

Baked at 350 Degrees

"It is God who works in you to will and to act according to his good purpose." *Philippians 2:13*

With a spaghetti pie meal in hand, I was out the door to deliver supper to a friend whom I wanted to bless. I delivered the meal successfully but hours later, I discovered that my wedding band and diamond ring were missing.

Not only was I feeling the heat of a summer day, but also the heat of life. Ever since God called us to embrace two orphans into our home, life felt like a hot, humid day. Continuing to live with two little scarred girls seemed more than what I wanted to deal with on a daily basis. Our once peaceful family of four had been replaced with intense drama and offbeat discord.

Thinking back through the events of that summer day, I suddenly was horrified at where I thought my rings could have fallen off my finger. After rooting through the leftover spaghetti pie, to my surprise there was my wedding band among noodles and tomato sauce. But where was my diamond? I quickly called my friend who was ready to eat the spaghetti pie. A phone call back revealed that the lost was found.

In Matthew 23:11–12, Jesus' definition of greatness is to live last and serve others. Serving others flows out of the heart of what God's incredible love has done for us. We can't repay what He has done for us but we can say, "Yes" to whatever He asks us to do. For my family, it meant going to an impoverished, distant land to rescue two little girls. Ultimately, Jesus Himself went to a distant, impoverished place to rescue us. God knew exactly what we needed in our family to become more like Him—heat. God has been furiously at work in our hearts molding and shaping us at 350 degrees.

Father, help me to welcome the heat that You bring into my life knowing that its purpose is to stamp Your image on my life.

Rosene Hertzler is a member of Valley View Alliance Church.

Letting Go, Letting God

"For whoever desires to save his life will lose it, but whoever loses his life for my sake will find it." *Matthew 16:25 (New King James Version)*

Have you heard of the monkey whose paw was imprisoned in a vase because he wouldn't let go of the prize he'd clasped in his paw?

How like us, locked in worry, anxiety or frustration because the concern we are grasping in our clenched fist is too precious to release to God.

Our son was attending school in another state when on a visit I met the girl he was dating—and her mother. If that sounds something like a double date that is exactly what I mean.

I went home with anxiety and worry gnawing at my heart. What to do? I sensed that expressing my concern would only put more pressure on our son. I felt drawn to entrust the situation to Father's care without my interference. "But in my mind the possible consequences of not speaking a warning loomed darkly on the horizon of his future.

Gently persuaded, I yielded my valid fears to the care of my Father. From that point on whenever anxiety rose in my heart, I turned it loose and trusted God with my son's heart.

Within a few weeks I received a call. Our son had ended the unhealthy relationship and I had learned the joy of losing my grasp to His grip. Why would I ever think my concern is safer in my control than in His?

Father, I trust You to own and hold the cares of my heart. I know You will never treat lightly my confidence in You.

Ruth Ann Stauffer, Lititz, is wife to Al and with him enjoys their four children, seven grandchildren, leading a house church and prayer counseling.

My Significance Is in Him

"For you created my inmost being; you knit me together in my mother's womb. I praise you because I am fearfully and wonderfully made; your works are wonderful, I know that full well."
Psalm 139:13–14

In the 1991 movie *Grand Canyon*, chaos and futility reign in the lives of the characters. At the film's climax, the protagonist chauffeurs the distraught cast to an undisclosed destination. At journey's end lies the Grand Canyon, where the little group marvels at its splendor. Their response is one of awe, but their awe speaks of insignificance. In the greater scheme of life, their problems seem petty and are overshadowed by the magnificence of Mother Nature. Their woeful lives are viewed with a clearer perspective. *Who are they in the greater scheme of the universe?*

Fast forward a few years . . . there I was alone at the Grand Canyon, if one can be alone amidst throngs of tourists. As I stood gazing into the abyss from the South Rim, the memory of the movie travelers came to mind. I fully expected a similar experience, but this was not to be. Rather than feeling insignificant, I was overcome by the humbling realization of significance. The same God whose magnificent handiwork stretched before me was the God Who created and loved me. *Had not this trip been an unexpected, yet coveted, provision from my Father? Was not this same Creator the One who delivered me from unspeakable pain and sorrow?* Savoring these truths, I drank in the beauty before me, choked with gratitude.

Armed with a panoramic camera on a later trip to the canyon, I determined to capture both the awesome grandeur and spiritual revelation from the earlier visit. Mission accomplished. These photos surround me today at home and office. When stresses abound, I gaze at the majesty of the Grand Canyon and return there in spirit. I am refreshed and encouraged.

Thank You, Father, that my life is another product of Your handiwork and my significance is in You alone.

Sally K. Owens lives with her husband Don in Lancaster, where they participate in two home church groups.

Saturated

"Be not conformed to this world, but be transformed by the renewing of your mind, that you may prove what *is* that good and acceptable and perfect will of God." *Romans 12:2 (New King James Version)*

Opening day for trout season brought us to a peaceful mountain creek, in hopes of catching a whopper. While casting my line, I looked down into the depths of the murky water and saw a waterlogged tree stump lodged at the bottom of the creek. In that still small voice, the Lord began to speak to me, as He often does in those quiet times while fishing. I had come to the creek especially weary and heavy laden, with many overwhelming concerns and "prayer requests."

Looking at the waterlogged tree, I wondered how it had become so saturated and weighed down. It had totally lost all its natural properties to float and be the useful, productive piece of wood it was created to be. It was literally stuck there, in bondage, at the bottom of the creek.

It made me wonder, what am I soaking in? Am I filled with the Word of God and all His life-giving truth, or am I soaking up all the worldly lies, thoughts, attitudes and empty values aimed at me. They are all meant to weigh me down like this waterlogged stump, unable to float or to be what God created it to be: possibly a wooden table, where families share a meal in love, laughter and fellowship; or part of a home for the homeless; maybe even the wooden cross that carried our precious Lord's sacrificial gift of salvation.

I never did catch the whopper trout that day, but the prize I did take home was a new refreshing, thankful mind-set determined to be free of useless fears, and worry. At the same time, I was ready to soak up all God has for me and to be all I was created to be, for His glory.

Lord, I thank You for Your enduring truth in Your Word, and how You refresh us, heal us, free us and guide and direct us with Your loving words. Amen.

Shirley Ann Bivens serves in the children's department at Christ Community Church. She does Christian clowning as "CoCo the Clown" and is a full-time grammy.

.

Feast, Fly and Crow

"For in Him we live and move and exist . . . ." *Acts 17:28*
(The Living Bible)

I know we all need vacations at times. I love vacations as much as the next guy, but many times I see vacationers return exhausted and tired.

Why can't people seem to rest on vacation? Because they continue to be caught up in a whirlwind of activities from morning until night and never really get that rest and relaxation that we all say we need on our so-called vacations.

I can't think of a more restful and rewarding place in the world to go than right at my own doorstep . . . . and it's free. Early cool mornings, with my Bible and my coffee, I love to escape to our back deck. An umbrella-covered table and chair await me as I watch the sun come up in the glory of God's awesome creation! I listen to our neighbor's rooster crowing, announcing it's a new morning, then I watch the yellow and purple finches come to eat at the thistle bay hanging close by. Today a butterfly sat down beside me and I realized, once again, how much of the day I get caught up in distractions which blur out all these marvelous details God has made and given for our enjoyment. It all reminds me of the Creator and Redeemer He is!

I thought about the scripture that says, "Be still and know that I am God." (Psalm 46:10 Today Lord, help me to reflect on your faithfulness such as the sun that comes up every morning. Cause me to come to feast in your Word . . . sort of like eating at the "living bag." Help me to fly like that butterfly above the circumstances, trials and problems which I may face today. And yes, help me crow like that rooster saying, "this is the day the Lord has made, I will rejoice and be glad in it." (Psalm 118:24) My heart's desire is to tell and reflect the good news of God's love wherever I go and whatever I do.

With mornings like this, who needs a vacation?

Lord, help me to trust You and rest in You, as You teach me to feast, fly and crow for the glory of God and see Your Kingdom built.

Jeanette Weaver is a wife, mother of two, grandmother of six and serves with her husband Don at DOVE Westgate as deacons and small group leaders

Through Christ I Have Victory

"I have been crucified with Christ. It is no longer I who live, but Christ who lives in me. And the life I now live in the flesh I live by faith in the Son of God, who loved me and gave himself for me."
Galatians 2:20 (English Standard Version)

Jesus Himself has said that we are in Him and He lives in us. His anointing empowers our lives and the lives of others.

When we become *confident* in whom we are in Christ, transformation begins! As we pray in confidence we begin to see things happen that may not have occurred if we were timid. When we maintain confidence in His Word and stay focused on His will, our confidence overcomes fear and brings us into a place of holy boldness!

Hebrews 10:35 warns us not to throw away our confidence because it has great rewards. It is the enemy's plan to destroy it. He wants to rob us of our reward, and if he can tempt us into timidity, we will not fulfill God's plan for our lives. Condemnation and guilt that come from the sin are also enemies of confidence. We must resist sin and continue to walk as Jesus did. We are the righteousness of God!

I was personally tempted to throw away my confidence because of overeating. I really struggled and knew I couldn't overcome in my own strength. When Jesus prayed, He looked toward the Father and focused all his attention upon Him. He was able to walk in a confident authority that came from above. He instructs us to walk in this same authority.

I live and move and have my being in Him. The anointing Christ provides is everything I need to overcome! This is transformation! Through Christ I have the victory!

Father, thank You for entrusting Your limitless power to work in us. I open my heart for You to empower me to express the life of Christ today. Thank You for the confidence we have in Your transforming power. Amen.

Pat Denlinger is a prayer leader, teacher and licensed minister of Teaching The Word Ministries.

God's Workmanship

"For we are His workmanship, created in Christ Jesus unto good works." *Ephesians 2:10 (King James Version)*

The dream of every aspiring golfer is to play in the United States Open, the most prestigious golf event in the world. After going through four difficult, pressure-packed rounds of golf, I had qualified. I obtained one of the forty-eight coveted spots from more than six thousand attempting to qualify. My caddie, who had led me to the Lord six years earlier, and I were tearfully amazed how God had blessed us.

Arriving early the week of the event, I prepared by playing a number of practice rounds. While on the putting green, rubbing shoulders with the great players of the sport, Palmer and Nicklaus, I was in awe of everyone.

At the roped-off practice putting green, many spectators crowded near attempting to see their favorite player, hoping to obtain a coveted autograph. As I practiced near the edge of the putting green a group of young boys ran up to the spectator's rope, shoved their autograph books toward me, and asked for my autograph. I had never been asked for my autograph, and I must say I was a little shocked. As I signed my name on the page and passed it back, one of the boys in the second row asked, "Who is it?" The boy read my name and shouted, "Nobody," and off they went in search of a real star.

After reflection and laughter, I realized that we are not "nobodies." I contemplated how God values us. God sent His Son to die for us. In Christ we are victors, sons and daughters of the creator, saints. We have been redeemed, are inheritors, anointed, sealed, secure and significant. We are God's workmanship and citizens of heaven. In Him we are everything!

Lord, may we humbly walk in the path You have prepared for us, realizing that in You, we are complete, a vessel to be used to serve, ambassadors of Your love.

Mike Atkins is a former PGA golf professional, two time Lancaster open champion, member of the Worship Center and president of the board of directors for the Gathering Place.

Go Ye into All the World

"I will instruct you and teach you in the way you should go."
Psalm 32:8

My husband and I had just finished an enjoyable breakfast in Ocean City, New Jersey. As we crossed the street to begin the day's activities, he called out to the gentleman across the street. "I see you like to read."

I about flipped. Just because the man was carrying a newspaper didn't exactly mean he liked to read. Dan was always finding some way to engage someone in conversation so that he could give them a tract and then share the gospel with them. But this time it seemed like a poor approach to me.

As I got into our car, I felt an annoyance rising within me. *Did he always have to do this?* More than anything I just wanted to move on.

Suddenly, it was as though God Himself was speaking to me. In my heart I suddenly felt ashamed. My husband was attempting to serve the Lord and share His love. Every day Dan prays that God will lead him to someone, and here I was sitting in the car inwardly fussing. I asked God to forgive me, and then I prayed God would help him to have the right words to share with this gentleman. When I looked up, they were both standing on the corner, and I noticed that the man holding the newspaper was sobbing.

When Dan returned to the car, I heard the whole story: He had begun to share the tract when the man asked him if he was a born-again Christian. When Dan responded in the affirmative, the man said, "God put you on this corner for me today!" The man knew the gospel, but he had turned from it by choosing a path which was leading him into sin.

This encounter was the beginning of a commitment for that man to follow Jesus. The man on the corner is growing in the Lord and keeps in touch with my husband. At Christmas he sent a beautiful card and note which read, " I was back visiting Ocean City when crossing 'that' street, I remembered 'that' day we met."

Dear Lord, help us to always be ready to share the gospel with others.

Ruth Little is a retired elementary school teacher, who is appreciating the opportunity to help in reaching kids for Christ through the Weekly Religious Education program in public schools.

Divine Intimacy

"How beautiful you are and how pleasing, O love, with your delights!" *Song of Solomon 7:6*

We hear much about the necessity of having an intimate relationship with our God. What is that? How can a flesh and blood mortal be deeply involved with the all-supreme God who made us? What must we do?

Those of us who are married have a relationship with our spouse that is above any other person. It starts with a desire that grows until it consumes us. Our waking and sleeping moments are focused on our loved one in a way that supercedes the need for sleep, food, work and other parts of life. We sigh, we cry and we giggle. We must be with our loved one. But how can this be? God already knows everything that can ever be known about us. How can we know Him in such a deep way?

Spend time with Him in a solitary special place where the two of you can be involved with only one another. Share thoughts, dreams, highs and lows of the entire living experience. Talk to the Lord as you would a beloved one sitting next to you. He already knows your thoughts, but as you articulate them to Him, they become part of your life together. Don't be afraid to spill your deepest needs, your secrets and your wants. You will come to understand yourself more as these things come up.

There is no end to this, no finish. The process goes on and on. But soon you will absolutely delight in your times with Him. He will become more and more a part of you and you'll become deeper in Him. He will bring surprises and blessings that will overwhelm you.

This is true love.

Dear Jesus, we don't understand how You love us so much. Let us grow to love You so we may be intimately involved with one another.

Jackie Bowser is a member of DOVE Westgate Church, Ephrata.

Truth and Nothing but the Truth

"See to it that no one takes you captive through hollow and deceptive philosophy, which depends on human tradition and the basic principles of this world rather than Christ." *Colossians 2:8*

One morning years ago as I was doing my daily devotions, reading the Word and spending time listening to the Father, I became aware of a thought that continued to grow in my mind. It wasn't a new idea because I grew up in a Christian home; but somehow this elementary head knowledge took on new meaning as it shifted from my head and began to resonate in my heart.

It was as though I sensed God's desire for me to grasp this truth regarding His Word. He wanted me to know that his Word is truth and that it will always remain true. Time passes, but His truth remains. Generations come and go but the Word of the Lord stands forever.

Truth never changes. Philosophies, ideas, theories change but truth remains truth forever. It never grows old or becomes null and void. God's word remains true forever.

Truth remains constant regardless of man's ideas, knowledge or denial. Truth does not depend on what man thinks or feels or on what they do or do not understand. Truth , God's Word remains truth forever.

Therefore, the promises of God's Word remain true throughout our generation and all generations to come. Truth continues to set people free and never grows old, outdated, ineffective or useless.

Thank You, Lord, for illuminating this truth in a way that it connected with my heart. Help us to depend upon You and Your Word for our daily living. For we know all scripture is inspired by God and is useful to teach us what is true and to make us realize what is wrong in our lives. Truth transforms us and teaches us to do what is right. Truth is God's way of preparing us in every way, fully equipped for every good thing God wants us to do. Amen.

Rosene Ressler is a wife and mother of two wonderful daughters. She and her husband Merle serve in various ways at Weaverland Mennonite Church.

Man's Wisdom Versus God's Power

"When I came to you, brothers, I did not come with eloquence or superior wisdom as I proclaimed to you the testimony about God . . . . My message and my preaching were not with wise and persuasive words, but with a demonstration of the Spirit's power."
1 Corinthians 2:1, 4

I recall when my children were elementary school students sitting around expounding their wisdom to one another; often these discussions were hysterically funny. As they sat around discussing these "great nuggets of wisdom," some of the lunacy that I heard made for great comedy. Now, remember this is comparing the wisdom and knowledge of an eight-year-old with the wisdom and knowledge of a thirty-five-year-old; and to us the discrepancy is quite remarkable.

However, try to imagine the discrepancy in knowledge and wisdom between that thirty-five-year-old and an omniscient, eternal, omnipresent, and omnipotent God. The gap is so great that truthfully we can't realistically compare one to the other. How hard God must be laughing at us as we confer our great wisdom to one another. Just imagine how He must smile and say, "Well at least they're trying." But I believe that many times His smile must disappear if we become puffed up, arrogant and proud.

In our highly educated society, we are exactly like the Greeks that Paul talks about in this passage. They were philosophers and debaters. In our postmodern society of today where one argument has as much merit as the next, what really matters to many people is who can make the finest sounding argument relative to their theory.

But Paul says that "God chose things the world considers foolish in order to shame those who think they are wise. And he chose things that are powerless to shame those who are powerful. God chose things despised by the world, things counted as nothing at all, and used them to bring to nothing what the world considers important."

God grant me the wisdom and humility to know how great Your power is and how desperately I need it in my life.

Deryl Hurst is the executive pastor for DOVE Westgate.

He Has My Back

"And your ears shall hear a word behind you, saying, 'This is the way, walk in it,' when you turn to the right or when you turn to the left." Isaiah 30:21 (English Standard Version)

As a new Christian, I often found myself waiting on the Lord—looking to Him for the next steps in my life. Certainly, this submissive attitude is one that didn't come easily for me. I was so accustomed to doing my own thing that the idea of someone else being in control or calling the shots was a difficult concept to understand.

Given the fact that going my own way resulted in many wrong choices and serious consequences, I was more than willing to give God a chance at it! Seeking the Lord for His direction became second nature once I realized that my heavenly Father knows what is best for me and works even the apparent negative things together for my good.

How well I remember weighing out each major decision I faced (and many minor ones, too). As I have matured in my walk with the Lord, situations arise where God wants *me* to make a decision—to take a step of faith. Knowing my history of making wrong choices, I approached this new way of thinking very tentatively. I was so afraid of making the wrong decision.

It was at this time that the Lord encouraged me with the scripture above. I had the image of my Lord walking behind me, saying that He trusts me to make the right decision. It was almost more than I could comprehend. Quite literally, He "has my back"! The realization that God has confidence in the presence of His spirit in me has emboldened me and allowed me to progressively move in faith. Each step I take is confirmation of His leading in my life.

At times, I may waver in my faith but all I have to do is look at the way He has led my life, how He has encouraged me. I am renewed in my confidence in Him and in His life in me.

Thank You Lord for leading me and for having my back!

Peachy Colleluori and her husband Domenic have served on the staff of the National Christian Conference Center for more than twenty-five years.

Waiting for You There

"The thief comes only to steal and kill and destroy; I have come that they may have life, and have it to the full." *John 10:10*

Like the feeling of a child tugging on a parents arm to get their attention was how God was tugging on my mind. He wanted me to serve at the Bridge Academy Community Center in Coatesville in the fall of 2009 at their Wednesday afternoon "Mom's Club." Our loving, faithful Father was waiting for me there to fulfill some of His plans and purposes for my life, to "have it to the full"!

Not only have I had the rich blessing of coming along side the women there to love them and encourage them, but I have received a love from them like no other place I have ever been!

I have learned that if God calls you to go somewhere in your own backyard or to a village in sub-Sahara Africa and gives you the grace to be obedient, He will be waiting for you there. He will be waiting for you with open arms and blessings beyond compare! He wants you to experience the fuller life He has promised to those of us who love Him.

Dear heavenly Father, thank You for Your great love for us that You so richly bestow upon those who obey Your calling on their lives. It causes us to love You more and to keep our eyes fixed on You instead of falling prey to the thief who comes to steal and kill and destroy.

Darla Eldredge lives in Chester County where she waits upon the Lord to direct her paths according to His will and purposes for her life.

GAP Insurance

"for he guards the course of the just and protects the way of his faithful ones." *Proverbs 2:8*

GAP insurance stands for Guaranteed Auto Protection. The term GAP represents the gap in coverage between how much one owes on a vehicle and how much that vehicle is worth. I first learned about GAP insurance while shopping for a new vehicle after my husband was in a terrible car accident that totaled our car. As a result, we were forced to shop for a new vehicle and faced a difficult decision. "Was it wiser to buy an old vehicle that we could pay off quickly and then save the difference for inevitable repairs, or was it better to buy a more reliable vehicle with a sizable loan? We prayed, asked for advice and researched but were tortured with indecision. God seemed silent.

We talked to a salesperson about the loan we would need in order to purchase the vehicle we were considering. She also introduced us to GAP insurance as part of her presentation. We left the dealership still feeling uneasy. The importance of the right choice consumed our thoughts and prayers.

The next day during my devotions, I was praying about the issue and the Lord clearly spoke through his word. God assured me that He was the "GAP insurance." No matter the decision, God will protect us and provide for us. Our job is to seek His will and try to be faithful stewards. It is God who knows the future and will provide for our needs. Based on this assurance from God, we were then able to make this decision with peace.

Now with every decision, we seek God for wisdom and trust Him to be our Jehovah-Jireh, our provider of GAP insurance.

Lord, thank You for guarding my course, being my protector and my provider.

Sonya Lanford is a member of Ephrata Bible Fellowship, a home schooling mom and homemaker.

Getting It Right

"... the Holy Spirit—he will teach you everything and will remind you of everything I have told you." *John 14:26 (New Living Translation)*

The Holy Spirit has been doing new and extraordinary things in my life. I tend to be oblivious to much that is happening around me: probably the by-product of a hyperactive imagination. And rarely do I give spontaneous gifts. In fact I'm notorious for being late with birthday cards and presents.

Recently the Holy Spirit has been alerting me to giving opportunities: making me aware of situations that in the past would not have made the smallest blip on my radar screen but now park themselves in my path daring me to ignore them. In the last six months, I have hired a masseuse for a friend, matched friends with a possible ministry/career by hosting a dinner party, paid for the professional editing of a friend's manuscript and gathered a crew to plant a garden for a friend recovering from surgery.

Each gift given was a joy and delight, which is another anomaly for me since I excel at thinking rather than action. Each act met a need. I was confident I was following the Spirit's prompting.

And each (with the exception of the massage) fell flat!

The friends weren't interested in the career information, the money for the editor was paid back and recovery from surgery was so rapid my friend planted his own garden.

Which leads me to the second phenomenal change: God's grace and the Holy Spirit's ministry have allowed me to fail without judging myself or second-guessing my decisions. It has freed me to give again and again. In the past I would have viewed such dismal results as evidence that I could not hear the Holy Spirit and vowed to reserve my giving for the offering plate. I would have called myself an idiot and cringed with every memory of my giving attempts.

But not this time. I've got some more giving ideas. . . .

Sooner or later, I'll get it right.

Holy Spirit, keep my eyes open for opportunities to give. Keep my heart open to respond and my head from getting in the way.

Ruth Morris is a special projects writer for several ministries.

Transformed at the Cross

"Let us then approach the throne of grace with confidence, so that we may receive mercy and find grace to help us in our time of need."
Hebrews 4:16

The church I attended in the mid-1980s had little idea how to deal with a thirty-five-year-old woman choosing to divorce her husband. As much as it took courage, strength and determination, the cost of it led to losing the respect of most of my siblings and losing many friends. Letters of opinions poured in from family members.

My dad was furious and embarrassed of me. I saw my heavenly Father much like my earthly father. I felt judged on the basis of how well I followed all of the church practices and doctrines. I became very angry at God and was tired of seesaw judgments. Thus my rebellion toward God began.

It was in the church that I was hurt deeply, but it was also a church that helped to heal me. Sitting under teaching of the truth for lost, hurting and broken people, I've learned how to forgive others and myself and to accept God's healing of all my wounds.

My transformation began when I realized that God is a righteous judge who deserved my utmost respect. I've never been the same since the Sunday I envisioned in my spirit my Lord hanging on the cross and looking at me with the most loving eyes when He said He loved me and called me by all my last names. I felt His unconditional love, which in turn allowed me to completely trust Him and totally surrender my selfishness.

What is it you need to recognize and admit at the foot of the cross?

Thank You, Lord, that You are my High Priest and I can boldly come before You as my loving Father, full of grace and mercy.

Beaty Miller is a member of The Worship Center and a leader of the Women of the Word Bible Study.

Desire of My Heart

"Delight thyself also in the Lord; and he shall give thee the desires of thine heart." *Psalm 37:4 (King James Version)*

When I was growing up on a small farm in eastern North Carolina, I amused and educated myself by reading the family's set of encyclopedia. I became interested in mythology; so I dreamed that one day I would visit Greece and Rome. In high school, I fell in love with foreign languages.

My parents had always taken me to church, and in my teen years I made a serious commitment to Christ. I went to college planning to become a teacher of French and Spanish. During my freshman year, however, I felt that God was calling me into ministry.

That presented a dilemma. If I became a preacher in our denomination, I knew I would never have enough money to fulfill my dreams of traveling to other countries. Nevertheless, I told God I would surrender myself to the ministry, thinking that my future likely consisted only of pastorates in rural churches in my home state. I would never get to travel anywhere!

Now as I look back over what God has done, He has far exceeded what I ever dreamed about! My wife and I have ministered all over the United States and Canada and have led pilgrimages to Israel and other countries, including Greece and Rome! God has allowed me to preach in English and in Spanish on four continents!

God's grace enabled a farm boy walking down a dirt path to the mailbox to say "yes" to His plan for my life.

When we choose to love and serve Him, we discover that it was He who put those dreams in our hearts to begin with! Then He lovingly hides the fulfillment of our dreams along the path of obedience. Praise the Lord!

Thank You, Lord, for Your great faithfulness in fulfilling the dreams You place within us. Empower us to serve You in obedience.

Wayne West and his wife Ruth live in Rothsville. Through their ministry, Praise Unlimited, they teach God's Word and lead worship in churches, camps and retreats.

Photo by Mark Van Scyoc

September

God Is Omniscient, So Why Am I Surprised?

"May the words of my mouth and the meditation of my heart be pleasing in your sight, O Lord, my Rock and my Redeemer."
Psalm 19:14

How did the all-knowing Creator know that I would be declaring His praise today with a group of adult men on a hanging rock? Was this scene just an accident of time and place?

No, my God foreknew all things before they were even created and is not limited to time or space. He planned for me to speak out loud these words today. I expressed the desire of my heart in this passage to be pleasing to Almighty God. My voice and meditations were aloud— and intentional—to guys, many with life-controlling issues, and challenges.

These were men, like me, who all need the Rock and Redeemer. This steamy August day was a planned trip to Pinnacle Overlook hundreds of feet above the river. Fifteen men gathered to check out the beauty of nature and spend the day together off campus from Water Street Mission's LifeRecovery Program in Lancaster City. Birds sang praise to the Creator, the wind tickled my hair and the humidity saturated my shoes in the grass as I walked down the trail. Many times I had been to the big rock alone or with close friends and family. Today I was with a group of men that had never experienced time at this rock.

Did God know and plan for me to be with these guys and see a new view, a higher view, of the Susquehanna River at the Pinnacle Overlook and of Himself?

Lord, I know that You did plan today and I give You the praise for that beautiful snapshot of time and place in Your grace at the rock with some men that needed to experience You personally. You surprise me, Lord. You are the all-knowing Rock.

Jim Stanton is a program counselor at Water Street Mission's LifeRecovery Program. He and his wife live in Lancaster.

Am I Ready to Humble Myself?

"If my people, who are called by my name, will humble themselves and pray and seek my face and turn from their wicked ways, then will I hear from heaven and will forgive their sin and will heal their land." *2 Chronicles 7:14*

For two years I've had the privilege of serving as the chair for the Chester County Leadership Prayer Breakfast, hosted on the National Day of Prayer. When I made contacts to see who would join me on the leadership team, it was humbling. Our team consists of leaders of various ministries and churches. These leaders understand the value of being a people called by God's name. They walk out this scripture in their daily lives. Each of us desires to see our county humble ourselves, pray and seek His face and turn from our wicked ways. We long for God to reach out and touch us for revival in Chester County.

The comment we hear most is, "I've been to prayer breakfasts before but never like this one! This one actually has more prayer than breakfast!"

They are right! The majority of our time together focuses on scripture readings by various leaders in our county and then group prayer and prayer around the individual tables. I am amazed and blessed each year as I greet our guests early in the morning. They come ready to call out to our God and seek His face. Business leaders, prayer warriors, government officials, pastors, ministry leaders and many others join together for one purpose—to give God the glory, not man. This once-a-year event reminds us that we must seek God's face daily, humble ourselves at all times, pray and repent. This is the way to being forgiven and having our land healed. I am challenged by this scripture. Are you?

Father, Please teach us to set a portion of our day aside to be with You and to follow the steps this passage teaches. Our desire is for a healed land full of healed people.

Karen Pennell serves as chair for the Chester County Leadership Prayer Breakfast. You do not need to be a leader to attend; you just need the desire to pray for the leaders in our community and nation.

I Think Not!

"This is the day which the Lord has made; we will rejoice and be glad in it." *Psalm 118:24 (American King James Version)*

Lost just miles from my destination, I waited impatiently for my GPS to "recalculate." Finally arriving at the sprawling apartment complex, my joy dimmed as I searched hard for even one visible house number in a sea of red brick buildings. No one was in sight. As a lone car slowly approached, I rolled down my window.

"Could you point me toward apartment number 335?" I asked.

"Follow me," she answered. "That's my mom's house."

Had I arrived on the scene ten minutes earlier or ten minutes later, I would have missed that vital connection. Coincidence? I think not!

I definitely heard my sunglasses stored in a hard-shelled case hit the floor in the dark theater. My granddaughter and I crawled around for what seemed hours, and the cleaning staff joined our search. Nothing. After leaving my name and phone number, we headed home. I stopped by the theater a week later. "I'll bring out the lost and found box," offered the manager. Just as she was putting the box up onto her desk, she swiveled forty-five degrees and picked up a black eyeglasses case. "Are these yours?"

Yes! Thank You, God."

"I know they weren't here this morning," the manager said. "I never saw them until just now."

Coincidence? I think not!

I approached the salesclerk in a crowded department store with my malfunctioning watch. I had purchased it six months previously but had misplaced my receipt and the extended warranty. Was it a coincidence that the same watch was newly featured on a display that week? The clerk simply took the faulty watch from my wrist and handed me a brand -new one. No questions, no paperwork.

Coincidence? Luck? I don't think so! Having a relationship with God provides Him with the opportunity to enter our lives at will. He is the perfect "God of Miracles—our God of *coincidences!*"

Thank You, Lord, for coming into my life in even these little ways, proving over and over Your great love for me.

Janet Medrow is a deacon at Great Valley Presbyterian Church in Malvern.

Mirror, Mirror on the Wall

"Nothing between us and God, our faces shining with the brightness of his face." *1 Corinthians 3:18 (The Message)*

Each year our church takes a group of youth for a week of home repair with the Appalachia Service Project. Each year is different and we never know exactly what conditions to expect. This year we were in the mountains of West Virginia. We were staying in a condemned school brought to a usable condition as the center or "home base" for the summer volunteers and staff. We were to sleep, eat, shower and have evening gatherings and socialize there with the other church groups while we spent our week in West Virginia.

We settled in on Sunday night and enjoyed meeting new people. After a good night's sleep, I got up the next morning to brush my hair and teeth when I realized there were no mirrors in the bathroom. I didn't pack one and neither did the people I knew because in previous years there were always mirrors! I went to breakfast in the school's cafeteria with about sixty-five other people. I knew the only way I could tell what I looked like was to observe the reaction of people as I said good morning to them. If they looked shocked or laughed I knew something about my appearance was askew! It was the only "reflection" I had of myself.

I wonder what is reflected from the inside? What do people see when they listen to me talk or watch my actions? Do I ever reflect the character of Jesus? Not having a real mirror helped me see the true reflection to look for. I want my face to shine with the brightness of God and His love no matter what my hair looks like!

Father God, help us to live as if there are no mirrors because all that matters is how your love is reflected by your children on earth.

Karen Keller is a mom, mom-in-law, Nana and wife of Allen Keller, youth pastor of Olivet United Methodist Church in Coatesville.

Labor Day—Birthing a New Thing

"Therefore, my beloved brothers, be steadfast, immovable, always abounding in the work of the Lord, knowing that in the Lord your labor is not in vain." *1 Corinthians 15:58 (English Standard Version)*

My "retirement" came early, about eight years ago. As I looked back I saw many satisfying accomplishments, some great relational experiences and other benefits that could be called the "fruit of my labors." While having many opportunities to speak for the Lord and influence others in a positive way, there was an unsatisfied longing, not clearly identified.

I actually don't believe in retirement. I prefer instead to think of it as a redeployment or reassignment. When God opened a door for leadership in a ministry devoted to the development and restoration of leaders, it seemed clearly the call of God. The ministry brought together virtually all of the life and vocational experiences I have had. My past has truly been a season of preparation for the new thing God is doing at The Haft, Inc., in the people He has called together as a ministry team and in my own life.

To be retired, you have to have experienced what it is to be tired. Labor directed by any goal, other than the Lord Himself, will inevitably produce discouragement, weariness and even burnout. Labor done with the motivation of the Lord produces sustainable, enduring joy, and contentment. The dreams, hopes and desires conceived by the Holy Spirit in my heart and mind, nourished through sometimes painfully challenging circumstances, finally burst forth into that new thing that God has planned from the very beginning. I hope it will encourage you as you face your own labor pains.

Father, thank You that what you have planted in me will bring forth much fruit for your honor and glory. Thank You for the deep satisfaction and peace that comes to my heart from knowing this.

Bruce Boydell and his wife Joan equip individuals and emerging leaders of businesses and ministry organizations, through Lifespan Consulting and Coaching Services. Bruce is president of The Haft, Inc., and serves there with Joan as on-site ministry director.

He Provides

"Delight thyself also in the Lord: and he shall give thee the desires of thine heart. Commit thy way unto the Lord; trust also in him; and he shall bring it to pass." *Psalm 37:4–5 (King James Version)*

I was determined to complete my education but with limited income and fear of piling up loans, I was limited, or so I thought. I started at the local community college, but I was aiming for a bachelor's, not just an associate's degree. So, in 2007, I started looking for universities. There were many schools: schools that didn't have my major, schools that I couldn't afford and schools that would not accept some of my previous courses.

In 2008 I was offered a full-ride scholarship to a school in the Philadelphia area. I could live on campus, complete my degree and eat for free. Additionally, if I graduated from there, I could apply for another scholarship for graduate school. This sounded very good but there was one problem: children were not allowed on campus. If I rented an apartment off campus, I would need to take out loans to pay for it. My mother in Africa could take care of my daughter while I finished school, but I have always believed a child's place is by his or her mother's side. So I decided to stay where I was and simply wait on the Lord.

I prayed and searched, and then I decided to enroll in online classes at a Christian university. It seemed right this time, but it was expensive. I remember saying, "Lord, I'm going to enroll and trust that You will provide." He did just that. He supplied my need with three scholarships. I'll be graduating in a year and it's all paid in full.

This experience strengthened my faith and changed my thinking. I might be financially limited but my Lord will never be.

Lord Jesus, thanks for being Jehovah Jireh my provider. Please help me to always trust and depend on You.

Chou Gabikiny serves on the Global Impact Team at West Shore Brethren in Christ Church.

The Appeal

"You are the salt of the earth. But if the salt loses its saltiness, how can it be made salty again? It is no longer good for anything, except to be thrown out and trampled by men." *Matthew 5:13*

Have you thought about visiting the Dead Sea? The Dead Sea holds our fascination. The northern end is deep (1,300 feet) while the southern end is shallow (30 feet). The Jordan River flows into it, but no water flows out of it. It is the lowest body of water on earth (1,350 feet below sea level).

But why do throngs of people travel through the desert to "float" or "soak" in its waters? Because of its salt.

The salt content of the Dead Sea ranges from 26 to 33 percent, compared to 4 percent in ordinary salt water. That means it is extraordinarily buoyant. Swimming, in the usual sense, is impossible. Too many limbs remain aloft! What an unusual, and humorous, sight to see people floating around without inner tubes!

The salt content of the Dead Sea also holds an appeal for its health value. The therapeutic qualities of the hot sulfur springs and mineral water relieve muscle and joint problems, and the black mud beautifies the skin. What a contrast: luxury seaside hotels and spas surrounded by barren and bleak desert landscape!

Jesus says we Christians are salt. We are to create thirst just like the salt of the Dead Sea attracts other people. We are to be unique, unlike anything else on earth, so that we whet the appetite of others with our different "idea of having fun" despite our "desert" surroundings.

Then, as they are drawn to our unique response to life's circumstances, our salt should assure them of their infinite value in Christ. We should allow them time to "soak" in His grace as we listen carefully and help meet their personal needs through Jesus' healing words.

Lord, help me be like the salt of the Dead Sea, to attract others with my unusual contentment and with a personal interest in them.

Tamalyn Jo Heim's idea of fun is thirty-nine years of dating her own personal jet pilot Bob, whose call sign is "Maverick."

Faith, Heroes, Heroes of the Faith

"Consider him who endured such opposition from sinful men, so that you will not grow weary and lose heart." *Hebrews 12:3*

Standing in church during praise and worship time, I sensed the presence of God in a very powerful way. The closeness I felt made Him very real.

I started to melt into joyful tears as I thought of God building my faith. He does! Countless times I've gone to Him in prayer with some more serious than others but none-the-less problems.

In prayer, I could trust His faithfulness and know His character, which is that He wants good for me, but until the problem was resolved it remained a problem. This day in church, as I stood there free of many of the problems I had prayed and asked God to fix—He fixed them!

Then my mind went to heroes such as Glenn Bowers, a World War II veteran, who fought with the Black Sheep Squadron. Bowers had recently passed away. He had been a close friend of my husband. My husband often visited with Glenn in his home. Glenn would tell him, "The real heroes are the ones who didn't come home—the ones who gave their lives."

I remembered Bowers' quote on Sunday morning and thought about how it applied to the people with problems that God has not yet fixed, the ones still waiting to see good results. They were heroes of the faith. Day after day, month after month, sometimes, year after year, not seeing this problem fixed, yet still believing, by faith, God can and He will!

Heavenly Father, thank You for those times You build my faith and please help us all not to grow weary and lose heart when we don't see our problems fixed. Help us be heroes of the faith as we persevere.

Lisa Dorr is a wife, mother, author, editor and a public speaker who loves God!

Perspective

"Bring joy to your servant, for to you, O Lord, I lift up my soul."
Psalm 86:4

Perspective of life is in the eyes of the beholder, isn't it?

I had a particularly difficult week of which seemed like the wheels were coming off the cart in several difficult situations I was immersed in. In several other settings, persons close to me were going through a faith crisis that was incredibly painful.

Wearily, I sat down on a Saturday evening to rest, zone out and watch college football. One of the five top-ranked teams was moments away from losing the game which would eliminate them from any chance at the national title. The cameraman slowly panned the sidelines as the final seconds ticked off the clock capturing fully the agony of defeat. Fans were standing, embracing one another, weeping openly as tears streamed down their grieving and shocked faces.

Reflecting on the life situations very fresh in my mind, I wondered about perspective. The perspective observed on the sidelines seemed weighted so very differently from what was going on in the lifelines of those close to me. Losing an opportunity to win a national title was perhaps cause to grieve, but compared to what?

My thoughts were immediately challenged by the Holy Spirit as I was reminded of my weariness. Perhaps my own perspective was also skewed as I attempted to fix the burdens on my mind versus committing and releasing the heavy lifting to the Lord.

Jesus was well versed in modeling an appropriate perspective. How often through the Gospels, Jesus patiently and passionately redirected the energy, thought and the mission of those He knew best, the disciples. Jesus' own heart was continually focused on the Father. Perspective and ministry then flowed richly and beautifully as a result.

Lord, today may my perspective be in sync with your mission. Make me Your servant in thought, word and deed.

Brian E. Martin serves as lead pastor at Weaverland Mennonite Church in East Earl. He and his wife Shirley are parents of three married children, one young adult at home and two grandchildren.

I Trust Him

"This I declare about the LORD: He alone is my refuge, my place of safety; he is my God, and I trust him." *Psalm 91:2 (New Living Translation)*

God called me to read this Psalm some time ago. Unknown to me, He wasn't talking about it as a "morning" devotion but a lesson to be learned. As I read the Psalm, I felt the Lord tugging at my heart to memorize it. I knew it would be challenging, but I had no idea what was in store for me. My eyes were open to how much was packed into it, so I decided to journal about it as well.

I started to write down what it meant to me. From verse one I broke down the words and their meaning in my life and by the time I got to verse two I was stuck. I spent a week on verse one to memorize it and verse two seemed to be quite the challenge. I found myself there for over two months! The verse itself was worthy of journaling a page or more each day. My problem was remembering the end, "and I *trust* Him." Each time I went to recite the verse I would say, "and I *will* trust Him." It was funny as I was writing about that I realized the word *will* is future tense. I have trust issues in my life from the past, and the Lord was showing me that I even had them with Him.

After two and a half months, a lot of journaling and talking with the Lord, I was able to recite that verse and say aloud, "and I trust Him." What a glorious feeling that was.

Later, I found myself telling a friend that I continue to struggle. He reminded me to reread my favorite passage: Psalm 91!

Thank You, Lord, for friends and their reminder of where we need to land. Thank You for Your Word that fills my soul, my life and my trust in You. I lay down my fears and put my trust in You, for You are my Rock, my Refuge, my place of safety! I love You, Papa!

Eileen Christiansen is a leader of Celebrate Recovery, a twelve-step, Christ-centered recovery program in Sadsburyville.

Grandpa's Moment

"I will say of the Lord: He is my refuge and my fortress."
Psalm 91:2

A family adventure in June 2010 took me to the tourist childhood dream world of Dutch Wonderland. I was grandpa to the delightful grandchildren that God graciously gave to my wife and me. After spending many hours enjoying the thrills of the roller coaster, log flume, carousel and water park we made our way to "the turnpike." The oldest grandson was now big enough to drive his younger brother in a replica antique car around the track. The remaining family members planned to follow them in cars.

Although anticipation and joy were contagious in our shared moments, heat and fatigue were starting to take their toll on all of us, especially on the younger children. One child was whining and did not want to stay contained to the sectioned long lines leading into the ride. I asked my granddaughter more than once not to cross beneath the divider, but she yielded to temptation and crossed again. This time I picked her up in my arms, sharing some sweaty moments. Her body snuggled up in my embrace and she seemed to enjoy Grandpa taking charge of the wait in the long line. This little girl's problems were cleared up by my comforting embrace, a refuge, until we got into the car and enjoyed racing around the turnpike track.

Isn't that how we as believers, God's beloved children, should relax and let Him do the holding when we are in our sweaty, long lines of trials and difficulties, waiting-for -something-to-happen moments? Will I let God hold me in my worries, trials, and unsure moments? Can I foresee us enjoying sweet fellowship as we ride around the track eternally? Do you?

Lord, let me rest in Your strong arms."

Jim Stanton is blessed to be married to Laurie, to be a dad and grandfather and a program counselor at Water Street Ministries.

Routine Faith Builders

"... having done all [the crisis demands], to stand .... Lift up over all the [covering] shield of saving faith, upon which you can quench all the flaming missiles of the wicked [one]." *Ephesians 6:13, 16 (Amplified Version)*

I had a routine mammogram and was not expecting anything unusual, which could mean a repeat in six months if there was a concern. This had been the norm for several years, so when I received the request to return for a different diagnostic test, I asked for prayer but I wasn't overly concerned. The technician showed me their concern, a pea-size something. Suddenly, I felt like a missile had hit me.

When the technician left, I asked God what to do. I needed to hear a good report from the Lord. I felt led to call my mother. She spoke God's truth and while praying for me she sensed the Holy Spirit's leading to speak, "Even if it appears to be something now it is nothing."

Standing with my shield of faith, strengthened and lifted high, I had my test pondering God's truth in my heart believing that this pea-size something was in fact nothing. When the results were shown to me the technician said, "It appears to be nothing, but a report will be sent after the doctor reads the test."

The report came and it read: *no sinister involvement found, appears to be nothing.*

What God ministered to me later, when the flaming missiles of the wicked one came at me, my shield was raised, and it did not kill me or wound me. What I felt was only the jolt of the shield being hit while quenching the sinister involvement.

Father, thank You for Your good report and those You have prepared to speak words of faith in season regardless of evil reports. Thank You that the trials and testing of my faith are just routine faith builders.

Debbie Davenport, Living Truth Fellowship, serves as a leader interceding and equipping others for kingdom purposes in various roles at Cornerstone Pregnancy Care Services.

Comforted by a Child

". . . weep with those who weep." *Romans 12:15 (English Standard Version)*

Andrew was a toddler when I first got to know him. From the beginning, I felt a special affection for this little guy.

When Andrew was ten years old, my husband died from injuries in a bicycling accident. Andrew's family was very good to me and included me in their large family gatherings. I could always count on a hug from Andrew whenever I saw him. That was a great gift for a lady like me with a broken heart.

Nine months after my husband died, the church held its annual service in remembrance of those who died in the previous year. It is always a very emotional service. As the pastor reads the name of the one who died, the church bells toll and a candle is lit in honor of the deceased.

I sensed someone had quietly slipped into the pew beside me. I looked and said, "Oh, Andrew." He looked at me with eyes so full of concern. I took his hand. As the service continued, I was in tears. Andrew put his arm around my shoulder, gently comforting me. At the conclusion of the service, family members are invited to go to the front of the church and receive a candle and a flower. I looked at Andrew and asked if he would go forward with me. I rejoiced that God was using Andrew to help comfort me.

We left the service and Andrew walked me to the exit. I hugged him and thanked him for being there with me. It was a bitterly cold November day. Andrew looked at me and said, "Stay warm."

My heart was warm and comforted because one of God's children had a heart as big as the world.

This year, Andrew is fourteen years old and I am privileged to be his mentor. Sometimes I think that is backwards. Andrew has been an example to me of the power of reaching out to a hurting heart.

Dear Lord, thank You for the children, for in them we truly see the glory of God.

Nancy S. Gibble, St. Paul's United Church of Christ, Manheim, is a writer, an avid reader and works part -time.

Clinging to a Promise

"Let us hold unswerving to the hope we profess, for he who promised is faithful." *Hebrews 10:23*

The dining room was filled with delicious aromas and the noise of teenagers arriving back from an outreach tired and hungry. I watched as the little woman we affectionately called "Mama Judy" bustled about, placing steaming bowls of food on the tables. She had fascinated me ever since our arrival in Lima where we were leading a group of teens on an outreach.

When the meal was finished, I took advantage of the pause in activity to engage her in conversation. I was curious to know more of her story. She talked about her darkest day—the day her husband walked out, leaving her with four young sons. She said, "I remember my boys literally clinging to my husband's pant legs, desperately pleading with him, 'Daddy, please don't leave us!' But he did and he never returned. I told my boys, 'Your daddy may leave you but there's one "daddy" who will never leave you.' And that's how I raised them—to always look to the One who would never abandon them."

Gazing at the peace on Mama Judy's face, I was overwhelmed with the power of her simple testimony. During our time in Peru, I had already met three of her four sons. One pastored a growing, vibrant house church. Another worked as a physician. We attended the wedding of Saulo who ministered to some of Lima's poorest children, living in shacks on the hillside. The fourth son was a spiritual father to numerous young men before moving to the States. God heard the cries of a young woman who didn't give in to despair in the midst of overwhelming circumstances. She clung to the promise of her Father to be a father to the fatherless. And He had kept His promise.

Lord, You are always faithful to Your Word. Help me to stand firm on Your truth today, regardless of my circumstances.

Nancy Barnett is an editor at House to House Publications and serves with her husband Tom in giving leadership to DOVE Christian Fellowship, Elizabethtown.

Tossed

"Praise the Lord. Blessed is the man who fears the Lord, who finds great delight in His commands . . . . Surely he will never be shaken; a righteous man will be remembered forever. He will have no fear of bad news; his heart is steadfast, trusting in the Lord." *Psalm 112:1,6–7*

"Love . . . always protects, always trusts, always hopes, always perseveres." *1 Corinthians 13:6–7*

Earlier this year, during worship at church, I watched a young father who was holding his young daughter. He was swinging her in time with the music, lifting her in the air, swooping her down, tossing her and catching her. At one point, she was lying across his arms, and he would toss her up a little then turn her—brown curls flying. I don't recall what song was being sung at the time, but she was laughing and delighted. She relaxed in her father's strong and loving arms. She had total confidence and trust that her father loved her and was protecting her. Therefore, she happily enjoyed this somewhat rough tossing about.

During the past ten years, and even before, I have felt tossed roughly by life. I did not laugh. I was not delighted. I struggled to believe that God knew what He was doing, and that I, my husband and my children would survive. The image of that girl in her father's arms, made me think about my response to my heavenly Father. I want to look at the somewhat violent ups and downs of my own life differently. I want to trust God more. I want to delight in Him as He swings or allows me to be swung up and down.

Dear Lord, thank You that You continue to speak Your truth into my heart. Thank You for reminding me that You are in control even when life seems to be shaking me. Help me to delight in You as You guide my life. Amen.

Karen Boyd is a contributing editor to *God Stories 6* and attends ACTS Covenant Fellowship.

Jehovah Jireh: the Lord Will Provide

"And Abraham called the name of that place Jehovahjireh: as it is
said to this day, In the mount of the Lord it shall be seen."
Genesis 22:14 (King James Version)

My house hunting caused worry and impatience. Since January I
had searched—brick with hardwood flooring, original kitchen and bath
and character of the past. House found, house lost. House found, house
lost. With my apartment lease expiring in July, timing was crucial.

As weeks ticked away, my prayers seemed unanswered. I reluctantly accompanied my real estate agent to yet one more house. I steeled
myself against disappointment. Yes, the house was brick with hardwood floors. And there were charming features such as a swinging
kitchen door and a terrace enclosed by a wall. Even the green and pink
tiled bathroom appealed to me. *But could this really be the house?*

The owners were missionaries and needed to sell their house prior
to leaving for Mexico. Supporters were praying with them for their
home to sell before their scheduled end-of-June departure date.

As you may have guessed, their home eventually became mine.
Many prayers were answered. Coincidence? I think not. Saturday, house
found. Monday, closing date set. Everything fell into place.

Another milestone was laid in my trust of God's providence. And
this experience is not rare. As I regularly scan the seasons of my life, I
rattle off a litany of God's provisions: family, friends, employment,
auto and on and on, with life in Christ being paramount. Each represents an example of divine providence. I am a grateful recipient of
God's extravagant gifts, and this home exceeded my greatest expectations. Does this illustrate that God always gives us what we want? Of
course not. But He does give us *His* best.

Years ago I carved a plaque proclaiming "Jehovah Jireh," which
means "the Lord will provide." Many life-changing events have occurred in the twenty years since that inscription was carved, but the
words remain a reality, even though such assurance was often realized
in hindsight. The plaque hangs perfectly over that swinging kitchen
door.

Father, thank You that You do indeed provide!

Sally K. Owens lives with her husband Don in Lancaster, where they participate
in two home church groups.

Obligations!

"So, dear brothers, you have no obligations whatever to your old sinful nature to do what it begs you to do. For if you keep on following it you are lost and will perish, but if through the power of the Holy Spirit you crush it and its evil deeds, you shall live."
Romans 8:12–13 (New Living Bible)

We all have them. Some of them are really good and some are quite taxing. We feel obligated to attend certain things or give financially to certain projects because of the relationships we have with the individuals involved. Even though they might say, "Don't feel obligated," we still do and respond accordingly.

Sometimes doing something because we feel obligated will build resentment in our hearts because we really don't want to do it but feel there is no way out. So resentment and frustration toward the situation and people involved begin to fester. It would be better not to do something and face the consequences than to do it and feel resentment in the end. Your true feelings will come out sooner or later, and your actions that you did from that obligation won't be appreciated anyway.

I wanted to pass on to you an obligation you no longer need to feel anymore. It is found in Romans 8:12. Paul tells us that we no longer need to feel obligated to follow the things that don't line up with the word of God. Sometimes the enemy lies to us and tells us there is no way out. That is a complete lie. We have been changed from the inside out. We are righteous! Old things have passed away and all things have become new. You have been set free from the past and all of its holds on your life by the power of the cross.

Next time you feel obligated to do something that may not be right, tell the devil you won't follow his lies anymore. Oh, and if you make a mistake, remember Romans 8:1–2, "So now there is no condemnation for those who belong to Christ Jesus and because you belong to Him, the power of the life-giving Spirit has freed you from the power of sin [wrong obligations] that leads to death."

Lord, set us free to know Your will and help set our focus on you.

Ron Myer is assistant international director of DOVE Christian Fellowship International.

A Prayer Answered

"In the day of my trouble I will call to you, for you will answer me."
Psalm 86:7

I had just returned from a two-week mission trip to Brazil. It had been an awesome experience, and I was flying high! Little did I dream that within a few days I would be lying in the hospital, recovering from quadruple bypass heart surgery.

When I awakened in the ICU following surgery, I was painfully aware that my lungs were filling up with fluid. It felt like I was drowning, yet I was powerless to call for help. I was certain I was about to die. Finally the alarms sounded, and a nurse rushed to my aid.

A fear like I had never experienced before set in. This fear became relentless. Every time I began to doze off, I would suddenly jerk awake in a panic, feeling like I couldn't breathe. Consequently, I couldn't sleep. Night after night this continued and the sleep deprivation began to take its toll. I grew weaker, instead of stronger.

One evening, the entire "Brazil" team came to visit me. They gathered in our bedroom because I was too weak to go to the living room. When they offered to pray for me, I told them about the fear and how it was preventing me from getting rest. I knew it was an irrational fear, but somehow it had overtaken my body and won out over my reasoning. The group prayed *specifically* that I would be delivered from that fear. After they left, and for the first time since surgery, I got a good night's sleep! That paralyzing fear was gone and I could rest peacefully.

I haven't seen every prayer answered so immediately, but that experience motivates me to keep on praying. I ask *specifically* for what is needed and leave the outcome to God.

Father, thank You that You hear my cries for help and answer! May I be reminded today that nothing is impossible for You!

John Charles is director of Abundant Living, a family counseling ministry in Lititz.

A Simple Smile

"A cheerful look brings joy to the heart . . . ." *Proverbs 15:30*

I felt like a drill sergeant! I loved my four children dearly, yet it seemed I did little more than bark out orders all day long. "Pick up your clothes! Put that away! Stop pestering your sister! Don't talk like that!" My words streamed out, stern and harsh and I could tell they made my family irritable and cranky. The mood in the house had become grim.

I needed the Lord's help. I asked Him to enable me to set a more positive example and tone for the family. But what did I really expect Him to do, magically morph me into June Cleaver?

It was not an audible voice, just His gentle whisper that penetrated my thoughts. "Just do this," He seemed to say. "Each time you address a family member, begin by saying that person's name, and as you say the name SMILE!"

"Way too easy. It'll never work," I argued. Then an old memorized verse popped into my mind: "A cheerful look brings joy to the heart."

"Okay, I'll try it, Lord!"

Two weeks later my husband came to me. "I don't know if you realize it, but the whole atmosphere in our house has changed. I think you're doing something different, but I'm not sure exactly what."

Could simple smiles have brought about such a great transformation?

I have concluded that a pleasant look generates two results: Not only does it relax the listener, predisposing him or her to respond favorably, but it also changes the attitude of the speaker. I discovered I can no longer talk with an angry, offensive tone while wearing a smile. A cheerful grin releases my pent-up frustration and softens my heart.

Isn't it like the Lord to create *one* tool to change *two* people! This had become a double-whammy effect.

Lord, thank You for inventing such a simple instrument, with such great potential to change lives! Help me honor You today and SMILE, SMILE, SMILE!

Sharon Charles assists her husband John, director of Abundant Living, a family counseling ministry near Lititz.

Transformation

"And we, who with unveiled faces all reflect the Lord's glory are being transformed into his likeness with ever-increasing glory, which comes from the Lord, who is the Spirit." *2 Corinthians 3:18*

My daughter was recently baptized at a pool that has lots of butterflies. After the baptismal service, she picked up a unique black, white and blue butterfly and wanted to keep it as a pet. As we walked to the car we talked about the transformation process a butterfly goes through and how it compares to baptism and the Christian walk.

Butterflies are amazing creatures that speak of God's amazing transformation in life. They start out as caterpillars that are not very attractive and are only able to crawl. Going through metamorphosis or the transformation process, they are no longer caterpillars but have been transformed into butterflies.

How does this process compare to our own spiritual journey? We start out crawling in our spiritual walk, often going through a process of development that takes time and patience. Oftentimes the struggle to develop isn't fun and comfortable. If we trust the Lord to develop us and are open to the Holy Spirit's leading, He is faithful to complete it.

Breaking forth from the cocoon is a great representation of God's deliverance from bondage, being born again and of baptism. They all represent something new, something transformed and of something changed, that can never go back to the previous image. What are we being transformed into? In the Christian walk I believe that image will be the transformation into the reflection of Jesus Christ.

We all have cocoons that God sometimes uses in our transformation process. Sometimes just like the cocoon, it appears as if nothing is happening. On the inside though there is transformation taking place. As we trust God, He takes us through the process, breaking us forth into something new, something beautiful, something only He could do to take us to new heights.

Father God, we praise You for taking us through the transformation process and taking us to new heights in You that reflect Your glory.

Diana Sheehan is blessed to be married to Robert and loves being a stay-at-home mom to three children. They are members of DOVE Westgate.

Free from the Curse

"God turned the curse into a blessing for you because the Lord your God loves you." *Deuteronomy 23:5*

When I was a young girl I made a vow that I would never let my mom get close to me like I saw her reaching out to my older sister, because I figured that if I wasn't worth her attention now I'm not worth it when I get older.

To the day she died in 1998, when I was thirty-nine, we were not close because I had hardened my heart.

About two years ago I had a dream in which my mom and I were snuggling together on the couch and giggling like adolescents. I believe that dream was the beginning of my healing.

Since then God began to soften my heart and I began to feel the pain coming through the hard crust that went deep.

Going to all-women functions were the hardest for me. I often felt alienated and alone.

I went to a women's retreat in early 2010 and the pain I was feeling was so intense I knew that if I allowed one crack to open wide enough for anything to get through, everything inside of me would gush out and there would be no stopping it.

A couple of months later I began attending a women's Bible study, taught by Beth Moore via video. Hearing her speak and seeing her passion for other women touched me deeply.

One night, after about the fifth session, I was driving home and suddenly the dam broke. I began to cry and sob loud, hard gulping sobs, and in the midst of my tears I cried, "Lord, I feel like my heart just burst wide open and everything is pouring out!"

Amazingly, I felt no pain, only a beautiful, cleansing release!

Mother's Day had always been painful for me in the past, but this year I knew I had made peace with my mom and I celebrated!

Lord, thank You for freedom from the curse! Amen.

Dolores Walker, God's beloved daughter, attends DOVE Westgate Church.

Doors Will Open —Walk Through

". . . but the Lord was not in the wind: and after the wind an earthquake; but the Lord was not in the earthquake: And after the earthquake a fire; but the Lord was not in the fire: and after the fire a still small voice." *1 Kings 19:11–12 (King James Version)*

At the end of 2008 I felt the Lord whispering to my heart that doors would open and I should walk through. At the time I was an executive for a large company. I marveled at how God took "me" a little farm girl and mother of four to a high-level position overseeing 240 million dollars. I always felt God preparing me for something bigger. I wondered if God was speaking of a promotion at my current job or calling me into something else. I struggled with unrealistic expectations, the long hours I was forced to work and I realized I was requiring the same of my direct reports.

In the spring of 2009 the corporation downsized and I was laid off. Because I had this word tucked in my heart I knew God was in control. Many of my co-workers were devastated but because I had heard God's still small voice, I had a sense of expectancy. For seven months I enjoyed my time off and in December 2009, I learned of an opening with Global Disciples whose mission it is to reach 2 billion souls around the world who have never heard the gospel. Lord could this be the door to a more fulfilling job? I quickly contacted them, interviewed and started in January 2010.

Through my life and career I have seen God's favor on me. Not because I have magnificent qualifications and college degrees. I believe His Word when He says he has given me the tongue of the learned. If we listen and trust in His still small voice, He will direct us in life and in ministry to believers around us and caring for the lost.

Lord, thank You for your still small voice. I trust You to lead me. Thank You for Your extravagant goodness to me. I am blessed, amazed and appreciative of Your loving guidance in my life.

Carol Roach is director of advancement at Global Disciples empowering churches and their mission-sending entities to train and send their local workers into the least reached areas.

One Small Group Makes a Difference in Kenya

"So let each one give as he purposes in his heart, not grudgingly or of necessity; for God loves a cheerful giver." *2 Corinthians 9:7 (New King James Version)*

When I first saw a Trees for Africa project card I thought, "How can our small group participate in this?" Christmas was fast approaching and I knew that many people find themselves in a financial crunch during the holidays. But I also knew that we all would be spending money on gifts, flowers, baking wonderful desserts and cookies, sending cards, etc. Surely we could spare a few dollars per family or individual to help our brothers and sisters in Africa with this pressing need. Couldn't we raise $100 that was all it would take to start a tree nursery in Kenya? So I handed out small plastic Christmas buckets to each family or individual in our cell group at our annual Christmas party and just asked that we collect our change throughout the Christmas season and next three months. Some folks collected just pennies; others collected all of their change—quarters, dimes, nickels and pennies. We brought the buckets to a small group meeting in March.

One of the guys "planted" a tree in the center of a galvanized wash tub, placed it in the center of the room where our small group was meeting and we all dumped our change into the tub. Some young people in the group volunteered to count all of the money. Final tally: $99.60!

What a faith builder! By all contributing a little, we reached our collective goal in just four months—with only our pocket change. We decided to take our buckets back home and to collect our change to start a tree nursery in Uganda!

Father God, we are so blessed by You. You provide all that we need and more than enough. Let us look for opportunities to seed into Your Kingdom and let us give hilariously. In Jesus' wonderful name. Amen.

Mary Prokopchak leads the Bossler Road small group of DOVE Christian Fellowship, Elizabethtown.

How to Shrink Problems

"O magnify the Lord with me, and let us exalt his name together.
Psalm 34:3" (King James Version)

Finances are tight. My income as a freelance writer and Amish taxi driver fluctuates from week to week. It would be so easy to fuss and worry about whether or not I will earn enough this week to pay the bills. But that approach leads to nothing but fear and stinginess.

If worrying were an Olympic event, I'd have a shot at the gold. I can imagine all kinds of disasters. My emotions react as if those "what ifs" are already reality until I'm filled with stress and anger.

But now God has shown me how to use those worry skills in a new, much more positive way. When I am faced with a problem that looms over me like a thunderhead, I spend time thinking about the names of God, especially the ones that answer the situation I'm stewing about. The longer I concentrate on who God is, the greater He becomes in my heart. I don't stop until my imagination has magnified the name of the Lord to a size much larger than that black cloud threatening me. Only then do God's promises replace my situation as the reality I see and expect.

So when finances look bleak, I focus on Jehovah Jireh whose grace is sufficient for me. I imagine his vast storehouse of provision. I remind myself that he knew this day was coming and made provision for it long ago. I think about El Shaddai who is more than enough. I place my situation side by side with the magnificence of the universe. I review how God has kept me in the past and I rejoice in His name which is like a ruler's signet ring guaranteeing His promises. I see Him with His hands outstretched toward me and so plentifully filled with good things they drip and spill. I see myself cradled in the Good Shepherd's arms as he cares for me just as I love to hold my little dog and feed him treats.

My problems shrink as God is magnified.

I will magnify You, O Lord, and invite others in joining me to praise Your name.

Ruth Morris is a special projects writer for several ministries.

New Four-Letter Words

"May the words of my mouth and the meditation of my heart be pleasing in Your sight, O Lord, my Rock and my Redeemer."
Psalm 19:14

Having had little Christian upbringing, my life was modeled around the world I lived in. Profanity and obscene four-letter words were standard speech for me.

Amazingly, values change when Christ enters your world! When my twenty-three-year marriage dissolved, it rocked my sons' and my world. Something had to change. I prayed that God would change my husband, but learned the only person I could change was me. What an awakening! What a reality! What a new season of life I had to face.

What changed in my life? Why Christ, of course! I needed to find emotional stability so that I could be the mom and head of the household I needed to be.

A dear Christian lady gave a brochure to me on a divorce recovery ministry at her church. Truly, this focused support group saved me and my kids! The teachings were right on target; the facilitators were compassionate and prayer warriors extraordinaire! I found myself absorbed in reading the Bible, listening to teaching tapes and Christian music, attending small groups and special Christian women's events, walking in Christian circles and making new godly friends. My old life was disappearing before my kids' eyes and my life was beginning! That was fourteen years ago! Today, these friends still have a very important role in my life and my oldest son is saved by grace. (I'm still praying for the youngest!)

My new life is encompassed with new four-letter words such as love, hope and care. When God restores you, He doesn't restore you to what you were before; He restores you to what you have always been in Christ!

Father, I thank You for changed lives. May I forever remember Revelation 12:11, which tells me that I am an overcomer by the blood of the Lamb and the words of my testimony.

Sandy Atkins is a member of The Worship Center and a facilitator in Divorce Care.

Grace and Truth

"Speaking the truth in love, we are to grow up in every way . . . . into Christ." *Ephesians 4:15 (English Standard Version)*

I've often heard the words *grace* and *truth* used together when describing how the Christian life should be lived. What does that look like? Does that mean we should overlook sin because of God's grace?

Almost two years ago I started working at the Lydia Center. The first time I experienced the pain of watching a woman prematurely leave the program, I was devastated. It seemed to me that we could serve her better if she stayed in the program. However, I have seen God's redemptive grace displayed through the grace and truth process.

A few months ago "Susie" left the center because of her actions. A week later she was allowed to come back for a meeting to determine if she was ready to resume the process of life transformation. The community allowed her to return. During her time away God had spoken to her and ministered to her. She had time to think about the things that really mattered. Without being allowed to separate from her situation here, she would not have felt the consequences of her actions and experienced God's love in spite of her failure.

All too often I am tempted to play God and interfere with His plan for others. I choose to ignore the sin in someone's life because I don't want to get involved or I want to save them from the consequences. But I am learning that God calls us to speak grace and truth into those around us. To ignore the truth of sin and not allow its natural consequences to occur is not true love, it is rescuing. God wants to use the difficult experiences in our lives to draw us to Himself.

Father, give me the courage to trust the people in my life to Your care. Remind me that Your plan for them is bigger and greater than anything I could imagine.

Donna Doutrich works at the Lydia Center, a division of Water Street Ministries.

Little White Mouse

"Behold what manner of love the Father has bestowed on us, that we should be called children of God!" *1 John 3:1 (New King James Version)*

On an extremely cold New Hampshire winter evening, I was sitting in my car waiting for traffic to clear when I noticed a tiny white spot on the side of the road. Realizing the little white spot was a mouse, I watched as he too appeared to be waiting for the traffic to clear. Compassion welled up in my heart and I so wanted to help the little fellow get across the busy street.

I remembered this little mouse one evening when my heart ached as I again failed the Lord I loved. Having spent too much money on myself, I could only give a thirty-dollar gift certificate to dear friends for Christmas. Sitting in my car, I wept and prayed, "Father, please tell me that You have some of the compassion in Your heart for me that I had felt for the little white mouse."

God chose to send His answer via a sympathy card I purchased for a friend. The message was clear: God's love for me is full of compassion and tenderness! As I held the card I lifted my eyes heavenward with a thankful heart. Today, years later, I remember that lesson. Why?

Recently a beloved family member was diagnosed with a degenerative neurological disease. This casts uncertainty on our plans to return to pastoral ministry. So today, my Father is giving me the opportunity to rely on His tender love and compassion even though anxiety tries to control my heart and mind. Feeling as fragile as that tiny mouse, I cry out for the Lord's help in my time of need and exchange my anxiety for His loving-kindness. Every day I must entrust myself to His shepherding love and skill.

Abba Father, I am grateful for Your compassionate love lavished on me in Christ Jesus my Lord.

Susan Marie Davis and husband Karl are members of Calvary Church, Lancaster.

Jesus, My Healer

". . . I pray that you may enjoy good health and that all may go well with you . . . ." *3 John 1:2*

When I think back to how I was living my life many years ago, I think of the time I ended up in the hospital with a six-centimeter cyst in my chest. The doctor decided to do a biopsy to see if the cyst was cancerous. Thankfully it was not and the doctor was able to shrink the cyst. But at my follow-up checkup, the doctor told me there was no guarantee that the cyst would not come back.

At the time, I was smoking and living a life that was not pleasing to God. During the next several years, the cyst started to grow back. Last year a test revealed that the cyst was four centimeters. At that point, I didn't care what happened to me.

Eventually I became homeless and had no place to go. I thought I was going to have to live on the streets. One day my aunt and uncle happened to drive past me. They said it was God that led them to me. They took me in and while living with them, I rededicated my life to Christ and started going to church again and reading His Word.

I believe that through this situation God has been working in my life. He has even made a difference in my physical health. The last time I had my cyst checked, the doctor told me the cyst had shrunk. I believe that could have only happened through Christ and my obedience to Him. I trust Him for my continued good health.

Dear Heavenly Father, I want to praise and thank You for being my healer and Savior.

Debra is a resident at the Lydia Center, a division of Water Street Ministries.

I Am His Daughter

"You will seek me and find me when you seek me with all your heart." *Jeremiah 29:13*

My life was in a downfall. I was at the bottom of my pit with the dirt caving in. I kept looking for something to fill the void in my life that I was missing. I called myself a Christian but I was not living the life of a Christian. I thought I would fill that void in my life through different men and being rebellious. I discovered that was not the answer.

I was left feeling worthless, like no one wanted me. I didn't feel good enough to be loved or accepted. I knew that I needed to make changes. But I didn't know how to do it.

I came to a Christian program where I was given tools and shown how to work on becoming who God says I am. In Him, my identity is His daughter and He loves me unconditionally and accepts me.

While working through the wounds from my past, I discovered I really did not have Jesus Christ in my life. On January 14, 2010, I accepted Jesus into my heart. Since then I found I am accepted, loved and wanted through Jesus. On June 25, 2010, I was baptized and have never felt such peace in my life. My son has remarked on the changes he has seen in me.

This is all possible through Jesus Christ, and having complete trust and faith in Him. I have given Him total control of my life. I know now that anything can happen with Jesus by my side.

Dear heavenly Father, I want to thank You for the changes You have brought into my life. If it wasn't for You, Father, I would still be empty and feeling down about myself. I know through You nothing is impossible. You fill my heart with such peace and a sense of fullness in my life.

Abbie is a resident at the Lydia Center, a division of Water Street Ministries. She attends Community Fellowship Church in Lancaster.

On My Own Strength

"I can do everything through Christ who strengthens me."
Philippians 4:13

Two years ago I was desperate, broken and open for change. I had tried time and time to break free of my addiction on my own but to no avail. It seemed as though I couldn't find a way out of that lifestyle, no matter how hard I tried. I heard about a place called Lydia Center and it was a Christian program.

I really was mad at God and didn't want anything to do with Him, but I also knew I was out of control and headed for death if I at least didn't give the program a try.

I arrived at the Lydia Center feeling self-righteous and believed everything that I had accomplished had been done on my own strength. I wanted instant healing. But it didn't happen that way. It took God to bring me back to reality to know I couldn't do anything—and expect to be happy and content—without Him!

Since learning to depend on God, my life has changed for the best. Without Him I wouldn't be where I am today both emotionally and spiritually. Whenever I go back to trying to do it on my own, I pray to God to give me the strength to continue to move forward and help me through any situation.

Some days I just want to praise and thank You, Lord, for the little simple things in life.

Anita is a graduate of the Lydia Center, a division of Water Street Ministries.

October

Fighting with the Right Person

"Submit yourself therefore to God. Resist the devil, and he will flee from you." *James 4:7 (King James Version)*

One of my teenagers was giving me some attitude and yelling at me. I am ashamed to say I was yelling right back. I consoled myself with the fact that at least I was yelling the truth: "You're fighting with the wrong person! Why won't you yell at Satan for causing you this grief?"

I got the foot stomp and eye roll and smugly knew I'd gotten through.

It wasn't but a few days later as I was throwing laundry in the washer, I felt the enemy telling me things that were demoralizing. Knowing I was alone and practicing what I preach, I boldly told him to go away and claimed God's promises. I felt satisfied, but also a check in my spirit. I had addressed him in a loud voice the same way I do with my kids when I'm really upset. He deserved it—they didn't.

Although they are my children and therefore need to submit to me, I realized they are also my siblings in Christ. I would never talk to my adult Christian brothers and sisters that way. To top it off, when I'm yelling at them it's really not because of their behavior, the origin is because Satan is niggling at me about my own worries and fears.

Too often, we are fighting the wrong person. The enemy has no power over us, but he sure can bother us if we let him. He's also efficient, killing two birds with one stone. In the case when I'm yelling at the kids, he knows I'm trying to fix my own inadequacies by myself, instead of claiming God's power to renew me. Plus, my children end up feeling shamed and probably scared.

Oh, to be so full of God that we are continually abandoned to His ways!

Father, I confess I separate myself from You in little actions every day. Help me to fight the one who rejoices in that by allowing Your Truth to incapacitate him.

Carolyn Schlicher attends DOVE Christian Fellowship in Elizabethtown.

What Is It?

"When the Israelites saw it, they said to each other, 'What is it?' For they did not know what it was. Moses said to them, 'It is the bread the Lord has given you to eat.'" *Exodus 16:15*

"Man-hu, man-hu. . . ." "What is it? What is it?" These were the very words of the Israelites as they came forth from their tents the morning after God's promised manna covered the desert.

The very word *manna* is rooted in the essence of "whatness" or "what is it?"

Imagine several million mouths fed to the full every day for more than forty years. This "what is it," was a gift of life from the very hand of God. God had prepared the people for the first manna and they did not recognize it. Jesus references this same manna in following the miraculous feeding of five thousand men in John 6. He then declares Himself to be the Bread of Life.

God had prepared the people for the new Manna for centuries. Again people scoffed and asked, "what is it, who are you?" Sadly many disciples left Jesus by the droves, vehemently rejecting Him despite filled stomachs from the miracle the day before. The Manna, the Bread of Life stood in their midst. They disdained and rejected the Manna given them for eternal life.

Not much has changed really since these two significant events occurred. The human heart can be incredibly hard, can't it? Jesus still asks the question of us as He did the twelve disciples that day. "You do not want to leave me do you?"

Will your response echo Peter's, who boldly declared, "Lord to whom shall we go, you have the words of eternal life. We believe and know that you are the Holy One of God."

Praise God, Jesus is Life.

Lord, refresh me anew with the amazing truth that You are the Bread of Life. May I be filled completely in You today.

Brian E. Martin serves as lead pastor at Weaverland Mennonite Church in East Earl. He and his wife Shirley are parents of three married children, one young adult at home and one grandchild.

Two-for-One Special

"My sheep listen to my voice; I know them, and they follow me."
John 10:27

While vacationing at the shore, I excitedly prepared to go out with my friends. As I was getting ready, I heard the Lord speak to me. "Carol's mother is being taken to the hospital. She will panic and want to take the two and one-half-hour ride home. Tell her not to. Tell her to trust Me and all will be okay."

I stopped what I was doing completely taken aback by what I had heard. Now I wondered, *how do you approach your friend with that kind of information? I mean we are so far away, her mother is eighty-nine years old, and what if my mind is playing tricks on me?*

I was so bewildered at that point and even when I asked the Lord for assurance that it was Him who was speaking to me – I heard nothing. I left the room and went out to the living room, when Carol's phone rang. She got up abruptly and left. I could tell by the look on her face that it wasn't good news, so I followed her. When I asked her what was wrong, she said her daughter called saying her mother was being taken to the hospital! I could barely stand. I blurted out what the Lord had just spoken to me. We cried, we prayed and of course our faith was tested and stretched as we waited.

The next day we heard that her mother was okay and at home. I call this a "two-for-one special" because my faith grew as well as Carol's because I questioned what I had heard. I had to trust Him that it was His voice, and He was the One instructing me. I went through my own set of doubts, but I came to know that information came from nowhere else than from above.

Thank You, Father, for speaking to us, increasing our faith and trust meanwhile showing us that You do have everything under control.

Eileen Christiansen is a leader for Celebrate Recovery, a twelve-step Christ-centered recovery group in Sadsburyville.

Singing over me

"The Lord your God is in the midst of you, a Mighty One, a Savoir! He will rejoice over you with joy; He will rest (in silent satisfaction) and in His love He will be silent and make no mention (of past sins, or even recall them); He will exult over you with singing."
Zephaniah 3:17 (Amplified Version)

While in a season of what seemed like great assaults to my physical body, I experienced a short time of not being able to feel movement from the waist down. I am a very active person, so this was a pretty hard blow. I could feel myself falling into a pity party. I was appalled at myself to what was coming from my heart. Ahhh! God was revealing the hidden things in my heart!

Two particular events stand out to me. First, I received a book marker that had been my deceased aunt's. Actually, I had given it to her when she was struggling with God's love for her. It had pressed flowers and a scripture from Jeremiah 29:11, "plans not to harm you . . . ." I felt God's love go directly to my heart. The second thing, my pastor's wife Michelle called me that same day when I felt at my lowest and sang a hymn over me. I can't tell you today the title of the hymn, but I can tell you that God used it to speak peace into my soul and a hope for my future.

God was singing over me during that season. He was right there with me mighty to save me, loving me and not mentioning my sin. He rejoiced over me as I got better and healed my physical body.

Father God, You lovingly bring us to truth in the inward parts, rejoicing over us with singing. You know our futures and they are good! Thank You.

Debbie Davenport, Living Truth Fellowship, serves as a leader interceding and equipping others for kingdom purposes in various roles at Cornerstone Pregnancy Care Services.

Am I Wise or a Wise Guy?

"Who is wise and understanding among you? Let him show it by his good life, by deeds done in the humility that comes from wisdom."
James 3:13

"Thank you for helping me! You have so much wisdom! How do you know so much?" This is a comment I hear many, many times when helping directors of nonprofit ministries and organizations. Each time I'm asked, I am reminded of where I've been, and where the "wisdom" has come from.

God has been my personal Mentor in my journey of nonprofit ministry. He has given me audiences before the faith-based and secular worlds to share His principles on godly character, planning and trust. Through these opportunities I've also been able to share my personal relationship with Christ. I've learned that I cannot do HIS ministry without Him. I've learned that working in my own strength doesn't get me very far. I've come to realize that when I turn to Him for direction, His ministry grows beyond my wildest imagination.

Over the past decade I've been sharing my "learned" wisdom with directors across the nation and around the globe. It's exciting to see God speak to each one as I share insights that were birthed in prayer and past experiences. The dictionary defines wisdom as discernment or insight. When God is your Mentor it's amazing the amount of wisdom and insight that is just a prayer away! I've learned to trust in His direction, even when it doesn't make sense to me. His ways are much higher than mine. He is the giver of true wisdom. The question is, "Are you willing to receive it?"

Thank You, Father, that You give us opportunities to help others around us. Teach us to use wisdom that comes from You in all situations of our lives.

Karen Pennell is the chief executive officer of Chester County Women's Services Medical, a life-affirming pregnancy care medical ministry in Chester County. She understands "It's all about the relationship!" and recognizes that God has a purpose for each person she meets.

Captured Thoughts

"Inasmuch as we refute arguments and theories and reasonings and every proud and lofty thing that sets itself up against the true knowledge of God; and we lead every thought and purpose away captive into the obedience of Christ, the Messiah, the Anointed One."
2 Corinthians 10:5 (Amplified Version)

Gossip has never been a substantial problem in my life. Not like I've never been involved, but like God has allowed me to understand that talking about others negatively is not acceptable, even if it's true.

A minister once called someone lazy. Later, the Holy Spirit told him He was offended that the minister called so-and-so lazy. "But it's true," said the minister. "You're talking about My family," replied the Holy Spirit.

We are not equipped to judge others when we do not know everything.

However, one day God showed me judging others in my mind was just as self-righteous as gossip. I would presume to know why others did certain things. I'd think, "I bet they just wanted to . . . ." or "I know what they're trying to do . . . ." would be a common thread in my thoughts as I looked on their actions or words. The Holy Spirit reminded me we are not equipped to judge others when we do not know everything.

In reading the book *The Shack*, the scene that impressed me the most was when Mack was asked to be "the judge." Not only did he know he wouldn't do it, he knew he couldn't.

Ever since that day, the Holy Spirit has been faithful to remind me when I am even tempted to think, "I know what they are trying to do . . . ." God has helped me take thoughts captive and repent when necessary.

Father, thank You for helping me change my thought life. Continue to help me stay yielded to You.

Sharon Eberly, DOVE Westgate Church, serves with her pastor husband Lester at Westgate.

Topsy-turvy Life

"In addition to all this, take up the shield of faith, with which you can extinguish all the flaming arrows of the evil one. Take the helmet of salvation and the sword of the Spirit, which is the word of God."
Ephesians 6:16–17

Life can get extremely busy. It may be with matters relating to the family or maybe it is work, which too affects all of us in one way or another. But then again, you may be like me: I have numerous health problems that occupy much of my time. Not that I can help it, but there are appointments to go to, blood tests to be drawn, occasional surgery and problems yet to appear.

Seems logical then, when life is all topsy-turvy, that the place to go is to the Lord. Am I right? However, I am guilty of often being too busy, and it gets in the way of the most important instructions given by the Great Physician. Sometimes I am too busy to spend time in His word, and therefore, I forgot to take up the sword. You see, when we are so busy, and least expecting it, Satan is at the ready with his flaming arrows. When we aren't ready and don't take up the sword (the word of God) to cut right through those arrows, Satan can make inroads into our lives. Defeat, irritation, depression, worthlessness and the list goes on and on. I know. It happened to me when I wasn't vigilant.

So what's the prescription?

Pretty simple, actually. Daily reading, studying and verbalizing God's Word. Before you know it, those fiery arrows will be put out, Satan will be defeated and you will be victorious in your daily walk. If an apple a day keeps a doctor away, then reading the Bible each day helps keep Satan at bay!

Lord, may we never get too busy to spend time each day with You! May we hunger and thirst for you! Thank You, Jesus, we trust in You.

Barb Shirey, DOVE Westgate Church, retired R.N., disabled but enabled through Jesus.

Joy in Heaven

"The he calls his friends and neighbors together and says, 'Rejoice with me; I have found my lost sheep. I tell you in the same way there will be more rejoicing in heaven over one sinner who repents than over ninety-nine righteours persons who do not need to repent.'"
Luke 15:6–7

I find it interesting that the only time the Bible informs us that we can bring joy in heaven is when a sinner is born again. I expect there is joy in heaven whenever God's people walk in faithfulness to their Lord but the only time the Bible explicitly states we cause rejoicing in heaven is when a person repents and accepts Jesus as their Lord and Savior.

What a privilege we have to bring joy to the angels in heaven. Let's witness with both our words and our deeds. Francis of Assisi said in essence, "Witness 24/7, if necessary, use words." That's like saying, "Be sure to wash, if necessary use water." We need to employ both deeds and words. If Jesus would have come and not informed us with words we would still be lost.

Share Jesus so others can be transferred from the kingdom of darkness to the kingdom of God's dear Son. (See Colossians 1:14).

Father, I thank You for sending Your Son who lived a perfect life and informed us how we can enter the family of God. Lord, help me to be a faithful and fruitful witness. Amen.

J. David Eshelman served as pastor and church planter for fifty years with the Mennonite Church. He is a church consultant and has written a devotional, *Living with Godly Passion*. He and his wife live in Manheim.

Puppy Trust

"And may you have power to understand, as all God's people should, how wide, how long, how high, and how deep his love is."
Ephesians 3:18

When Buddy, a poodle/terrier mix, arrived at my friend's house, he didn't trust people even though he hated being alone. After being rejected or abandoned by several owners, he preferred to curl up at the foot of the bed—close but not too close. Eventually, Buddy learned to know my friend's family better. He realized that they weren't going to hit him with a fly swatter (his worst nightmare). He knew that his food dish wasn't going to be empty, and he learned that he was welcome to cuddle. He moved up from the foot of the bed to lie beside them.

Then came the day he decided to totally trust them. They awoke to find him lying tight against them, on his back with hind legs sprawled like a frog's and front paws folded on his chest. The most vulnerable position a dog can choose. But the only possible position if you want tummy rubs.

I'm a lot like Buddy. I've been taught things about God that made me fearful and reluctant to get close. But as I've learned to know Him as the God of grace—to know I have peace with Him and have no need to fear—I have been inching my way closer and closer. What a tremendous relief to know that God poured all the wrath that I deserved on Jesus. I can only imagine what the love of God feels like, but one day soon I'll experience for myself. (I'm hungry for the people version of a tummy rub.)

Buddy has absolute confidence in his family's love and welcome. If a dog can learn to trust his family, I can do it with God. I will not be out-trusted by a puppy!

I've been told that one of the words for worship in the Greek is the word picture of a dog greeting his master at the door.

We cannot love Who we do not trust. We cannot trust Who we fear.

God, please give me the power to understand the vastness of Your love toward me.

Ruth Morris is a special projects writer for several ministries.

Wisdom

"If any of you is lacking in wisdom, ask God, who gives to all generously and ungrudgingly, and it will be given to you." *James 1:5 (New Revised Standard Version)*

When I was a teenager, I wanted to find wisdom. But in the atheistic environment where I grew up, no one knew where that wisdom was located. I have no idea why, yet, somewhere deep down in my heart, I knew that God, in Whom we did not trust, might have known the answer.

I began to seek Him. When I met Christ, I realized that He was the bottomless well of wisdom. Later I learned that He was Wisdom Himself. Also I realized that learning from Jesus meant learning to be wise.

Today I understand that learning to be wise is a lifelong process. In a way, it has been similar to my studying English as a second language. In both cases I had to begin from the beginning. A good textbook where the rules are explained was also needed. Then many exercises were required. Mistakes and disappointments were plentiful. But that is where perseverance became crucial. The more I practiced it, the more professional I became in speaking and writing.

I find the book of Proverbs especially helpful in my understanding of wisdom. It also teaches me many life lessons: how to act in my family and society; how to avoid mistakes, sins and dire consequences; how to live a life pleasing to God. No, it doesn't mean I've become Ms. Perfect. God knows that, but He honors my effort. Furthermore, He is patient and generous to share more of His wisdom with me— if only I ask.

Jesus, help us to become wise. In Your name, we ask. Amen.

Yulia Bagwell, Beth Yeshua, serves at the Community Bible Study and translates for *The Upper Room* devotional magazine.

Yielding to God's Will

"But they that wait upon the Lord shall renew their strength."
Isaiah 40:31 (King James Version)

All of God's children are a continual work in progress. Gradually as we begin to let go and let God, we release our faith allowing God to do some powerful work in our lives.

The hard part is yielding to God's will. We cannot see the big picture, so oftimes what we determine is God's will for our life does not make sense in things that happen to us.

The next time something happens that doesn't make sense, I encourage you not to question God or turn your back on Him. This could be a test to see how ready you are to receive a change in your life, or it could be another step in the process of preparing you for what God has in store for you. If you patiently wait and obey God's bidding, you will not only receive what God has planned for you all along, but you will be better equipped because you accepted the setbacks, the disappointments and even the heartaches that came your way.

Looking back you will see how you grew from each of those experiences. Good or bad, much can be gleaned with an open heart to God.

Each day as you travel the road of life, listen to what God is saying to you, and then be obedient to His Word. If you practice these principles, before long there will come a time when you realize you are not displaying the same response you would have made a few days, months, or even years ago. It is then that you will realize God has been slowly transforming you all along the way.

Lord, help me to let Thy Will, not my will be done. In Jesus' name. Amen.

Janet Young is proprietress of Over the Teacup, Camp Hill.

Love of Steel

"Love never fails . . . ." *1 Corinthians 13:8*

It was a Valentine's Day assignment for my youngest. "Interview members of your family or others and write down their definition of love." I was in the kitchen as he asked one of the girls in our house how she defined love. She responded with visions of roses, soft music and candlelight. All of the things you would find in a Hallmark card.

My son then turned to me and asked, "Dad, how do you define love?"

In the inspiration of the moment, I told him that love is a steel ball. The steel ball is surrounded by a tough rubbery substance. The tough rubber is covered with a beautiful but fragile coating. The outer coating is the sexual draw. That part of love can be the most beautiful thing in the world, but it is fragile. Garlic toast for lunch, or a sneeze at the wrong time, and it shatters into a million pieces. The rubber coating is the friendship that we all long for.

If you were to ask me who my best friend is, I would not have to think twice. Nobody comes close to my wife Brenda in that category, but sometimes even the friendship is beaten away by the daily wear-and tear of life, and we find our love down to the steel ball. The steel ball is the unconditional agape love that is at the core of God's love. It is that part of our vows that take us "through sickness and health." It has nothing to do with attraction, and nothing even to do with friendship. We all, at some point, find our relationship down to the steel ball. It is not a sign of failure, but a reminder of the foundation we have to rebuild our love on.

Father, thank You for the agape love that You have loved me with, and help me to radiate that love to those around me.

Steve Hershey is a teacher and speaker at White Oak Church of the Brethren. Steve and his wife Brenda have opened their home to young adults.

Unexpected Blessings

"God can do anything, you know—far more than you could ever imagine or guess or request in your wildest dreams!" *Ephesians 3:20 (The Message)*

My husband Michael found himself suddenly unemployed on October 5, 1979, which was also his thirty-third birthday. How would we manage? What would Christmas be like for our children this year? These were all worries that raced through my mind.

As we began to deal with joblessness, friends shared Proverbs 3:5–6: "Trust in the Lord with all your heart, lean not to your own understanding, acknowledge Him in all your ways and He will direct your paths." Our paths were definitely not our chosen ones!

November was truly a month of thanksgiving as we experienced our daily needs being met in ways beyond our wildest imagination. Anonymous financial gifts, groceries, needed clothing and even a turkey was delivered right to our door. Not understanding her choices, our neighbor brought chocolate syrup, Michael's favorite soap, peanuts and Pepsi. Essential needs, no, but unexpected delights, definitely!

Some would say Christmas had not yet arrived, but for us it began on October 5, with my husband's pink slip birthday gift.

As December approached, the blessings continued to pour into our home. Cuddly baby dolls and red velvet dresses arrived for our two young daughters. Even a coveted pair of clogs was given to our oldest daughter. To our amazement, a beautiful homemade wreath was anonymously hung on our front door, while a freshly cut evergreen was delivered to the back door. Of all our Christmas trees over the years, this one remains the most memorable!

Did the blessings stop December 25? Hardly! The Lord provided a job for my husband in January 1980, and the miracles continue even today, as our hearts remain open to receive God's daily gifts.

Try reminiscing through your treasured memories and discover how God has moved in your life as well.

Lord, enable us to see You working in our daily lives and give us the courage to go and share as Your Holy Spirit leads.

Susan Kulka is a wife, mother and grandmother. She and her husband Michael attend The Worship Center.

Even in the Fog

"And my God will meet all your needs according to his glorious riches in Christ Jesus." *Philippians 4:19*

My husband and I recently took a trip to Nova Scotia. We did not follow a planned itinerary so each day was an adventure without a designated destination to reach by evening. We were free to explore without a time schedule to meet, but we still had a few bumps along the way. One of these happened on our way to Cape Breton, which is located in the northern part of Nova Scotia. The road runs along the top of steep rock formations bordering the sea. The scenes on postcards were absolutely beautiful so we looked forward to admiring the gorgeous scenery and were confident it would be worth driving about one hundred miles out of the way.

The morning we started the drive, fog rolled in on the northern coast. The fog became so thick that we could not see God's beautiful creation. The hundred-mile drive seemed quite long and my husband and I felt quite tense from the eye strain.

The journey reminded me that in our lives, the fog rolls in sometimes and we become so focused on the circumstances that we forget that God is in control. In the fog, we look intently for road markers and the center line. We look for familiar markers to assure us that we are on the right road. Sometimes it takes a little fog to remind us to get our eyes on the Father. In the fog or out of the fog, our Lord wants us to intently look toward Him. He wants us to put our trust in Him and Him alone.

As we ended our hundred-mile trip, the fog lifted. Our search for dinner brought us to a restaurant at closing time. We were blessed by being seated at a table and the assurance not to worry about the time. As we ate our meal, the Lord even topped it with a special dessert—a beautiful perfect rainbow framed through the window. Once again, God reminded us how much He cares for us. He is always with us and wants us to focus intently on Him.

Father, thank You for being Lord. Thank You for being my provider and thank You for reminding me to stay focused on You—even in the fog.

Judy Bowlby, DOVE Westgate, teaches at Donegal High School.

There Is a God

"For my thoughts are not your thoughts and My ways are not your ways . . . ." *Isaiah 55:8*

I don't understand God's ways, but I do know He exists. I have a Jewish friend whose grandmother survived the holocaust. After coming out of a concentration camp, she was questioned by her friends who told her to deny God, since He obviously must not exist.

Her answer to them, "No, I am certain there is a God, but I do not understand His ways," spoke a lot of truth to my heart.

This past year, we lost our son in a terrible car accident. In addition, I totaled my car and life's daily stresses just seemed too much to bear.

Several months after my son's death, I was deeply depressed. I remember walking through the parking garage of a hospital, en route to an interpreting job, when I, in desperation, asked God to show me some sign of His love to me. Almost immediately, I felt this warm sensation on the top of my head. It turned out to be a pigeon's droppings!

I laughed to myself and said, "So, that is what You think of me, God!"

Nonetheless, the humor of the moment broke my depression, and I was able to laugh.

I still don't know why God allowed all these things to happen, but I somehow knew that I was loved!

A Native American friend told me that in her culture, getting pigeon droppings on one's head is considered a "blessing." I'm still not sure if I want that kind of blessing again, but I guess God Who knows all and sees all had that timed perfectly for me!

At any rate, I am still learning to trust Him. And, perhaps someday, He will reveal His eternal purposes for me.

Lord, help me to know that my times are in Your hand, and that You do care about our daily grind. Help me to walk in obedience and love and help me appreciate Your sense of humor.

Jim Schneck is a freelance interpreter for the deaf and the husband of Rosalee.

Always Run

"Trust in the Lord with all your heart and lean not on your own understanding; in all your ways acknowledge him, and he will make your paths straight." *Proverbs 3:5, 6*

"*Always* run to God, *never* from Him!" became my family's number one phrase during a difficult time. We knew we needed Him and that we could depend on Him, and that He was the only one who could fix things.

We can all choose to run toward something: drugs, alcohol, prescription drugs, food, a counselor, a friend; the list can go on and on. But what happens when we do? Sometimes things feel better—for awhile, kind of like a Band-Aid was put on a wound. Sometimes nothing happens and it just keeps hurting. Sometimes it leads us in a terrible downward spiral, only to take us farther away from God.

If we *always* run to God and *never* from Him, we can trust that He wants good for us— all the time. Now, that doesn't mean instantly! His timing is not our timing and His ways are not our ways, but He does always want good for us, and so, He will make it right in the end – if we trust Him through to the end! He says He will bring to completion the good work He's begun and all things work together for good. These are just two truths to hang onto in times of need. We can trust Him. He is trustworthy. He loves us more than anyone ever could and He always will.

So, how about it: Do you want to make the catchy phrase your own today? Do you want it to be more that a catchy phrase for you and your family, but instead a truth that you can hang onto? Come on, together, let's *always* run to God, *never* from Him!

Lord, thank You that You can be trusted. Thank You that You are bigger than anything anyone of us will ever have to face and thank You that because You love us and because You are near to us, we never have to face things alone. Thank You that we can always run to You. Please help us never to run from You.

Lisa Dorr is a wife, mother, editor, author, public speaker and most of all a child of God.

Honor Your Mother

"Honor your father and your mother, so that you may live long in the land the Lord your God is giving you." *Exodus 20:12*

Before my mother's eighty-eighth birthday on October 17, 2004, my sister and I felt that it would be a good idea if my three brothers and their spouses joined us and our spouses to celebrate her birthday in a way that we had not done earlier. We had given a large party for her family and friends on her eightieth birthday. So in 2004, we decided that instead of each of us siblings taking her out to eat separately, we would all meet at her apartment to celebrate our mother's special day with food, gifts and a birthday cake.

Mother lived alone in a first-floor apartment and was thankful that she did not need to go to a nursing home or an assisted-living facility. She was happy that we surprised her in this way, as four of her five children arrived about the same time. Mom seemed a bit distracted in our conversations and glanced at the door occasionally. When my brother and his wife arrived, she settled down and really enjoyed the fact that all of us could be there, like chicks around a mother hen. I remember her big smile and how pleased she was that day.

Little did we know then that on December 4 of that year, we would all be gathering for her funeral. Much later I realized that her birthday gathering was God's blessing to her. He had prompted my sister and I to arrange the day, and He knew that it would be a wonderful last birthday for her.

Even now in times of grief, like when I hear her favorite hymn or attend her church's annual picnic, I am thankful that my heavenly Father in His wisdom gave my mother what every mother desires, a special day surrounded by those she loves the most.

Heavenly Father, You know the times of our lives and You desire that we honor our mothers. Thank You for giving our family that special day together.

Sharon Neal attends Lancaster Evangelical Free Church, where she serves in children's ministry, the shepherding team and with women's Bible studies and occasionally volunteers with Susquehanna Valley Pregnancy Services.

Seeing Clearly

"Answer me when I call to you, O, my righteous God. Give me relief from my distress; be merciful to me and hear my prayer." *Psalm 4:1*

I was an addict and didn't know how to begin my recovery. I would cry night after night "God please help me."

I wanted freedom from my addiction, which was taking away everything and everyone I love from me. One day I got high and drunk and started asking for help again. I didn't want to start the process. I wanted a quick fixing. So I got into trouble and went to jail. While I was in jail, I started giving my life to God and reading the Bible. From jail, I went into a thirty-day program and another thirty-day program before entering a six-month Christian program. I wanted even more of Christ so I looked for a program that would take me deeper and I found the Lydia Center. God had more for me.

At the Lydia Center, I began to allow God to work in me. I began to see clearly that I was the problem. I looked inside at the reasons I did what I didn't want to do and why I repeated certain behaviors that went against my recovery. I began to see there was no quick fix. I had to want it bad enough to work for it. God wanted me to do the work with His help.

Now that I have put my will in God's hands, things have become clear. I see myself in the mirror as somebody that God loves. I am God's daughter and He is my Father. He brought back my sense of direction and my smile. I feel better and see different. I can be anything—or anyone—with God's help.

Thank You, God, for everything You have done with me. Help me to live a clean and sober life.

Christine is a resident at the Lydia Center, a division of Water Street Ministries.

The Lord Works in Mysterious Ways

"Delight thyself also in the Lord and He shall give thee the desires of thine heart." *Psalm 37:4 (King James Version)*

In 1992, my daughter was in a terrible automobile accident. She was thrown from the car and seriously hurt. Her three-year-old son was with her but he was unharmed. A man sat with her son until the ambulance came for her. We often wanted to meet the man and thank him for taking care of our grandson. Years later, we went with our son when he made settlement on his home and we met that man. The Lord knows and gives you the desires of your heart.

In December 2009, my brother was in an automobile accident on his way to visit me and later died. We witnessed to him for years but he never confessed to accepting the Lord. The next day as I was praying, I had peace in my heart that he made things right. Several days later we went to see the place of the accident. As we were taking photographs, a car pulled off the road and approached us. The Lord sent the woman that came across the accident. She and her husband were on their way to church so that I could talk to her. She asked me if he was a Christian and I told her I wasn't sure. She said as she was praying the day after the accident she felt such peace about it and that was the same day I had the peace in my heart. God is so good. He knows what we need and He knows just how to give it to us.

Father I thank You for knowing exactly what we need and meeting our needs. Help us to see You at work especially in times of trials. In Jesus' wonderful name. Amen.

Doris Showalter is a wife, mother, grandmother and great-grandmother and attends Mission of Love Church in Ephrata.

Not a Firefly

"Only be careful, and watch yourselves closely so that you do not forget the things your eyes have seen or let them slip from your heart as long as you live. . . ." *Deuteronomy 4:9*

Splat! There went another lightning bug on the windshield of my car. And what pops into my mind? "Gee, I'm glad I am not a firefly."

Think about this. The average life span of some insects is just days or weeks. I even saw in my research of this topic that there is one kind of fly whose average life span was only thirty minutes to one day! That is not very common, but in looking over lists of other animals, I discovered there are not many non-turtle kinds of animals that average more than twenty years.

So what am I saying? God loves old people more than those taken in their prime?

No, of course not. But in the grand plan of things, God has given us quite a long opportunity to make a difference in this world. Humans average about seventy to eighty years of life. But that is not to say we couldn't be nearing the end of ours now. Have you made the most of the time God has given you?

Lord, we have no idea when You will call us home, but please show us how to make a difference until then.

Tracy Slonaker is not a firefly, but a wife, mother and director of Christian education at Harvest Fellowship of Colebrookdale.

Brokenness Meets Brokenness

"The Lord is near to the brokenhearted and saves those who are crushed in spirit." *Psalm 34:18*

When I was invited to lead a devotional time with a group of homeless women living at the Water Street Rescue Mission, I really had no idea what to expect.

As they walked into the room, each one attempted to project strength and self-sufficiency, but I'm well acquainted with that mask from my own use of it before I had surrendered my life to Christ. Seeing beyond their masks, I sensed their deep sorrow and shame. Their darting eyes revealed their poverty of self-respect as they purposed not to look fully into my eyes.

What can I possibly say to comfort them? was my cry to Holy Spirit and His reply was simply, "Allow Me . . . ."

That made picking out the first song easy. I had written "I Can See You" in response to a previous assignment when my teacher had asked, "Do you see that woman in a heap, hiding in that corner?" In my mind's eye, I had seen her as clear as if I was in the same room with her. "Sing her out of that corner, My child," was God's request.

Thankfully, that song was the icebreaker that persuaded this small group of broken women to give me access to their lives. As I sang the songs from my collection that seemed to address the observable needs of their hearts, tears fell freely from battle-worn eyes.

Acknowledging my own brokenness was all it took for them to trust me with theirs. They could hear me confessing my own weakness and desperation for God through what I was singing, and they quietly yet wholeheartedly joined me. It was my great privilege to touch their lives. I carry them with me.

Lord, touching other people's lives is so much less complicated than I imagine it to be. We're all broken in some way, in need of forgiveness and restoration. When we meet in brokeness, we can fully embrace each other. Thank You for using my humanity to touch lives. I am grateful.

Kathi Wilson and her husband Mark are co-authors of *Tired of Playing Church* and co-founders of Body Life Ministries and members of University Christian Fellowship.

A Prophet Named Mike

"Do not treat prophecies with contempt. Test everything. Hold on to the good." *I Thessalonians 5:20–21*

"If you really studied the Scriptures and loved God's word, there is no way you would accept divorced and remarried people into our church!"

I can still remember the sting of that judgment. How could this person question my love for God's Word? I had served as youth pastor and was on the leadership team of our church, preaching and teaching regularly.

It was in the middle of this intense soul-searching and wrestling with the issue of God's redemptive plan for all people, even those who had been through the challenges of divorce and remarriage, that God sent a prophet named Mike to see me. I didn't know Mike, who was from a neighboring state. I'll never forget when Mike burst into my office and introduced himself. His next question was: "Are you open to the prophetic word of God?"

When I cautiously agreed, he told me that God knew the struggles I was going through, that I was going to enter a season in my life where my teaching would release light and life, not just the letter. As tears began to stream down my face, he continued to speak words of encouragement into my heart and assure me that God was near to me. Mind you, Mike didn't give me all the answers to my struggles nor all the solutions to the issue of divorce and remarriage. But Mike did prophesy the loving heart of God.

Scripture teaches that we should "not despise prophecies." I think this implies that we don't just latch on to any word that is given to us in the name of the Lord. However, it does mean there are some prophecies that need to be held onto and believed by faith. His Spirit helps us to discern what should be held onto and what should be released.

Lord, open us to hear Your prophetic word for faithful prophets and hold fast to Your truth.

Mike Zimmerman serves as associate pastor on the leadership team at Erb Mennonite Church in Lititz..

Buying a Car or Receiving His Blessing

"The Spirit of the Lord is upon me . . . . Instead of shame and dishonor, you shall have a double portion of prosperity and everlasting joy." *Isaiah 61:1, 7 (The Living Bible)*

My husband Bill was trying to buy a car that he wanted to be safe for me and would travel well during winter weather. I on the other hand just wanted a small economy car good on gas.

Bill is a thinker and very cautious. He waits and ponders until he is settled. The cars I wanted, I have to admit were not feeling as safe as the ones he was picking but my mind was on what I wanted.

God led Bill to buy a certain car for me, fully loaded, yet at a dealer's price. Seeing Bill's excitement for me to have this car, I conceded.

During this same time period, I had been asked to take a ministry position. I kept thinking of all the reasons why I was not the right person for the position yet I was already walking in it without the title. God was trying to bless me.

Revelation came. I recognized that I was fighting a double blessing and did not even realize it.

God was trying to bless me through my husband and my pastors, and I was fighting Him. Blinded to what was before me as blessings from God, I recognized that pride was keeping me from seeing the truth about my worth. I wanted what was less than God's best for me and my husband was showing me that in the car he bought for me. False humility was keeping me from the title of something God had called me to walk in for many years.

My husband saw it. My pastors and God all knew my worth. Now I was getting it.

Dear God, thank You that as Your children You offer us double blessing and honor. You removed the shame of our past and pride can't stay. You are so real and lavishing.

Debbie Davenport, Living Truth Fellowship, serves as a leader interceding and equipping others for kingdom purposes in her various roles in the body of Christ and at Cornerstone Pregnancy Care Services.

Faith Versus Circumstances

"Then the Lord said to Abraham, 'Why did Sarah laugh and say, "Will I really have a child, now that I am old?"' Is anything too hard for the Lord? I will return to you at the appointed time next year and Sarah will have a son" *Genesis 18:13–14*

I can relate only to that verse in a very small degree because my wife Mim and I also desperately wanted to have a son. When we had been married for several years and were in our mid-twenties, we decided it was time to have children. We assumed that it would be just that simple; and that children would come and all would be well. However, our first pregnancy ended in a heart-wrenching miscarriage. As difficult as this was, we were both still in faith that God was going to give us children. After navigating our way through much of the emotional trauma of that initial miscarriage, sometime later Mim became pregnant again. We prayed fervently for the health and safety and protection of the baby that Mim was carrying. However tragedy struck, and instead of a healthy child we experienced a premature stillbirth.

The emotional trauma of that original miscarriage paled in comparison to this experience. It was a painful, agonizing test of our faith.

About a year later Mim again became pregnant. To say that we were nervous, anxious and uptight would be a vast understatement. We desperately wanted a healthy baby and again prayed and interceded for that baby. Our small group and much of the church stood by us during this time in prayer and intercession on behalf of us and our unborn child. Nine months later our full-term, healthy son was born. It is almost impossible to describe the joy, gratification, relief, intense sense of peace and fulfillment that flooded us at the birth of our precious son.

But Abraham and Sarah's arms were empty. He was ninety-nine years old, Sarah about ninety and still they had no children. They had a direct promise from God; they were to have a child. But yet their arms were empty, and Sarah became cynical. But then God asks the question, "Is anything too hard for God?"

God thank You that nothing is too hard for You; build my faith, forgive my unbelief. I know that Your plan will be accomplished in my life.

Deryl Hurst is executive pastor at DOVE Christian FellowshipWestgate.

What's in a Name

"Everyone who calls on the name of the Lord will be saved."
Romans 10:13

I have one of those names. It's the type of name most everyone mispronounces or misspells. It's an easy name to make fun of. I have to admit, I always wondered if my children would accept or better yet, embrace such a different name. So far, so good. My wife tells me she wanted someone with a "classy" last name. If she thinks class describes our last name, I'm impressed. On the other hand, you just wouldn't believe some of the intriguing misspellings on mail that arrives at our home. Or, maybe you would because you have one of those difficult last names.

But no last name, no matter how different has been used as profanity, a form of cursing for more than two-thousand years like the Name. I found out that this Name was a popular Hebrew name until it was associated with a rebellious reformer who spoke candidly to the religious leaders of His day. But the scripture states that there is salvation in no other Name. Simon the sorcerer wanted the power in this Name. No other name can be associated with the forgiveness of sin as this Name. Healing is found in this one Name. This Name crosses denominational lines and geographical borders.

This Name was very intentional on the father's part, "...You are to give him the name *Jesus* . . . ." (Matthew 1:21) You and I can call upon this precious Name this day for all that is on our heart. Tell Him how much you love this Name and adore the One it is associated with — Jesus Christ, Son of God.

Father, thank You for the name that You have given us for it is far above every other name.

Steve Prokopchak is married to Mary for thirty-five years and is a member of the DOVE Christian Fellowship International Apostolic Council giving oversight to DOVE churches in various regions of the world.

Free Birthday Lunch

"If people can't see what God is doing, they stumble all over themselves; but when they attend to what he reveals, they are most blessed." *Proverbs 29:18 (The Message)*

To celebrate my father's birthday, I took a vacation day. He selected lunch at a smorgasbord, a family favorite. Visits to Lancaster area are deep in our family memory book where we visit the area spending time shopping, eating and enjoying fun moments. Over the years we enjoyed the trip to God's country viewing the picturesque beauty of rolling hills, farms and land space.

Upon the arrival we found altered seasonal hours and a dinnertime opening which led us to explore the many area eateries. Earlier that day I had prayed that God would allow this to be a very special day for Dad. I wanted the best for him and for a birthday memory, but it didn't seem like things were working out at all and not in the manner that I view as "God's best."

God was teaching me that He is in every component of life; he knows the deepest desires of the heart. A final decision put us across town to yet another familiar place. I drove Mom and Dad to the lobby door and I parked the car.

As I entered the lobby area, I saw the sign on the bulletin board, "Free Birthday Lunch." I had forgotten that Dad loved the honor of a free lunch celebrating his birthday but God did not forget. God knew that this was very special and important to my father. It mattered to him, and my prayer was answered.

Dear Lord, I praise You, for Your word says "every good gift comes from God. Thank You for leading us to every good thing that we need in our life. I give You all the glory and praise in Jesus' name. Amen.

Cindy Healey attends Calvary Assembly with her mother. Cindy is a freelance Christian writer.

Salvation Is a Miracle

"No one can come to me unless the Father who sent me draws him, and I will raise him up at the last day." *John 6:44*

We can never bring people to Jesus. The Father must draw them. It is impossible for a person to become a Christian unless this great miracle happens. We cannot persuade them or argue them into the kingdom of God because their problem is not an intellectual one. They cannot change their behavior and become like Jesus because they are born with a selfish nature. Only Jesus can bring about the new birth, the new life and the new godly nature. They are spiritually dead according to Ephesians 2:1–2 and the devil has taken them captive to do his will according to 2 Timothy 2:26.

The forces that hold people captive are far more powerful than our strength. There is not the slightest possibility that we can lead anyone to the cross unless Jesus is drawing them. It is only His power that can save them. But the good news is that we can be absolutely sure that Jesus will help us to reach the lost. The Word of God says, "God isn't late with his promise as some measure lateness. He is restraining himself on account of you, holding back the End because he doesn't want anyone lost. He's giving everyone space and time to change."

On the day of Pentecost the Holy Spirit was poured out on the disciples. Peter preached under the power of the Spirit and they cried out, "What shall we do?" Peter replied, "Repent and be baptized, everyone one of you, in the name of Jesus Christ for the forgiveness of your sins. And you will receive the gift of the Holy Spirit."

We need the Holy Spirit to witness. (See Acts 1:8.) We need the Holy Spirit to be born into God's kingdom. (See John 3:5.) We cannot do anything apart from the Spirit. (See John 15:5.)

Father, thank You for the Holy Spirit. As I witness for You, help me to depend on your Holy Spirit for words to say, for walking in obedience and for your Spirit to draw people to yourself.

J. David Eshleman served as pastor/church planter for fifty years and is church consultant for Eastern Mennonite Missions and Lancaster Mennonite Conference. He is author of *Now Go Forward: Reaching out to grow your congregation* and *Living with Godly Passion: Daily Reading for those with a passion to share Jesus.*

Jet Fuel No Longer Needed

"The message is very close at hand; it is on your lips and in your heart." *Romans 10:8 (New Living Translation)*

Silly me—for years I expected seeds still in a packet to produce the same results as those planted in rich soil. Not in a literal garden, of course, but still you'd think I'd know better.

Until recently I thought storing the Word in my head (seeds in a packet) was the same as the Word established in my heart (seeds in a garden). What a frustrating, futile, not mention foolish, enterprise that was. Oh, there was some fruit in my life as long as my willpower was running on jet fuel. But I had weaknesses that hung like leeches and failings that hovered like vultures.

What a difference when I learned how to plant the Word in my heart. No wonder King David made a point of hiding the Word in his heart to keep sin at bay.

Negative reactions that used to strike with the speed of a cobra no longer coil and hiss. My fear of people and their opinions have sloughed off like an old skin. And the panic I felt when confronted with new, difficult situations has been extinguished.

Both these changes happened without me focusing on my problems and weaknesses, digging around in my past or even praying for help. They disappeared as I established some foundational Word truths in my heart and concepts that I had no idea were in any way connected to my problems. Now, without thought or ramping up my willpower, my reactions in those same kind of situations are radically different, automatic and delightful.

I've discovered that what I plant in my heart grows and produces without conscious effort because what is in my heart flows and spreads into every corner of my life. What an incredible powerhouse: God's Word flourishing in my heart.

Holy Spirit, teach me how to plant more and more of God's Word in my heart.

Ruth Morris is a special projects writer for several ministries.

In Dying, We Gain

"For to me, to live is Christ and to die is gain." *Philippians 1:21*

A recent newspaper article confirmed that truth is indeed stranger than fiction. According to the report, a ninety-one-year-old widow, living in Bradford County, Pennsylvania, had her husband exhumed from his grave and kept him in a bedroom in her home for ten years. She explained her actions helped her forget that he had died. "I could see him. I could touch him," she said.

When her twin sister died several months ago, the widow also had her exhumed and kept her on a sofa in her home. The widow is quoted as saying, "I think when you put them in the ground, that's good-bye. In this way I could touch her and look at her and talk to her."

She went on to say, "I put glasses on her. When I put the glasses on, it made all the difference in the world. I would fix her up. I'd fix her face up all the time."

A psychiatrist who commented on the bizarre case said the research shows that people who aren't particularly spiritual or religious often have a difficult time with death because they fear that death is truly the end so they deny death. In this case, the widow got the bodies of her loved ones back and she felt fulfilled by having them at home, like she was beating death by bringing them back.

Most of us cannot identify with such rationale, but it does remind me that as Christians we view death quite differently than those who do not believe in God. Revelation 21 promises that when we go to be with the Lord, there is no more sickness, pain and worries. Best of all, we get to see Jesus face-to-face. He will wipe the tears from our eyes. And, we shall see Him as He is.

Dear Lord, thank You that the sting of death is eased by the knowledge that in dying, we gain. How wonderful to know that we will get to see You face-to-face forever and ever.

Lou Ann Good and her husband Parke are members of DOVE Westgate and enjoy ten grandkids, biking and reflecting on God's faithfulness.

Older than the Dinosaurs?

"Heaven and earth will pass away, but my words will never pass away." *Matthew 24:35*

Age is relative. And thankfully, its relativity helps us appreciate age.

In Lancaster County, old is defined by the Hans Herr House, dated 1719.

In the western United States, some ancient Pueblo villages were built in AD 750 When Bob and I traveled to Israel and Egypt, we discovered a whole new realm of "old." Some archaeological digs unearthed thirteen to twenty-plus civilizations stacked one on top of the other! Tourists walking the ruins of ancient Bethsaida view a first-century village. Jesus performed several miracles here, so we most likely walked on the very stones our Savior traveled! But let's go back farther.

In 37–31 BC, Herod built the great fortified Masada, a high plateau near the Dead Sea, as a palatial getaway fortress.

In 930 BC, King Jeroboam built a forbidden shrine, or high place, with the golden calf near Tel Dan, in northern Israel. Also at Tel Dan is an intact clay brick gate, the arched entry to a Canaanite city—most likely a gate through which Abraham and Sarah passed around 1,800 years before Christ.

In Cairo, Egypt, we viewed the Gezar pyramids (built in 2700–2500 B.C. or 4,600 years ago), the oldest and only surviving ancient wonder. The Khufu pyramid took 100,000 laborers about twenty years to push and stack 2.3 million blocks. Despite their monstrosity, all of the pyramids gradually lose height each year, a sign of the fragility of the things of this world.

Though we marvel at ancient wonders, they will not remain forever. In the beginning (before the pyramids), God's words spoke creation into existence, and His words are still applicable today, for tomorrow and eternity!

Lord, help us to revere Your preserved ancient words in the same manner we marvel at antiquated wonders of the world.

Tamalyn Jo Heim, despite what you hear from her four adult children and three in-law children, is not as old as the dinosaurs!

Go Where the Christians Aren't

"For God has not given us a spirit of fear, but of power, and love, and a sound mind." *2 Timothy 1:7 (New King James)*

I was raised to believe that if I wanted to be a good person, I had to surround myself with good influences. Good influences meant Christians. Everyone else was, well, not a Christian.

Years later I was a disgruntled thirty something wondering why my life, my Christian life, felt so empty. The problem was that I was put on this earth to do God's will, but I couldn't find anything to do. It was like I gave the Lord my life and He didn't want it.

"What do you want me to do?" I cried desperately in my prayers. That night He spoke loud and clear.

"If you want to do My work, you must go where the Christians aren't."

What did that mean?

The next day I drove past a farm. The farm was well known because every October it was transformed into "one of the most haunted places on earth" to get a little extra money.

Acting positions fill up quick. Go get a job!

Was God kidding? I don't watch scary movies. I barely even like Halloween. It's so unchristian. But I turned my car around, drove down the dusty driveway and asked the owner for a job. I started in July working construction, something else I didn't know how to do.

Slowly I got used to skeletons and scare tactics. I started to make friends. Good people, but not a Christian among them. I stuck out like a sore thumb. Eventually they started asking questions. What makes you act like that? What's someone like you doing here?

For the first time in my life, I was a true evangelist. God knew what He was doing all along.

Abba Father, thank You for being right. Please help me and all who read this to step out of their comfort zones and go where the Christians aren't to see Your love in action.

Amy Swanson is a graduate of Philadelphia Biblical University.

November

God's Protection

"The Lord will keep you from all harm—he will watch over your life; the Lord will watch over your coming and going both now and forevermore." *Psalm 121:7*

My wife and her two sisters decided to plan a visit to Alaska this past summer and included us three brother-in-laws in the adventure.

One of their planned stops was Denali National Park. Upon arriving, I spent some time reading about the park which included instructions on what to do if one were to encounter a grizzly bear.

These tips were meant for backpackers hiking deep into remote areas of Denali Park: 1."Don't run! A grizzly will think you are prey and can outrun you at speeds up to forty miles per hour. 2. Don't climb a tree. Bears are very good tree climbers. 3. Stand your ground. Raise your arms and shout.This makes you look bigger than you really are and will probably scare the bear away."

The following day, we hiked eleven miles on a wide and well used trail to a historic cabin still used by park rangers today.

One-half mile into the trail, we heard a shout ahead of us. A grizzly appeared around the next bend only thirty yards away.

We froze in disbelief! I remembered what I had read and yelled to our group of six not to run and to raise their arms and start to shout.

Wow, did we shout! But the bear kept coming down the trail. When he got within ten yards of us, he growled and turned to our left and disappeared into the woods. The park ranger at the historic cabin, whose yell we heard, had yelled when the bear had poked his head into the cabin window. The ranger reported our sighting to headquarters. We six were quite shaken as we thought about what could have happened.

That night we six gathered in our hotel room and thanked God for His protection. We believe that God had posted an angel on the trail to turn the bear at the ten-yard mark.

I wonder how often God protects us from danger or harm without us having the faintest clue of how close we come to catastrophe.

God, thank You for Your protective hand that shields us from harm. Thank You for loving and caring for us even when we are unaware.

Joe Nolt attends DOVE, Elizabethtown.

Transformation

"Now we look inside, and what we see is anyone united with the Messiah gets a fresh start, is created new. The old life is gone; a new life burgeons. Look at it! All this comes from God . . . ."
2 Corinthians 5:17 (The Message)

A beautiful symbol for this verse is the black and orange monarch butterfly. It is amazing how it glides on the air currents seemingly without effort and yet has the strength and endurance to migrate to a valley in Mexico every autumn. Utterly astonishing!

But this was not always true for the butterfly. It began as an earthbound caterpillar clinging to a green leaf for all its worth and eating its way into the utter darkness of a cocoon. Only after months of seclusion was it transformed into the graceful butterfly it was always meant to be.

This miracle can happen for us as well if we surrender completely to the Lord. Give up clinging to what used to be and simply ask the Holy Spirit to live in us. He will feed us, guide us and provide the power to burst forth from our earthbound cocoons to be transformed into the people He created us to be—freely gliding on the winds of the Holy Spirit.

Dear Jesus, please come and live within me and by Your mercy and grace transform my life.

Susan Kulka is a wife, mother and grandmother. She and her husband Michael attend the Worship Center.

Wonderfully Loved

"You hem me in—behind and before; you have laid your hand upon me. Such knowledge is too wonderful for me, too lofty for me to attain." *Psalm 139:5–6*

The words of the surgeon cut deep like a scalpel and hung like cold icicles in the briefing room. My wife and I sat in silent shock as the surgical team carefully articulated immediate next steps. The avalanche of medical vocabulary and decisions needing immediate response was overwhelming. The "c" word, cancer, was not in our everyday vocabulary nor was it in our appointment book.

The weeks that followed were like a dream. Plans and priorities quickly accelerated yet remained focused as we anticipated our daughter's upcoming wedding in the midst of it all. In my flesh, I found myself wanting to be buried in busyness to avoid embracing the journey that lay ahead for my wife. In my spirit, I found myself rooted in faith yet trembling inwardly.

My wife and I invited our family and pastoral leadership team for anointing with oil. Healing and grace was manifest that evening in a multitude of ways. It was a powerful evening, but her cancer still remained and was surgically removed as scheduled.

A beautiful expression of God's love and peace was provided through a simple vase. This vase was filled with individual flowers given to my wife by each participant that evening. Miraculously, time and again, as these flowers faded throughout an extensive recovery period, someone would show up at our door with a fresh bouquet having no knowledge of "the vase" that needed refreshed. God was so good and His timing was incredible.

Every day is a gift for every one of us. If God takes the time to trouble Himself counting the hairs on our head, how much more does He consider what burdens our heart?

Lord, today, remind me that I am Yours, and that I am wonderfully loved by You.

Brian E. Martin serves as lead pastor at Weaverland Mennonite Church in East Earl. He and his wife Shirley are parents of three married children, one young adult at home and two grandchildren.

No Longer Blind

"In that day the deaf shall hear the words of the book, and the eyes of the blind shall see out of the obscurity and out of darkness." *Isaiah 29:18 (New King James Version)*

I was working with a deaf and blind man one afternoon in a backroom of a large state institution when a nurse interrupted me and claimed she had worked with four deaf and blind patients at the State Hospital for the mentally ill.

I was skeptical but asked Carrie, a deaf friend, and a social worker to check the facility's two-thousand residents, where they found Nellie. She was elderly, but walked with pride and not with an institutional shuffle.

Carrie spelled "hi" into the palm of Nellie's hand. Nellie gasped, as if she had been shocked by a sudden awakening. Slowly, she spelled back, "I have not talked to anyone for the last nineteen years. What's going on in the world? Who is president?"

I found out later that Nellie had been born with vision problems and hearing problems. She became totally blind at the young age of eleven and totally deaf by the time she was twenty. After her father and mother died, her relatives committed her to a mental institution, which tragically robbed her of nineteen years of freedom!

After some heavy advocacy work, a year later, I had the privilege of escorting her out of the institution into a new life of freedom. We were walking to the car and suddenly Nellie stopped, took a deep breath of the fragrant outside air and began to slowly, but firmly, fingerspell: "I am free!"

Nellie's story does not end there. After several months of freedom, I asked her what helped her keep her sanity for those nineteen years without communication. Without hesitation, she told me that the Lord Jesus gave her strength and comfort during those dark days. Spiritually, she was not blind.

Nellie passed away several years ago. But, she now sees and hears with exceptional clarity!

Father, thank You that the blind shall see and we shall be free.

Jim Schneck is a freelance interpreter for the deaf, the husband of Rosalee and a doctorate student.

No Longer Fearful of Death

"No eye has seen, no ear has heard, no mind has conceived what God has prepared for those who love him." *1 Corinthians 2:9*

I have been a registered nurse for thirty-three years, although I say retired for six years. Nurse friends used to kid with me by saying that death seemed to avoid me. Patients would seem to cling to life, lasting if only for minutes until I had left the building. That was how it seemed until it all came crashing down a couple of years ago.

My dear mom had become ill with bladder cancer. The turn of events that followed happened with dizzying speed. She had surgery, remission, moved to Florida to retire with my sister and husband, and then the cancer returned with a vengence. Within a few very short months, Mom was very ill and suffering beyond belief. Her mind was gone except for brief moments of clarity. Pain wracked her body.

Suddenly, I became acutely aware of what lies ahead for the believer after death. All of us—sons, daughters, husband and friends prayed that God would take her into His arms and give her eternal rest. My last act as a true nurse was listening to my own mother's heart as it slowly, purposefully, stopped beating, and I had to pronounce her time of death. Mom, in that moment in time, leaped from this earth into the place that "no mind has conceived." Angels exhalted! The heavens rejoiced! Another loved one had gone home! Only her body remained.

Father, thank You for allowing me the greatest opportunity I could ever experience: removing any fear of death from my heart. For in that moment, I knew Mom was at peace—the peace that passeth all understanding.

Barb Shirey, DOVE Westgate, retired R.N., disabled but enabled through Jesus.

Releasing to Him

"So do not fear, for I am with you; do not be dismayed, for I am your God. I will strengthen you and help you; I will uphold you with my righteous right hand." *Isaiah 41:10*

When my daughter graduated from high school and was accepted at a college in New York just a few short years after September 11, 2001, I found myself facing a new battle with fear. I imagined a large bull's-eye target painted over the Empire State Building (which is where the college was located), just waiting for the opportune moment for another terrorist attack. The darkness of that picture haunted me. What was I releasing her to at this new stage in her life? Big, bad and dangerous New York City!

One day as I was praying, the Lord spoke to my heart. *You are not releasing her to New York, or to terrorists; you are releasing her more directly into My hands. And I am in New York City, just as I am here. My hands will carry her, guide her and protect her. They are not too short to save, but are strong and mighty on her behalf.*

What better place could she be? If He was calling her to New York and His hands were guiding her there, she was in the best place she could be—much better and safer than if she stayed in Lancaster!

Lord, I'm so glad Your thoughts are not my thoughts, limited and given to fear. May my thoughts become more like Your thoughts, lifted above what I see with my physical eyes. Thank You, that as the I AM, You are truly in every place—Your Spirit guiding, Your hand protecting and Your love covering. Thank You for being Immanuel— God with us, no matter where we are.

Cindy Riker is a wife, mother, homeschooler and leader at Change of Pace Bible study.

Light in the Darkness

"You are my lamp, O Lord; the Lord turns my darkness into light. With your help I can advance against a troop; with my God I can scale a wall." *2 Samuel 22:29–30*

Do you ever feel like you are at your wits end and do not know where to turn?

Life can be full of challenges and opportunities where we need God's help to see the way forward. It is comforting to know that we can turn to God to bring light and understanding into the dark and confusing situations we sometimes face.

Often we can get so focused on the challenge itself that it becomes a wall that keeps us from moving forward. Instead we should be viewing it as an opportunity for God to move on our behalf and help us overcome it. There is nothing like a challenge or two to help build our character and a miraculous answer to prayer to build our faith.

Just imagine for a minute how much more difficult it must be for those around us who are not believers. Perhaps God wants to use you today to shine His light into their lives. Remember you have a great hope that you can share with those around you. Your words of encouragement may bring the breakthrough they need in their lives.

Dear God, I pray for Your light to shine into my life and give me the grace I need to face challenging situations that may arise today. I pray that You would also use me as a source of encouragement to those around me.

Mark Van Syoc is a programmer analyst, freelance photographer and a member of DOVE Westgate in Ephrata.

God Got My Attention

"You will seek me and find me when you seek me with all your heart. I will be found by you," declares the Lord, "and will bring you back from captivity . . . ." *Jeremiah 29:1–14*

After more than twenty years of addiction, depression and self-loathing, I found God who was caring and compassionate. Or should I say He found me?

I was at the end of myself. I was homeless with no hope of a future. The only solution I believed was suicide. This is when God started to reveal Himself to me. I found emergency shelter where I stayed for six weeks. During this time I got into drug and alcohol treatment and searched for a program that would be right for me. I applied at various programs and was not accepted.

I was almost to the point of giving up when I was not accepted into one of the programs due to my physical disabilities. I called the woman back about making accommodations for me. She said they could not do that, however, she gave me a name and a telephone number to call. I called and was accepted into the program. Here is where I learned that God was not a punisher but rather loving and faithful. I also came to know Jesus as my Lord and Savior.

Today, I have a better understanding of why certain things have happened in my life. If they hadn't happened, I believe I would still be lost. Sometimes in order to see God, He must do things to get our attention. I am eternally thankful that He got mine.

Thank You, Lord, for getting my attention and being a God of love and not a God of punishment.

Elaine is a resident at Lydia Center, a division of Water Street Ministries. She attends Community Fellowship Church, Lancaster.

What Am I Collecting?

"My soul finds rest in God alone. . . ." *Psalm 62:1*

While attending an art exhibit with my family, we noticed a collection of jars. Each jar was individually labeled with a year and inside the jars were nail clippings. The exhibit was aptly titled "Nail Clippings."

Later my young son commented while looking at the scars on his legs, "Look, Mom, I'm collecting scars not scabs!" Recently, while watching my son play soccer on his school team, I was reminded of that time he had said he collected scars because a boy sitting near me at the game had scars covering one side of his face from his ear to his neck. The thick scar tissue deformed his ear.

As I reflected I thought about my scars. The ones on the inside seemed to be at the heart of my reflection. I wondered if my covered wounds and hurts would look like the boy's face if I could pull them out of me for a closer visual examination.

Turning this over for further wisdom and clarity it struck me that God has an evacuation plan for our internal scars. We can bring them into the light of His love and in that safe place our loving shepherd Jesus can minister to us. For me, I've experienced that God's evacuation plan takes place in the context of centering prayer. This is a prayer of simple consent in which I give my "yes" to healing and transformation. While silent in prayer, centering each day, I sit and consent to being attentive to God's presence and gently turn away from thoughts and cares of the day as they come across my mind. In this practice over many years, mystery and miracle intertwine. God the master healer does His work while I sit and give my consent.

Lord, praise You for the way you heal us. Remind me that the deformities that attach to my spirit are no match for You and can be evacuated in your presence even as I find rest alone in your being.

Susan K. Shiner, mother of four boys, married twenty-two years to Jeff is serving in Songs for the Journey Ministry to the actively dying and as a Love In the Name of Christ intake volunteer.

Am I a Sponge or a Sieve?

"A man's steps are directed by the Lord. How then can anyone understand his own way?" *Proverbs 20:24*

This year the ministry I serve in Chester County celebrated their twenty-fifth anniversary. I have been blessed to be their director for the past nine years. I clearly remember the day I first heard God's call for this season of my life. I remember saying, "Not now Lord. I'm enjoying life and I love being home after a couple of decades in corporate America." After a lot of discussion—well, mostly me discussing and God waiting patiently—I began the new journey He had for me. Although I've served in management positions in corporate America and in leadership positions in church, nothing, I repeat nothing, prepared me for the journey God was calling me on.

Although there was a learning curve in my past ministry and corporate life, I learned things very quickly. Age can soon make a person very humble! Beginning a new journey in my forties certainly was different than beginning adventures in my younger decades. While things used to come easily to me, now I needed to concentrate, read, seek counsel and observe other successful non-profit leaders. God was so faithful and always put the right resource in my path, just as I needed a new piece of knowledge. Each time He brought me new information I had two choices: absorb it like a sponge or let it go in one ear and out the other like a sieve. I chose to listen! At God's knee I learned marketing, public speaking, the importance of relationships and more. Over the past several years God has given me numerous opportunities to pass on my knowledge and experience to other nonprofit leaders. See, you are never too old to learn new things!

Thank You Father that You provide all we need for the calling You place on our lives. Faith is strengthened in the journey!

Karen Pennell is the chief executive officer of Chester County Women's Services Medical, a life-affirming pregnancy care medical ministry in Chester County.

Peace Despite Sorrow

"And let the peace of God rule in your hearts, to the which also ye are called in one body; and be ye thankful." *Colossians 3:15 (King James Version)*

November 2007 was one of the worst years in my life. My mother was in a crosswalk and was struck and killed by a motorcycle.

How could that possibly happen? Although the cars on the other side of the crosswalk had stopped for her to cross, a motorcycle had quickly turned without noticing her.

I got the call at work. Anger, bitterness and resentment came quickly to the surface.

My co-workers were wonderful. They drove me home, called my husband and offered me all the time off that I needed.

How could I be thankful for what had occurred? Would life ever feel normal again? Lying on my couch at home, I felt crushed and yet sensed the peace that only God can give.

It took me a long time to be able to forgive the man responsible for my mother's death. But I recognized that some good did result from her death. It brought my brothers and sisters closer together and we continue to meet once a month for a family meal. I know my mom would be happy about that.

Celebrating holidays are the hardest. The first Thanksgiving without my mother was really difficult. I missed her running around the kitchen taking care of the meal and telling us all what she wanted us to be doing. Although I would never say I was thankful about what happened, I realized the truth in my older brother's statement that said it best: "Mom died because Mom would never have wanted to be laid up and unable to walk or get around."

I've learned that life goes on and God is good!

Father, I know that Your grace is always sufficient. Thank You for Your peace that even in times of trial is so evident. You are good.

Christine Harsh and her husband Roger attend CBC in Marietta where she serves in the nursery. Christine is also a Susquehanna Valley Pregnancy Service volunteer.

Include International People

"I saw a large crowd with more people than could be counted. They were from every race, tribe, nation, and language, and they stood before the throne and before the Lamb." *Revelation 7:9 (Contemporary English Version)*

In my fifty years of pastoral ministry I was blessed with many wonderful relationships with people from many nations. I miss the cultural diversity when there's only one nation, culture, sex or race present in a group. Heaven is pictured as an international community all focused on Jesus.

Make special effort to build relationships with people of different races and nationalities in your life and in the life of your congregation. Your Bible studies will be enriched. Your concept of God will be enlarged. Your diet may even be enriched! One thing sure is your worship will become a foretaste of heaven.

Jesus made no mistake when he created diversity. I am greatly grieved and embarrassed that Sunday morning is the most segregated hour of our week.

"Christ brought us together through his death on the cross. The cross got us to embrace, and that was the end of the hostility. Christ came and preached peace to you outsiders and peace to us insiders. He treated us as equals, and so made us equals. Through him we both share the same Spirit and have equal access to the Father," it reads in Ephesians 2:17-18 (The Message).

Jesus is our model. He went through Samaria even though the Jews had no dealing with the Samaritans. He chose to go this route to break down the barriers because Jews usually avoided Samaria by crossing the Jordan and traveling on the east side to get to Galilee. Jesus was intentional. We too must be intentional to overcome these barriers. Welcome international people into your life and church. Many of them will teach us new levels of faithfulness to our Lord.

Jesus, forgive me for being so provincial. Help me go out of my way to develop friendships with those of different cultures and nationalities.

J. David Eshleman served as pastor/church planter for fifty years and is a church consultant. He is author of *Now Go Forward: Reaching out to grow your congregation* and *Living with Godly Passion.*

Inferior Talents?

"The man who had received the five talents brought the other five. 'Master,' he said, 'you entrusted me with five talents. See, I have gained five more.' His master replied,'Well done, good and faithful servant! You have been faithful with a few things; I will put you in charge of many things. Come and share your master's happiness!' The man with the two talents also came. 'Master,' he said, 'you entrusted me with two talents; see, I have gained two more.' His master replied, 'Well done, good and faithful servant! You have been faithful with a few things; I will put you in charge of many things. Come and share your master's happiness!' Then the man who had received the one talent came. 'Master,' he said, 'I knew that you are a hard man, harvesting where you have not sown and gathering where you have not scattered seed. So I was afraid and went out and hid your talent in the ground. See, here is what belongs to you.' His master replied, 'You wicked, lazy servant! So you knew that I harvest where I have not sown and gather where I have not scattered seed? Well then, you should have put my money on deposit with the bankers, so that when I returned I would have received it back with interest. Take the talent from him and give it to the one who has the ten talents.'" *Matthew 25:20–28*

Some time ago I was thinking about the talents that I have. It seemed to me that some talents are more important than others. Talents for organization or business seem much more important than my talents of being able to paint and draw. At times, I feel as if my talents are so inferior that I don't even want to use them.

After studying the verses for today's scripture, I came to recognize that all talents are important. Here's my thought: I don't want to come to the end of my life and hear the Lord say to me, "I gave you a talent and what did you do with it?"

God wants me to use my art. He has given these talents and I don't want to hide them.

Thank You, Lord, for giving each of us talents. Help us to be good faithful stewards of the talents You have given us.

Donna Van Scyoc is a wife to Mark and mother to Brighton. She gives private art lessons and loves being creative and hanging out with creative people.

Victory in Jesus

"With God we will gain the victory, and he will trample down our enemies." *Psalm 60:12*

For the past eight years, I have been a part-time missionary to Haiti. I traveled there several times a year to work in Montrouis for Life Connection Mission as well as at a little church school in Charrier. I've led numerous teams there to serve in missions. I love Haiti and the Haitian people. Serving them is my passion and I thrive on adventure.

For the past several years, my personal life has been an adventure as my youngest son was diagnosed with bipolar disorder. This mental illness affects his emotions. They are either extreme highs or extreme lows. In this world, every day is an adventure.

I've struggled with guilt, heartache and judgment from those who do not understand the suffering of mental illness and how it affects the patient as well as the family. Then there is the question, why? And, what could I have done differently? I was beating myself up.

Through it all, I've spent many hours in God's Word and in prayer and know God is faithful. He will not leave me and He will not leave my son. He loves me and He loves my son. My son is the workmanship of God's hands, created specially by God for His glory.

I've given my son all the tools I could to make wise choices and decisions in life. I did my best. Now it is up to him. He may make good choices or bad ones. The fact is they are up to him. He is in God's hands. I will trust that God will have victory and trample down my enemies.

Dear God, thank You for strength to face each new day, You are faithful and I find strength in that. Lord, I give You my worries and my fears. Thank You for the victories You give me, big and small. I place my trust in You. In Jesus' nam. Amen.

Cynthia Zimmerman is a board member of Life Connection Mission, Montrouis, Haiti. She attends New Life Fellowship Church, Ephrata, and is married to Rick Zimmerman.

No Second-Guessing

"Let the peace of Christ rule in your hearts . . . ." *Colossians 3:15*

I was seventeen years old and trying to decide which university to attend after graduation from high school. I had narrowed my options to two colleges: one in Toronto, Ontario close to my home, the other in Indiana, a seven-hour drive away.

I had discussed the possibilities with my parents, my pastor and numerous Christian friends. I had read all I could find about both schools. I prayed fervently that the Lord would help me make the right choice and finally I settled on Indiana. I began finalizing plans to attend that school.

But then came the second-guessing: "Had I made the right decision? What if I made a mistake? A wrong choice could mess up my entire future. After all, at college many individuals meet the person they one day marry. And, while there, many come to decide on their life work. So, if I was at the wrong place, I could totally miss God's best for me." My anxiety increased daily.

Then a friend shared Colossians 3:15 with me and explained that the word *rule* is similar to the word *umpire*. "You sought godly counsel, researched your possibilities, prayed for the Lord's direction and used your mind to make what you believed to be a good decision. Now you need to allow God's peace to call the shots in your heart!" he advised.

He was right. As I chose to invite God's peace to *officiate* in my life, the unruly emotions settled down and the misgivings disappeared. What a welcome transformation! I moved ahead in peace, confident that the choice made was the correct one.

Lord Jesus, I invite Your peace to rule in my spirit today. I will not dwell on what could happen, or on what might have been. Please give me Your wisdom as I make necessary choices and then help me to relax, with Your peace in charge!

Sharon Charles assists her husband John, director of Abundant Living, a Christian counseling ministry in Lititz.

Where You Lead, We Will Follow

"The Lord had said to Abram, 'Leave your country, your people and your father's household and go to the land I will show you.'"
Genesis 12:1

I really don't know how Sarah did it ... how do you continue to move ahead "to the place I will show you?" I was feeling a bit like Sarah as our family contemplated yet another move in order to follow what we felt God was calling us to do. Now, moving was not a new thing for our family; in fact we've moved every three to six years since my husband and I were married in 1982.

It all started when my husband Clair agreed to be part of a group discerning a transition in ministry in Columbia, Pennsylvania. He was adamant that this was not a place he was called to, but he would be an advisor to the group. Enter the rest of the family. Clair invited us to join him in visiting some of the local restaurants and businesses. In a very short time, we began to fall in love with this beautiful, historic city beside the river. These visits became more frequent and our love for Columbia and its people more sincere. Through a series of "incidents," we began to clearly get the idea that God was calling us to move to Columbia and finally we said, "We'll go."

Selling a house and buying a new one in these tough economic times looked impossible. Yet, approximately twenty-four hours after we'd made the decision to move to Columbia, we had an interested buyer (no, I didn't skip the part about putting the house on the market ... we didn't). The day we made settlement on our old house, a fellow believer wrote an email stating that he felt the Lord was asking him to sell us his house and he lived at one of my favorite locations in Columbia (yea, that's what we said too).

Thank You, Lord, for Your guidance in our lives. Help us to hear Your voice today and to obey.

Beth Good and her husband Clair are church planters, living in Columbia.

Agape Love

"But the Fruit of the Spirit is love, joy, peace, longsuffering, gentleness, goodness, faith, meekness, temperancy: against such there is no law. . . . If we live in the Spirit, let us also walk in the Spirit."
Galatians 5:22–23, 25 (1599 Geneva Bible)

For years, one of the primary ministries given to me by the Lord was visiting and praying for the sick in the church, hospitals, rehabilitation centers, nursing homes and private homes. In all the many years the visits, prayers and His Healing Hand reached others. But, for the past many months my wife has been in and out of the hospitas for a heart condition and a hip operation after a fall, and then many days for therapy.

Visits during my wife's hospitalization were always special. I spent hours just sitting looking at her as she slept, helping her eat, praying and talking with her, watching her during her therapy sessions, talking to her doctors and crying out for the most excellent care for her. I felt deeply for her when she was in pain, but comforting her was very special.

God gives each of us His agape love to share and to express with our spouse. It is unselfish love that comes out when we serve our spouse.

Is it different visiting and serving her? The answer is yes. Scripture teaches for me (and all of us) "Love the Lord your God with all your heart and with all your soul and with all your strength." (Deuteronomy 6:5). Love can be known only by the actions it prompts.

We cleave (cling) to our spouse. That is the difference. It is that clinging love of oneness that prevails. It is divine and agape love.

Lord Jesus thank You for Your caring love and for You healing my wife. You are the way, truth and our life. Thank You, Lord. In Jesus' name. Amen.

Bob Burns serves as pastor and shepherd of Spiritual Growth Ministries, a guiding ministry to church leaders in areas of spiritual growt, and he ministers at Spring Valley Church of God.

Carole's Alabaster Jar

"Mary took an expensive perfume; she poured it on Jesus' feet and wiped his feet with her hair. And the house was filled with the fragrance of the perfume." John 12:3

Carole is a woman transformed. Hunched over a cart of her earthly belongings, she shuffles as she walks, staring straight ahead. She wears several jackets regardless of the temperature, a thin coat of red lipstick and polished nails. Her long graying hair has been brushed. Her favorite color is pink.

Carole used to sit alone in the cafeteria. Lice visibly crawled through her hair, her clothing soiled. She rarely spoke.

Through time—and love—she received shampoo treatments for the lice. She started wearing fresh clothing. She accepted the cart a stranger offered her.

Carole spends her days in the Community Homeless Outreach Center. She sleeps on a mat on the floor of the Outreach Center at night.

Daily she visits my office. She makes a list on borrowed paper of items for sale that I might wish to purchase. She wishes me "Sweet dreams."

Last summer Carole purchased two large buckets of ice cream and served the men and women in the Outreach Center. It was a ninety-degree day. She patted the men and women on their backs and encouraged them. Staff lined up for a scoop of Neapolitan.

Yesterday Carole was sitting on the steps outside my office when I left for lunch. I lost my balance as I stopped to sit with her and fell against her knees. We laughed together at my clumsiness. We discussed the best treatment for my daughter's cold.

I considered her as I sat at her feet, on the steps a little lower than her. I considered how she ministered to me out of concern for my daughter. And with ice cream . . . I considered how she looked more like Jesus than I did sometimes.

Lord, help me sit on the ground and risk getting dirty for the sake of the kingdom!

Debbi Miller, Water Street Ministries, lives in Lititz with her husband and children.

Ugly Scars

"But he said to them, 'Unless I see the mark of the nails in his hands, and put my finger in the mark of the nails and my hand in his side, I will not believe.'" *John 20:24–29 (New Revised Standard Version)*

When I peeled off the Band Aid from my neck I was shocked. A bloody scar was quite visible. Humiliated and ashamed to carry such a mark in public, I hid myself in the quiet room. But there my sorrow only multiplied.

"Lord, why?" I sobbed and wept all evening until I finally fell asleep. When I woke up the next morning, I remembered that my scar would be permanent. Sadness gripped my heart and clouded my new day. At the same time, somehow I began to recall God's many miracles connected to this scar: His lavishing love and care through many people, His provision for my trip and surgery in America and the success of my deadly tumor removal and renewal of my life.

"Lord, but what about this ugly scar?" I still felt pained when looking in the mirror that reflected the scar stretched from my left collar to the right one. And then I froze. A feeling of awe overfilled my heart— the ugly scar seemed to smile at me! At that very same moment thoughts about Jesus overfilled my mind. *Weren't His scars ugly? Yet when Thomas saw them he confessed that Christ was his Lord and God.*

I cannot know how Jesus must have felt bearing those ugly scars, but I was humbled by the pain and the cost of His sacrifice for my sake.

Then my scar is really no big deal, I was about to conclude. Instead, I confessed, "Jesus, it is! At least for me, for when I lose my heart and faith, remind me You are the God of miracles whose smile is carved on my body."

Jesus, thank You for being the God of scars, pains and sorrows. Amen.

Yulia Bagwell, Beth Yeshua, serves at the Community Bible Study and translates for *The Upper Room* devotional magazine.

Dreams and Visions

"... I reveal myself to him in visions, I speak to him in dreams."
Numbers 12:6

One of our four teenagers was definitely making wrong choices. I preached, begged, bargained, threatened, nagged and did everything I could to try to convince my son of the error of his ways. He did not argue. He did not talk back. He did not become angry. Instead, he simply ignored me. His lack of response frustrated me even more.

I thought it was our duty as parents to force him to comply, to live for the Lord, but nothing we did or said changed him. I feared where his choices would lead him.

One night while praying for him, I had a vision of a huge bonfire in front of me. Jesus stood beside me and in his arms was a baby who I knew represented my son. Without a word, Jesus stepped forth to go into the fire. I grabbed Jesus' arm and cried, "Not my baby. Don't make him go through the fire."

Three times, Jesus stepped toward the fire and each time I grabbed his arm and screamed for him to stop. Finally, Jesus turned and pried my fingers from his arm and said, "He must go through the fire, but I promise you, I'll carry him in my arms."

The vision faded. But I knew that I needed to be willing to let my son go through a purifying fire and face his own consequences. I sensed the Lord asking me if I wanted my son to turn his life over to Him even if it meant that he would lose his popularity, even if it meant that he might be permanently injured. Did I want my son's salvation enough to say, "Do whatever you want to do with him, Lord."

To surrender my child to the unknown was not easy for me. But it was comforting to know that Jesus promised to carry him through in his own arms.

I stopped nagging my son and started trusting God to carry him through the fire. Amazingly, within a few weeks, my son fully committed his life to Jesus and today has a ministry in helping other teenagers discover a meaningful relationship with Jesus.

Lord, thank You for speaking to us, the slow of heart, in visions and in dreams.

Lou Ann Good and her husband Parke appreciate the amazing adults their children have become.

Everything We Need

"His divine power has given us everything we need for life and godliness through our knowledge of him who called us by his own glory and goodness." *2 Peter 1:3*

Recently, I was part of a medical mission trip to Haiti. It was the first medical mission trip in which I had participated. Weeks before I had asked God to use me wherever I was most needed. I was unsure of what to expect. Things were chaotic when our group arrived in Port-au-Prince Airport. It took time to collect eighteen large suitcases filled with medical supplies and the team's personal belongings.

When we left the airport, it was raining and continued throughout the two-hour trip to the compound where we were staying. When we arrived, the walkways were flooded and we had to drag the luggage through standing water. It was hot—very hot! Our dorms were without air-conditioning. As soon as we arrived, we attached mosquito nets around our beds to keep out the mosquitoes. I was tired from the day's trip and frustrated in trying to attach the mosquito netting. Finally, in desperation I called for help. A kind person offered to help and I crawled into bed and cried silently to God, "What have I gotten myself into? If I am going to be of any use this week, it's totally in Your hands."

The next morning I awakened at 5:30 a.m., got up and had strength, energy and perseverance throughout the week to do the jobs I was asked to do.

All praise goes to God, the Father. I did many things that week that I was surprised I could do. It's amazing when we put our life in God's hands, how He gives us everything we need to complete the job. God says when he calls us to serve Him, He will give us everything we need to complete the work.

Thank You, Lord, for Your provisions. You are ever near and You are waiting for us to call to You.

Sandy Weaver is a licensed practical nurse and member of Ephrata Community Church.

Potty Training

"I am the true vine, and my Father is the gardener . . . . every branch that does bear fruit he prunes so that it will be even more fruitful."
John 15:1, 2

With the start of our family, my husband and I dreamed of moving. We prayed and searched the Scriptures and one day we were certain God was calling us to move to a house at a specific location. Then, God suddenly said, "No, not now."

Our daughter was three years old at the time. When we would suggest she use the potty, her response was "no thank you." Even the promise of underpants with glittery gem stones did not alter the polite rejection to our potty pleading.

One evening, I showed the undergarments to our daughter one last time. "I want to give you these pretty underpants, but you are not ready for them. When you decide to use the potty, you may wear them." I slid the glittering undergarments into the drawer and gave my sad daughter a goodnight kiss.

I walked into our bedroom to find my husband looking betrayed. "Why would God do that? Why would He lead us and allow us to follow only to say no." God spoke to my heart in an instant, "Underpants!" I said. My husband looked confused. "God wants us to potty train before he gives us underpants." I went on to explain the conversation I had with our daughter just minutes earlier. God wanted to prepare us for the gift he had in store for us.

We endured a painful time of pruning. God cut away discontentment, selfishness, apathy and lusts of this world. After the cutting, God touched us with healing and forgiveness. We "potty trained" for over two years and then, once again we heard the call to move. God pulled those "shiny underpants" out of the drawer and provided a new home just blocks away from the original house before the pruning began.

Lord, thank You for being a good gardener. Help me see the bounty of Your pruning sheers.

Sonya Lanford is a homeschooling mom and homemaker. The Lanfords attend Ephrata Christian Fellowship.

My Hummingbird Friend

"Be anxious for nothing but in everything by prayer and supplication with thanksgiving let your requests be made known to God."
Philippians 4:6 (New Revised Standard Version)

I was sharing with a friend, how I was really struggling with the journey my husband Phil and I were on with a recording project. As I was relaying the frustrating details, I was also sharing how I had given this to the Lord and was resting in Him. At some point in our conversation, she stopped me and simply said, "You remind me of a hummingbird." (Both of us share a love for the fascinating little creatures.) So being compared to one caught my full attention. When she explained, I was a bit humbled. "You think you are being still but your wings are going a mile a minute."

God's truth spoken through my friend caused me to see I wasn't resting as I believed. My "wings" were still flapping. I was anxious and troubled. According to Psalm 46:10, God wants me to truly be still and know that I am God. In response, I chose to take a deep breath and trust Him.

I have come to understand that being still doesn't mean I am to do nothing because His Word in Philippians 4:6 tells me to pray hard and bring my anxiousness to Him. That is my part. But then, Praise God, the rest is His part. Philippians 4:7 promises, "And the peace of God, which surpasses all comprehension, will guard your hearts and minds in Christ Jesus. Amen."

Oh how I have felt His peace and experienced Him guarding my heart, especially when I've stopped flapping my wings. I love watching those little birds when they occasionally stop and perch on my bird feeders while eating. Now that is the comparison I want of myself to the hummingbird.

Dear Jesus, I so desire to live in your stillness constantly knowing You are God. Thank You for Your peace. I trust You.

Cyndi Garber considers herself blessed to be a wife, mother and Nana. She serves in various ministries at Lives Changed By Christ, Manheim.

God Amazes Me

"Trust in the Lord with all your heart . . . ." *Proverbs 3:5*

The mudslide started with a note. He was leaving us. My heart sank as I watched our daughter's tears. LOSS.

Separation came then divorce papers arrived. The court dates were set . . . more loss. Lack of work and income with bills to pay, we were forced to move out of our home—loss again. Three weeks later the letter arrived. An emergency court order was filed stating the return of my daughter back to her dad—loss at it's ultimate.

I ended up at Water Street Mission the day before Thanksgiving. Suffering from chronic depression, overwhelmed with life's losses and missing my daughter. Feeling lonely and lost in a shelter with the holidays coming, I cried!

"God please help me!" I prayed. I could not do this alone. He heard my prayer, saw my tears and felt my hurt. He showed compassion, answering my prayer with much needed support through staff, family and friends. My God sent angels surrounding my life each step of the way. Holding tight onto my firm foundation of knowing my God is real and bigger than any of this mess, I put total trust in my heavenly Dad. Walking forward with faith and hope I accepted God's perfect will to be done in my life.

During the past six months I've struggled with health issues, emotions, separation from my daughter, but God filled my body with strength, energy and the courage to persevere. I accepted the awesome opportunity to gain my GED through Water Street's Learning Center. With the help of super teachers I graduated. All the glory is to God! God knows the desires of my heart and continues to amaze me. Prayer is power. I've learned to ask and trust. He is in control and will make my path straight.

Thank You, Father God, for loving me unconditionally. You know all about loss. You walked the earth as a man. You died for our sins. You rose again. You reign over all. Lord, I will trust You. Use my life to complete Your will. Thanks, Dad!

Deb has four children, seven grandchildren and is reconciling with her husband and daughter.

Thanksgiving

"Those who go out weeping, bearing the seed, for sowing, shall come home with shouts of joy, carrying their sheaves." *Psalm 126:6 (New Revised Standard Version)*

My Ukrainian, urban parents had to move to a village. To survive there you must have a garden and some livestock. Keep in mind, all labor there is manual: breaking the ground with a spade, carrying buckets of water from the well, watering the seeds with a cup, weeding and eliminating harmful insects by hand. After all, labor not, eat not.

At first, my parents and I worried much. But then we began to learn to seek God's favor for all those matters. For instance, when it was a drought that could kill the crop we'd pray for the rain. When it rained hard we'd pray for the sunshine. If a storm broke out, we'd ask God for His protection. And when the harvest was reaped, and there was so much to eat for many days, months and even seasons ahead, we thanked and praised God for His mercy.

Many ungodly villagers wondered about the secret of my parents' abundant harvesting. Yet nobody believed that while laboring in the garden, my parents and I learned to thank God "in season and out of season." Truly, we thanked Him for healthy chicks and ducklings; for growing tomatoes and watermelons; for giving us new eyes to see His power and presence, provision and protection. And when hardships seemed to be unbearable, we just thanked Him for what He was and what He'd already done.

Laboring in spiritual fields, we may grow weary and discouraged, too. We may even lose hope and faith. But if we lift our eyes and voices to the Most High, He'll hear us. And He'll answer. Moreover, in His timing we will reap our harvest, carrying the fruits of our labor from the fields of His kingdom.

Lord, bless us and help us to work in the fields of Your kingdom, glorifying Your name in all seasons. Amen.

Yulia Bagwell, Beth Yeshua, is a housewife-caregiver, a writer, and a translator for *The Upper Room* devotional magazine.

Praise

"I will praise the Lord at all times. I will constantly speak his praises." *Psalm 34:1 (New Living Translation)*

One reason David is known as the man after God's heart is because he was continually praising the Lord. The word *praise* appears in the Psalms approximately one hundred eighty times. That's more than the word appears in the remaining sixty-five books of the Bible.

Praise is sometimes translated "Hallelujah." George Frederick Handel in composing *The Messiah* repeats the word *Hallelujah* approximately one hundred and fifty times. It has been said that when he finished composing, he wept for some time because he'd seen the face of God. Praise puts us into the presence of God because the Lord inhabits the praises of His people. David's final Psalm includes eleven commands to praise the Lord. He says we are to praise Him for his acts of power and His surpassing greatness. We praise him with the trumpet, harp, lyre, tambourine, strings and symbols. We praise Him with the dance. Everything that has breath is instructed to praise the Lord.

When we first encounter Jesus we want to praise Him for his gift of salvation. As time passes, we tend to lose our first love. We need to discipline ourselves to praise him. To practice his presence we need to praise Him. David says, "I will constantly speak his praises." Praise affects our attitude. Attitude affects our relationships and productivity.

Praise propels us into His presence. There will be many times when you don't feel like praising God. Feeling must not control us. When praise becomes a discipline, you learn to praise Him even in times of adversity.

Praise invites His presence into your life—into the seemingly impossible situations. That's when you know Jesus is present, putting the situation in a totally different perspective.

Lord Jesus, You are worthy to be praised. I choose to praise You continually. Amen.

J. David Eshleman served as pastor/church planter and is a church consultant for Eastern Mennonite Missions and Lancaster Mennonite Conference. He is author of *Now Go Forward: Reaching out to grow your congregation* and *Living with Godly Passion: Daily Reading for those with a passion to share Jesus.*

Reset

"We toss the coin, but it is the Lord who controls its decision."
Proverbs 16:33 (The Living Bible)

We live in a fast-paced world, to say the least. I was reminded of that while flying out of Harrisburg on a quiet, early Saturday morning. All seemed to be going well: on-time flight, no security concerns and the pilot even stated that we would be leaving earlier than expected. Wow! This trip across the United States into Canada would be a cinch.

And then the unexpected happened: the plane's computer began malfunctioning. It had to be "reset." Not just once, but several times. Not only would we not be leaving early, we would be arriving late in Washington, D.C. Everyone's connections would be extremely tight, if not missed. Frustration, impatience and anxiety broke loose among the passengers.

As humans we often want everything to work in a quick and timely fashion, but God often calls us to push the "Reset" button of our spiritual lives. "Be still and know that I am God" is not just a biblical slogan or a nice Sunday morning sermon topic, but rather it is a life-sustaining prescription for keeping us mindful that God is in control of this world and our lives.

For an on-time arrival in heaven, remember to push the "Reset" button of life on a regular basis.

Please Lord, reset my heart and mind, on a daily basis, so that I don't remain in a spiritual descent.

Dr. Sandy Outlar and his wife attend Wheatland Presbyterian Church.

The Simple Truth

"He does not take his eyes off the righteous . . . ." *Job 36:7*

My wife expressed concern over the behavior of our two pre-school sons.

"Often the youngest one is screaming angrily so I correct him, but I'm not always sure that he caused the ruckus. Sometimes I think his older brother was the instigator. But by the time I intervene, he's acting like a perfect angel. I guess I need to be more alert so I can catch him in the act."

Then I got an idea. And I believe it was God-inspired.

I began stating a simple spiritual truth to my oldest son. Numerous times each day I would swoop him up into my arms and announce enthusiastically, "Oh, I love you so much! Do you know that God loves you so much too! And do you know that God is watching you ALL the time! He cares for you and so His eyes are always on you! Where did you just come from? Your bedroom? Do you know that God saw you there? He sees you when you ride in the car, or play with your toys or sleep in your bed. God is so good to watch over us!" Then I would set my son back on his feet, pat his head and send him on his way.

After about two weeks of repeating this basic theological truth dozens of times, my wife reported major improvement in the boys' interaction!

Such a simple truth: God sees me all the time! As I worked to instill that truth in my son, it became permanently engrained in my own spirit. And it began to change me: how I used my time, how I spent my money, how I treated my wife and children, even how I drove my car!

Father, thank You for watching over me. Help me remember that Your eyes are on me every moment. May You be pleased with what You see in me today!

John Charles is director of Abundant Living, a Christian counseling ministry in Lititz.

I'll Not Leave You as Orphans

"I will not leave you as orphans; I will come to you." *John 14:18*

During my last trip to Kenya, my heart was sensitized to the youth who were fatherless, orphaned because of AIDS and other tragedies. The Lord burdened me with a message: "A bruised reed he will not break." (Matthew 12:20) Many around us feel deserted, helpless, destitute, unwanted, unloved, rejected, vulnerable and all alone . . . even those whose parents are still living! You don't have to be an orphan to feel like a bruised reed.

There is good news and healing for those who need it. Jesus promised the gift of the Holy Spirit. "I will not leave you as orphans; I will come to you." The Church, Jesus' body, is called to partner in this ministry of restoration. Two young Kenyan ladies whose dads died some years ago provided the inspiration for this song.

> *Jesus has asked the Father, The Father has given you*
> *The gift of His Holy Spirit, The Helper and Spirit of Truth*
> *Counselor and Comforter, God has made His home in you.*
> *So lean hard on Him, remembering this Word of Truth.*
> *Rejected, shamed, forgotten, filled with loneliness*
> *Let us hear the heart of God for the fatherless*
> *That pure religion, undefiled helps orphans in distress.*
> *Will we turn our hearts to them and say, "Yes!"*
> *So when it seems no one is there to speak in your behalf*
> *And you ask, "Who hears me when I cry?"*
> *God is watching over you, protecting your very life.*
> *You're under His care! You're the apple of His eye!*
> *Chorus*
> *You may feel like an orphan, But, God will come to you*
> *With His love as a Father and a family, too.*
> *Nor can we leave you as orphans, we will come to you*
> *With the love of the Father and a family, too.*
> *Hear these Words of Jesus, They are life to you*
> *"I'll not leave you as orphans; I will come to you!"*
> *I'll not leave you as orphans I will come to you*
> *With the love of the Father and a family, too!*

Father, let those who are or feel like orphans know the presence of Your Spirit today. Grant me grace today to care for orphans in distress.

Daniel Wagner serves as senior pastor of Towerville Christian Church in Coatesville and as president of the Ministers Alliance of Coatesville .

Signing Up Willingly

"But God demonstrates His own love toward us, in that while we were yet sinners, Christ died for us." *Romans 5:8 (New American Standard Bible)*

I was riding home from yet another counseling appointment with a family member. I was exhausted mentally, emotionally and physically after an intense hour of watching the loved one cling to self.

I felt angry. Inwardly I reasoned: *They just don't appreciate how good they have it! They are already the center of attention and act as if they are starved for more. We are trying to be patient, we are spending our money, we are doing everything right, but they don't choose to change.*

My eyes would have gotten wet with that last thought if I believed I had enough energy enough to blink back the tears.

I complained, "When I committed to this duty, I didn't know it would be so hard. I didn't sign up for this!"

I'm old enough to know that nobody signs up for the hard times. People get married without realization of the depth of that commitment. Couples have babies not realizing the overwhelming involvement it will take for the rest of their days. Every day, people get sick with terrible illnesses that they worked hard to ward off with good nutrition and exercise.

I lingered in the thought that everyone has it hard at one time or another. A new thought entered my mind. *The only person who ever signed up for their hard job with a thorough knowledge of what would happen was Jesus.*

I paused.

That's right. Jesus came down to earth knowing He had to die. He spent His whole life knowing that a gruesome death awaited Him and even that it would go unappreciated by some for all time. He did this with the infinite wisdom it would complete the work of restoring us to a right relationship with God. He signed up for it—willingly.

Father, help me! I can't do the hard times on my own. I pray for Your patience to be revealed in my life.

Carolyn Schlicher lives with her family in Elizabethtown.

December

Comfort Quilts

"Praise be to the God and Father of our Lord Jesus Christ, the Father of compassion and the God of all comfort, who comforts us in all our troubles, so that we can comfort those in any trouble with the comfort we ourselves have received from God." *2 Corinthians 1:3–4*

We use whatever method and resource God puts into our hands. Ever since I was a little child (making by first quilt at age six, with my mother's help, of course), I have been sewing things for people. Since I am given fabric from different places, I want to use it to comfort people. Sewing quilts for Project Linus is a blessing to me and provides some comfort to the children going through traumatic experiences. As I sew, I pray over each quilt. I pray that Jesus will comfort that little one when he or she receives the quilt.

This year, there was a call for "comfort tops" for the earthquake victims in Haiti. In response, I sewed larger quilts and prayed for each recipient to not only receive the blanket for physical comfort but also be consoled in Jesus' loving arms.

We all have experienced losses of various kinds in our lives. It's part of living on this planet. I personally have lived through some losses such as miscarriage, my brother's death and the passing of my dear grandpas and grandmas. Losing a job I cherished and suffering through the loss of a friendship that could not be mended were all experiences through which I needed consoling. As I give myself more and more to Jesus who comforts me, I want to comfort others and encourage them to find solace in Jesus.

Dear Jesus, please comfort each one both close by and far away with Your hand of love and nearness so they will find You and live for You. We look forward to rejoicing with them in heaven.

Marlene Buckwalter attends DOVE Westgate Church. She has taught home science and related subjects to junior and senior high school students. Since she and her husband have raised two daughters for the Lord. Marlene has time to sew and enjoy their five grandkids.

One of the World's Mightiest Transactions

"... I tell you the truth, this poor widow has put more into the treasury than all the others. They all gave out of their wealth; but she, out of her poverty, put in everything—all she had to live on." *Mark 12:43–44*

One day Jesus sat down in the treasury area of the Temple with his disciples. They observed many rich people passing by and flaunting their giving. Along came a poor widow, contributing two very small copper coins, worth about a quarter of a cent. What was significant about her contribution? She had given all! That gift—small as it was—proved to be one of the world's mightiest financial transactions.

Years ago, I was preaching renewal services in another part of the state. During the week, as the pastor and I did some visiting, we visited an elderly widow in a nursing home. As soon as we came into her room, this widow's eyes lit up as she said, "Oh, Pastor, I've been expecting you! I have a dollar left over out of my security check, and I want to give it to you for the work of the church. Maybe next month I can give you a dollar and a half.

That gift—which came not out of surplus or abundance—certainly did not go unnoticed by our Lord. I have a hunch that the gift of one dollar—given out of sacrifice and a heart of devotion—became a mightier transaction than that of the man who, later on that week, slipped the pastor a check for $1,000. The man was well off, and so what he gave the church was not really given out of sacrifice.

The bottom line is this: True giving isn't measured by the size of the gift, but rather by what's left over after it is given.

Grant, O Lord, that my giving may be done sacrificially and out of a heart of devotion. In Jesus' name. Amen.

Paul Brubaker serves on the ministry team at Middle Creek Church of the Brethren, Lititz.

Citizenship

"Let us therefore come boldly to the throne of grace that we may obtain mercy, and find grace to help in time of need." *Hebrews 4:16 (New King James Version)*

My husband Domenic and I love to visit Washington, D.C. We appreciate our country's history and have enjoyed numerous trips there. In all of our visits however, we have never had the opportunity to tour the White House.

Our son and his family came for a visit from Arizona recently and that was one of the things our granddaughters wanted to do while on the East Coast. No problem, right?

My recollection was that all we needed to do was pick up tickets when we arrived in D.C. and show up at the time indicated. That was before September 11. Understandably, security has been increased to protect the president and I quickly discovered that this would not be an easy task.

I contacted my congressman and was informed that it was advisable to obtain the tickets six months in advance of the visit. I didn't have that long to plan. Thankfully, my son was able to get tickets through a business contact.

The tour was limited to very few public areas and rooms in the White House. There is no way that we could just walk in and chat with the president; telling him our problems or asking him for a favor. Theoretically, as United States citizens, we should be able to do that. But such access is reserved for the rich, powerful and influential. What a stark contrast to the accessibility we have to the Creator of the universe! Scripture tells us that we have the same access to the Father as the Son. He is available to us 24/7. We are encouraged to "just drop in" for a chat or to bring Him the most impossible of requests. Not only that, we should do so with an air of authority befitting the most influential of citizens. We are just that, citizens of heaven and joint heirs with Jesus.

Lord, I am both proud and privileged to be an American, but glory more in the fact that I am a citizen of the kingdom of God.

Peachy Colleluori and her husband Domenic have served on the staff of the National Christian Conference Center for over twenty-five years.

Divine Patience and Me

"Be careful for nothing, but in everything by prayer and supplication with thanksgiving let your requests be made known unto God. And the peace of God which passeth all understanding shall keep your hearts and minds through Christ Jesus." *Philippians 4:6–7 (King James Version)*

My life was turned upside down when my husband left. Depression and self doubt became constant companions. Where had I gone wrong? I wondered.

Disillusioned I set about trying to mend the gaping holes left in the fabric of my life. However, the tears refused to be mended. Finally mentally and emotionally exhausted, I came to the end of what I couldn't do and found the beginning of what God could do.

My transformation occurred at a Bible study, where weary and totally spent, I collapsed at God's doorstep and He invited me in. I discovered God had waited patiently for me to come to Him as He felt my every pain and longed to comfort me. The moment I felt God's presence, every care lifted from my shoulders while I bathed in the warmth of His love. I also discovered that I'd never known the meaning of true peace until I surrendered all my burdens to God.

Surrendering is an ongoing battle because I'm still human, but as I walk a new path in life I feel God's presence. He places His hand in mine and gives me the strength to face each new day.

Dear Lord, please be a beacon of light to those in need of a lighthouse on the stormy seas of life. Help them to find the peace and unconditional love that I have found in You. And thank You for not giving up on me when I was drowning.

Sandy Arnold is a member of Rossmere Mennonite Church and helps with Mennonite Central Committee projects.

God's Plans

"'I know the plans I have for you,' declares the Lord, 'plans to prosper you and not to harm you, plans to give you hope and a future.'" *Jeremiah 29:11*

When I was in my thirties, I was a believer in Jesus Christ and my life was going well. I had a great job and was relatively content. One day after a twelve-hour shift, I came home and was met with devastating news. One of my family members had been arrested.

As details trickled in, I functioned in a fog. How could it be? Where was God in all of this?

There was deafening silence from God. What were His plans?

Very soon after the arrest and subsequent trial, I began having trouble sleeping, cried frequently and had a terrible sense of dread that often swept over me. I was diagnosed with depression and anxiety. I was sent to psychiatrists and had my medication changed.

God felt farther and farther away and I became desperate. What were His plans? I spiraled deeper into depression and began having panic attacks. Medications were ineffective and my family was at the end of their rope. My faith in a healing, loving God was shaken.

For the first time in my life, I began choosing to drink alcohol to quiet the anxiety. One night after mixing many of my pills with alcohol, I was found unconscious. During my hospitalization I met a new doctor who immediately gave me a different diagnosis. After that episode of hitting rock bottom and in the ensuing months of being unable to hold down a job because of continued drinking, I was strongly encouraged by family members to enter a recovery program. I did.

The work to change my heart is underway as I evaluate and take steps to open myself up to God's truth and care. There is freedom from addiction and peace when striving for conformity to the image of Christ.

Dear Lord, thank You for having a plan for my life and in your own time revealing it to me.

Tina, whose name has been changed to protect family members, is a resident at the Lydia Center, a division of Water Street Ministries.

Showing the Gospel of Christ by Example

"For God, who said, 'Light shall shine out of darkness,' is the One who has shone in our hearts to give the Light of the knowledge of the glory of God in the face of Christ." *2 Corinthians 4:6 (New American Standard Bible)*

For years I have tried to speak the gospel of Christ to my brother, but he just couldn't accept it. Many times I would ask him to pray, especially when my husband was critically ill over a three-month period.

My brother and I had grown up in a traditional Jewish home. He supported me when I accepted Jesus as my Savior thirty-one years ago, even when my Jewish parents disowned me for such as abominable choice from their viewpoint. My brother remained agnostic only dipping into a Catholic church where his wife was attending.

"Well, I guess your God isn't answering prayer," he said when my husband went into a coma. I assured my brother, "My God is a loving God whose ways may not be our ways but He is in full control."

Murray, his wife and his whole family traveled from Chicago to be with me the week of my husband's burial and memorial. Food, flowers, notes, phone calls, visitations all came flooding in that week, and during the memorial service everyone surrounded him and his family with the love of Christ.

"I have never seen anything like this," he told me later that week. "Your friends are so caring and giving. You've got quite a church."

"You see," I said with love, "that's the way the church of Christ should be and has been to me for the past thirty-one years. I couldn't have made it through this grueling trial without them." I smiled then nudged my brother, "Well, I guess you had to see it to believe it—God really does answer prayer. You just got a taste of heaven on earth."

Lord, I know seeing You is believing You. Help me to be an example of Christ both to my brother and those all around me. Amen.

Jan Dorward is a Messianic Jew who resides in Ephrata where she attends DOVE Westgate Church. Jan loves to write. She presents Messianic Passovers.

The Least of These

"He will have compassion on the poor and needy, and the lives of the needy he will save." *Psalm 72:13 (New American Standard Version)*

Vanessa is one of the most interesting young ladies I have ever worked with as an interpreter for the deaf. At the time I worked with her, I estimate she was about sixteen-years old. Vanessa had been placed in an institution for the mentally retarded as a young child, due to her severe temper tantrums and supposedly profound mental retardation.

We were told that Vanessa had an IQ of zero since she was untestable and seemed to be totally deaf.

Could Vanessa learn anything? Was she teachable? It seemed like nothing could reach her except her love for food. Teachers at the institution began to show her signs for food items such as cookie, candy, French fries, hamburgers and potato chips.

Amazingly Vanessa learned some signs and began to sign them when she wanted something. We even were able to get her to sign phrases such as "I want cookie, please." Then we began a long series of lessons that attempted to teach Vanessa not to throw a temper tantrum whenever she pleased. (Admittedly, that took much longer!)

Vanessa seemed to be profoundly deaf. She neither startled in response to any loud sound nor did she ever use her voice to imitate any sounds. Imagine our surprise when one day we discovered that she had perfect hearing! Behind a screen in the classroom, we opened a bag of potato chips—and she came running!

Vanessa never learned to speak with her voice, but she did learn to communicate by using sign language. Her entire world changed because of that.

Vanessa is proof that even the "least of these" have value in the eyes of God.

Thank You Lord, that You have compassion on those who cannot communicate. You reach out to them in wonderful ways. You have not forsaken them and they are precious in Your sight. Help us to see You in them.

Jim Schneck is a freelance interpreter for the deaf and the husband of Rosalee.

Hidden in Christ

"For you have died and your life is hidden with Christ in God."
Colossians 3:3 (New American Standard Version)

My daughter, Christiane, lives in an apartment where she became acquainted with her next-door neighbor, "Mr. C.," a retired older gentleman. In time, she noticed that he stayed mostly indoors, and it appeared that his rarely seen family was coming to visit quite regularly. Christiane learned from his daughter, that Mr. C. was recently diagnosed with terminal lung cancer. She was faced with a decision: should she insert herself, uninvited into his world, to bridge the divide of her world and his? A few days passed as compassion compelled her to eliminate the gap. She quickly found herself in his favor and her visits made a difference in his well-being.

Christiane visits him daily now, comforting him and being the tangible expression of God's love. I'm also praying for Mr. C. Even though I've never met him, there's undoubtedly a connection between me and the Father who loves us with an undying love!

The Lord has made us to be a blessing. The trick of the enemy is to divide us by releasing a fear of the unknown or the uncertainty of how we might be perceived by others. Being "others" conscious rather than "self" conscious draws us out of and beyond ourselves.

Those whose lives are hidden with God are graced and empowered to give gifts, riches and the nature of Christ which God has placed within us. My daughter is the one at Mr. C.'s bedside; however, both of us have the privilege to be the tangible expression of God. Our lives are hidden with Christ in God and are a blessing to be a blessing.

Lord, thank You that we have the opportunity and privilege to be the tangible expression of God's love to those whose paths we cross.

Reyna Britton serves others through her work at Lancaster General Health as director of accreditation; leadership-development and life-transitional coaching; voluntary nurse chaplaincy role; and a teammate to her husband Duane, senior pastor of DOVE Westgate Church. The Brittons live in Ephrata, have three children and six grandchildren.

Trust Me

"Trust in him at all times, O people; pour out your hearts to Him, for God is our refuge." *Psalm 62:8*

On November 1, 1999, something happened that changed my family's lives forever. It started as a normal day, but about 2:30 p.m., my husband Lester and son Nate came home early after working on an electrical job in Lancaster. After getting out of the work van and walking toward the house, Lester suddenly fell over on our stone driveway and had a grand mal seizure.

Nate burst through the front door and yelled, "Call 911."

I did. Shocked but with prayers in our hearts, we gathered around Lester until the ambulance transported him to the hospital.

Little did we know what the next year had in store. After many tests, the doctors discovered a cancerous brain tumor the size of a quarter with fingerlike projections.

I had many questions such as God where are You and why don't You do something?

We have five children ranging in ages from six to nineteen years.

I argued with God. "We can't handle this right now." I sensed God saying, "Trust me and remember, I will never leave you nor forsake you."

There were many ups and downs that year, but we continued to cry out to God for Lester's healing. Healing did come, but not the way we planned. Lester went home to be with Jesus November 9, 2000.

Life is not easy, but one thing I have learned is to take one day at a time. God's grace is there. When I can't understand God's hand, I trust His heart.

Lord, help me to trust You.

Sharon Kurtz is a widow, mother of five, grandmother and member of Petra Christian Fellowship.

As Is

". . . to the praise of the glory of his grace, by which He made us accepted in the one he loves." *Ephesians 1:6*

"As is." When you purchase a used car, it usually has that disclaimer. Or you buy a piece of furniture with a nick or an appliance with a scratch and you get a good price because it sold with the damage, "As is."

"As is" seems to infer a risk and that something is defective, not worth as much. It implies that the buyer should beware because whatever condition exists are accepted with all its faults.

I believe with all of my heart that God accepts us as is. He has never demanded I be perfect, but I have perfectionist tendencies which make it difficult for me to accept myself, as is.

Instead of trying to do things right and be right I am on a journey of learning to accept my imperfections—to change what can be changed, to accept what cannot be changed and to develop the wisdom to know the difference. I will accept myself in "as is" condition!

Father, thank You for accepting us in the Beloved, help us to love and accept ourselves, so we can better love and accept others.

Sharon Blantz serves as pastor of care and support at the Worship Center.

DECEMBER 11

Christ Took the Beating for Me

"But He was pierced through for our transgressions, He was crushed for our iniquities; The chastening for our well-being fell upon Him, And by His scourging we are healed." *Isaiah 53:5 (New American Standard)*

Frustration seems to always be lurking just around the corner, since I am at the age where my short-term memory takes regular vacations. How could I forget that a recently purchased fan sat on my kitchen floor, waiting to be taken out of the box? After all, the weather was hot and the air movement would bring welcome relief. However, snipping away at the plastic that was wrapped around the cord, I inadvertently cut the cord. My excitement in finding the fan turned to disappointment. Then the temptation made its ugly appearance: "Go ahead. Punch your forehead." Instead, by the Lord's tender mercies, I telephoned the store where I purchased the fan, and an electrician was glad to repair the cord.

Periodically over the years punching my forehead was a way I punished myself. Having grown up in a harsh environment with continuous words of disapproval, it has been extremely difficult for me to comprehend the love and grace of God. The sufficiency of Christ's redemptive work on my behalf was equally difficult to grasp. To my emotionally troubled soul the definition of grace appeared as unmerited favor. My gracious heavenly Father provided the turning point. How?

The Holy Spirit brought conviction to my heart. I was distressed to learn that my forehead punching was actually an insult to my beloved Lord and Savior, who experienced grotesque suffering so that my sins would be forgiven and taken away. Therefore, I rejected this punitive action and experienced God's love and joy at a deeper level. Also, I have been enabled to treat others more graciously. What a great salvation the Lord Jesus has provided!

Lord Jesus, You alone are my light and my salvation. May my life be a song of thanksgiving to You.

Susan Marie Davis and husband Karl are members of Calvary Church in Lancaster.

Abba's Provision

"It shall come to pass that before they call, I will answer, and while they are speaking I will hear." *Isaiah 65:24*

During the years after my devastating divorce, I learned many valuable lessons about Abba God's provision. These lessons were not easily learned. Sometimes He orchestrated similar tests in order to instill greater trust. However, at other times during this single-again experience, He used situations that I orchestrated to remind me of His ever-present care and provision.

The reason He had to build trust in me was due to both my childhood experience with my father and my marriage to my former husband—both of whom were unable to provide a secure and stable lifestyle. Promises were broken, abuse was prevalent and provision was often meager. Such a lifestyle encourages self-sufficiency and the building of a huge wall of control to assure self-protection. By early adulthood, I was an expert at self-preservation.

One of the most powerful and meaningful lessons I learned about Abba's provision and love occurred when I willfully chose to purchase something without having first prayed about it. During a one-day bus excursion, I saw a full-price skirt I just had to have. Within hours I experienced buyer's remorse, for I had no idea how I was going to pay the charge card debt when it came due. I agonized over my willfulness, repenting before the Lord. As is always the case when we cast our cares on Him, He removed the guilt and I began to expect His provision.

Imagine my joy when a check for overpayment from a former utility arrived in the mail just before the bill was due! Yes— it was for the exact amount due, and should have been mailed months earlier but was held up due to their internal glitch. God's timing is always perfect. His love is always unconditional. Hallelujah! What an awesome God we serve!

We thank You, Lord, for Your answers before we ask and for overwhelming us with Your love continually.

Denise Colvin is happily remarried to a wonderful man Rich, who is a pastor. Together, they serve at The Villa Chapel in West Reading. Denise is the blessed mother of four lovely daughters who have filled her quiver with ten grandchildren.

Provision and Timing

"You will eat the fruit of your labor; blessings and prosperity will be yours." *Psalm 128:2*

Working in the school district as a learning support aide was something I enjoyed very much. Helping the students and working with the teachers as a team was very fulfilling for me. I had wanted this job and prayed to get it. So what was going on with me? Day after day, I started to feel discontent. My mind would wander to all the things I wanted to do—at home. Finally, after much prayer, it got to the point where I knew I needed to resign.

Now at home, I was able to be involved more at my church. I began singing on the worship team and soon I was leading a Bible study. I enjoyed cleaning my house and being available for morning prayer at my house. I also had time to work on the book God had laid on my heart to write. I thought often of the job I left behind and missed it, but knew I needed to be home in this season.

Next, and unexpectedly, my father got very ill. I was able to be with him in the hospital overnight and for many days at a time. Something I would not have been able to do if I were still working outside the home.

My book got published and my dad got better. Just as I was about to hibernate for the winter, I got a call from the school asking me to come back to work! I excitedly accepted. On my first day back to work, my hubby called and told me he had been let go of his job of twenty-six years. We were shocked but marveled at God's provision and timing!

The very next day, my hubby was offered, not one, but two jobs. He has picked one and is very happy and I am happy working at the school. Oh! And my book, *Every Little Detail*, is blessing many, as we've gone through three hundred and are ready for a second printing.

Lord, thank You for Your provision and Your timing. You always know what's best for us, and when we can't see it for ourselves we can trust Your faithfulness.

Lisa Dorr is a wife, mother, editor, author, public speaker, but best of all, God's child.

An Unsung Hero

"Blessed are the merciful, for they shall be shown mercy."
Matthew 5:7

It was a bittersweet ending to a long-awaited cruise. We stood dumb-founded as hundreds of passengers hurried to claim their luggage. In the midst of the swarm of people and luggage, a woman lay sprawled on the floor. She was semiconscious, bleeding from the nose, not moving an inch.

My husband Greg was amongst the unfortunate, having been sick from a flu that had spread among the ship's passengers. The last day was the worst, even for the healthy. We wanted to get off the ship and head home. The panic of people trying to get off the ship horrified me—chaos at its best. We were herded into a huge room to claim our luggage and there she lay. This precious elderly woman was flat on the floor, facedown in a pool of blood and not a soul had stopped to help her.

I have always known Greg as a man of mercy, so it didn't surprise me to watch my pale husband drop his bag, get down on his knees and begin to stroke her blood-stained hair. I heard her name was Anna as Greg encouraged her to talk. Twenty minutes later a medical team finally arrived pushing people aside who had stopped to gawk.

"You can leave now," a paramedic informed Greg. It was hard for him to go as he gave Anna one last squeeze assuring her she'd be okay.

My husband never asked for a thank-you or even acknowledged in the limo ride to the airport that he was the "kind man" who had helped that lady everyone was now talking about, but Anna knew. A few days later, when we were both feeling well enough to unwrap our souvenirs, there, at the bottom of the bag Greg had dropped next to Anna, was a brown luggage tag with Anna's name on it. We don't think it was a mere coincidence it got into Greg's bag, but the best way a grateful lady could say thank-you to an unsung hero.

Dear Precious Jesus, help us to open our eyes to needs all around us. Give us the compassion and mercy to help others in their times of trials. Amen.

Jan Dorward wrote this in memory of her husband who recently passed away. She attends DOVE Westgate Church and loves to write.

God's Call

"He who has been forgiven little loves little." *Luke 7:47*

Justice & Mercy is a faith-based corporation focused to do criminal justice reform in the state of Pennsylvania, creating opportunities to put biblical principles into public policy.

Bishop E. Daniel Martin asked me to get involved with John Rush who was doing aftercare and mentoring people coming out of prison. My immediate response was, "No!" My wife and I were committed to not becoming involved in social programs because I considered social programs much less important than evangelism and discipleship.

I had missed the call of God before, so to be sure I wouldn't miss it again, I told John I would give him every Tuesday for six months for God to show me a need. I thought, *in six months I will prove we have the best court system, and there are no innocent people in prison.*

After the six months, I was shocked and disappointed. I had become very troubled about how dysfunctional our system was as it relates to the truth on how we arrest, judge and incarcerate the poor. When I sat down with wardens and asked what they would do if they met God today, they would say that was a hard question and then blame the system. Then legislators would blame it on the born-again Christians who wanted bad people locked up.

My discovery was that we Christians feel we have never committed these crimes. Do we like to get people who go astray saved then say it's too much work to disciple them after they have committed crimes? The problem I have found is not the police, the courts, the prison wardens or the politicians, but may be those of us "good people" who love revenge rather than mercy. My desire is to change that.

Lord, I pray the church will love mercy, do justly and walk humbly with our God.

Tom Zeager, member at DOVE Westgate, president of Hershey Farm Restaurant in Strasburg and president of Justice & Mercy, a nonprofit Christian judicial and prison reform group.

Reflection of His Love

"My command is this: Love each other as I have loved you."
John 15:12

As the tears streamed down my patient's face, he looked at me and asked, "Why do you care about me?"

In 2004, I was working as a nurse in a well-known hospital serving children and their families. I loved being a nurse, but was feeling somewhat disconnected from my patients and their families due to the busyness of a staff nurse's schedule. I longed for the type of relationship I had with my patients when my family lived and worked in rural Kenya. In the small rural clinic, I felt much freer when verbally connecting my passion for healing with my faith. In the hospital, however, I felt that I had just enough time to, safely, complete my tasks and nothing more.

When I began working at Hope Within Community Health Center, I felt as if the Lord was giving me, once again, the opportunity to combine my passion for nursing with my passion for Christ. Time after time our patients comment on the respect and compassion they feel as they come to our clinic, opening the door to express the reason for my caring. These conversations are never forced or required, but when the opportunity arises, the staff is free to offer words of faith and hope. Such as, "Mr. M., God has blessed me with the opportunity to care for you. I want to be a reflection of His love for you."

Lord, please make me a reflection of Your love and mercy to those You put me in contact with today. Cause them to wonder in the fact that You care for them.

Beth Good is the director of clinical services at Hope Within Community Health Center. She and her husband are also church planters, living in Columbia, Pennsylvania.

Sacrificing for Others

"For I testify that according to their ability, and beyond their ability, they gave of their own accord." *2 Corinthians 8:3 (New American Standard Bible)*

One December, my four-year-old son learned about the city shelters where children were living. Joshua reasoned that because these children were not at home, Santa would not be able to find them. This troubled my child to no end, and I wanted to ease his mind about these children.

Touched by the fact that my son, an only child, had a heart for others at such a young age, I wanted to show him that simply caring was good, but action was better. He and I went through his extensive toy box. I encouraged Joshua to pick out the toys that he no longer wanted or played with and we would clean and disinfect them and take them to the Women's Abuse Shelter in Lancaster City.

To my surprise, Joshua not only picked toys that he didn't really want but toys that he treasured. My son was willing to sacrifice something important to him for the sake of total strangers.

Jesus tells us to esteem others higher than ourselves. I spent my life worried about establishing and exercising *my* rights and what was right for *me*. To see someone so young embrace and live this truth was humbling and planted seeds of caring and generosity in my life that continues to grow after all of these years.

Joshua is now sixteen years old. His friends will tell you that Joshua is the most caring and giving one in their pack, and they love and respect him for it. He walks in the Lord's calling to not only to pray for our suffering brothers and sisters, but to give.

Lord, teach us to give beyond our ability in demonstration of the love of Christ!

Tara Rice is resident assistant of Life Awakening.

The Faces of Christ

"... 'Lord, when did we see you hungry and feed you, or thirsty and give you something to drink? ... I tell you the truth, whatever you did for one of the least of these brothers of mine, you did it for me.'"
Matthew 25:37–40

I had an opportunity to serve with my church at an Ephrata Community Meal. Everyone and anyone is welcome to come on any given Thursday evening throughout the year for a free meal. Several churches in our area volunteered to cook, greet and serve meals to whomever would show up.

I was assigned to be the greeter. There were the homeless, people with mental and physical handicaps, young families, widows and widowers and people who just wanted to sense friendship. Every person there had the face of Christ. As I looked into their eyes and greeted them individually, I could feel their hurts, sympathize for their disabilities and almost cry for the young children who were happy to receive a decent meal. Yet, they were very polite and showered us with thanks and smiles.

I remember one particular lady who sat right by the entrance, criticizing and eyeing everyone who came through the door. She was a teaser, and her loud guffawing clearly showed her insecurities. I befriended her as I stood by the door, reassuring her that a lovely lady like herself couldn't possibly mean what she said about others.

"God made us all," I told her, "and certainly we are all beautiful in His sight, especially you." Finally, she got a glimpse of herself "in the mirror" and accepted God's love. My reward was a hug I received at the end of the meal.

The experience was an "eye-opener" for me as the gospel came alive when Jesus said "if you do this to the least of my brethren, you have done it unto me."

Dear Lord, I pray that every Christian has an opportunity to serve the needy so they can see Your face in theirs.

Jan Dorward serves and attends DOVE Westgate Church in Ephrata. She loves all the new opportunities and experiences God provides.

Worrywart Finds Peace

"Do not be anxious about anything, but in everything, by prayer and petition, with thanksgiving, present your requests to God. And the peace of God, which transcends all understanding, will guard your hearts and your minds in Christ Jesus." *Philippians 4:6, 7*

My husband and I have been married for almost thirty-three years. If you had asked my husband during the first 30 years of our marriage, he would probably have described me as a worrywart most of the time. You know the kind: worry, worry, worry, as if worry will actually change a situation.

Two years ago, I changed. I had been admitted to the hospital for a totally unrelated problem, but the doctor came into the testing room to tell me that my chest X-ray showed a mass on my rib. She suggested getting a CAT scan immediately on discharge. A pulmonologist came into the room minutes later, and things took on an even more dismal outlook. A trip to a thoracic surgeon, a tumor discovery with a possible cancer diagnosis gave me more worry, worry, worry. After all, worry was part of me, remember?

While preparing for the big day to have a rib resection, I asked friends, relatives and churches to pray. I immersed myself in God's Word.

What did I find through it all? Peace. God's peace. Peace beyond understanding as they wheeled me into the operating room. Three weeks later, I sat in the surgeon's office awaiting the biopsy results. At the moment I received the answer to the request I had made in prayer to God: Benign—a miracle!

That made two miracles, for you see God had guarded my heart and my mind in Christ Jesus.

Jesus, Thank You! Thank You for guarding our hearts, minds and souls when we place our trust in You. No need to worry, no need to doubt or fear. You are my everything.

Barb Shirey attends DOVE Westgate and is a retired registered nurse, disabled but enabled through Jesus Christ.

Spring of Water

"Whoever drinks the water I give him will never thirst. Indeed, the water I give him will become in him a spring of water welling up to eternal life." *John 4:13–14*

Jesus is picturing a vigorous fountain. Other translations read: a perpetual spring, living water or an artesian spring within or a gushing fountain of endless life. The water leaps up. Jesus is speaking of vigorous, abundant life. He is using water as a symbol of the Holy Spirit. (See John 7:39.) We are commanded to be filled with the Spirit, literally "keep on being filled" with the Spirit. (See Ephesians 5:18.)

If you find that the fountain of life is not springing up from within you blessing the lives of others, something is blocking the flow. Could it be that the flow has stopped or is only a trickle because you are not passing it on? Are you a dead sea? A dead sea produces no life.

Learn to pass it on. Jesus' life in you becomes a fountain that overflows, spilling out on those you meet. This river passes through you to others. Jesus said, "If anyone is thirsty, let him come to me and drink. Whoever believes in me . . . streams of living water will flow from within him."

If you are not living in the Spirit, God has so much more for you! Stay true to Him. Be obedient in every detail and you will experience the water that becomes a spring gushing up and overflowing to others.

Keep paying attention to the source. Remain in Jesus and you will bear much fruit. No one can block a river indefinitely. It will overcome every obstacle. Others may throw rocks in its path or try to dam it up but it will overflow to them.

Father, I thank You for your Holy Spirit. Thank You that I never need be thirsty again. Help me to overflow to the many thirsty people around me today. Amen.

J. David Eshleman served as pastor/church planter for fifty years and is church consultant for Eastern Mennonite Missions and Lancaster Mennonite Conference. He is author of *"Now Go Forward: Reaching out to grow your congregation* and *Living with Godly Passion: Daily Reading for those with a passion to share Jesus.*

I Have to Apologize for What

"Therefore, if you . . . remember that your brother has something against you, leave your gift there in front of the altar. First go and be reconciled to your brother; then come and offer your gift."
Matthew 5:23–24

I learned about the Jewish holiday Yom Kippur by watching the 1990s TV drama *Northern Exposure*. I was relieved that I wasn't obligated to make amends with every person with whom I'd been in conflict. The idea quickened my heart—how intimidating!

Years later, I experienced Yom Kippur powerfully when a Jewish woman I'd worked for apologized to me for a misunderstanding, as part of her observance. The fault wasn't even clearly hers. Her humble reconciliation is still impressed upon me.

Since then, I've learned I *am* held to that standard, though we Christians have no yearly observance to remind us. My relationships are of such concern to Jesus that he tells me to go reconcile before I worship! Seeing a Jewish woman handle people in a more Christlike way than most Christians do made me realize how much I, and perhaps the church in general, have been missing. It's not just about a to-do list—it's about a way of life that keeps you humble, close to the heart of God and continually looking to others with more concern than yourself.

The instruction even goes beyond apologizing for our wrongs—it says to reconcile with anyone who "has something against *you*"—no matter our lack of fault or even our interest. It's been an eye-opener about how I must interact (despite discomfort) and about how we are meant to live in community, constantly negotiating relationships instead of acting self-protectively to avoid conflict. Understanding God's priority for peacemaking has transformed my understanding of what it means to be Christlike and love others.

Lord, give us courage and wisdom to reconcile with those who have issues with us, honoring You in the process.

Renee Lannan, New Cumberland Church of the Nazarene, serves as a stay-at-home mother to two small ones.

Power to Determine My Course

"Guard your heart above all else, for it determines the course of your life." *Proverbs 4:23 (New Living Translation)*

The hot fudge sundae is half eaten, my stomach is beginning to protest the burden and ever since I ordered my treat my head has been yammering about the dreaded C's: calories, carbs and cholesterol.

Do I stop? No! Something compels me to eat every bite. When only a few drops of vanilla remain, I am in misery with a surfeit of food and guilt. Why couldn't I stop? My mind knew all the facts and reasons to quit. My body didn't even crave it. But my heart believed something that contradicted both mind and body. And when there is a difference of opinions, my heart has veto power.

Guarding my heart is the key to change, to victory or defeat. It is my responsibility to keep lies out and welcome truth in. I'm the one who must filter the thoughts and ideas that swirl around me, always vigilant never relaxing my defenses. The Holy Spirit is eager to teach me to recognize the good and the potentially deadly. All I have to do is listen and follow through.

How do I guard my heart?

1. Keep it soft and pliable through worship so I can hear God's voice
2. Protect it from hardening influences of unforgiveness, bitterness and worry
3. Refuse entrance to all ideas and lies that oppose God's truth
4. Uproot old beliefs that contradict God's truth
5. Deliberately plant God's truth.

When God says "above all else" he has an excellent reason for doing so. As the One who created us, He knows how much power He gave to our hearts—the power to determine the course of our lives.

Teach me to guard my heart. I want the course of my life to glorify You and demonstrate Your kingdom's power.

Ruth Morris is a special projects writer for several ministries.

Christmas Night Fellowship

"... I tell you the truth, whatever you did for one of the least of these brothers of mine, you did for me." *Matthew 25:40*

What a terrific Christmas evening at the Ephrata Church of the Nazarene. There were fifty people there, of which twenty were members of our church. We were blessed with live music, gifts for everyone, food and clothing for those in need, basketball games, prayer and great fellowship.

We were able to give a backpack to someone who was homeless. We were able to pray together and really make some good connections to help with housing, medical care and other needs. The recipient called me the next morning to say that it was the first time he could remember waking up not cold because he had the sweatpants and socks on from the backpack.

Two adults were excited to get two children's sleeping bags! They have no bed but had received some pillows for Christmas from other family members. Another family said they would not have had gifts for their children had it not been for this event. This is the true meaning of Christmas, to see the depth of appreciation from giving so little to someone who has nothing.

We ended the evening by lighting candles and singing "Silent Night." We sang all the verses and kept singing the first verse over and over. It was like no one wanted that time of pure worship in the presence of our Lord and Savior on His birthday to end.

Thank You, God, for Your goodness shown through many people.

Darlene Adams has been involved in street ministry since 1995 and attends the Ephrata Church of the Nazarene.

Our Christmas Tradition

"And Jacob the father of Joseph, the husband of Mary, of whom was born Jesus, who is called Christ." *Matthew 1:16*

We in the United States celebrate the birth of Jesus on December 25, the day we call Christmas. Each year of my wife's and my fifty-five years of marriage, we carry out a tradition on Christmas Day. We have a brightly decorated cake with the words imprinted with icing: "Happy Birthday Jesus!"

Following our dinner meal, we light the candles on the cake and our family sits around the table and sings "Happy Birthday" to Jesus. Then we blow out the flame on the candles and enjoy eating the birthday cake.

Visiting friends often join us to take part of this Christmas tradition.

Is this unique? We don't know, but there is joy as we celebrate the birth of our Lord each year in this manner. Join us!

Lord, thank You for dying for us, for coming to earth and for being our Savior, and for saving us, Your people, from sin. Thank You for the opportunity each year to sing "Happy Birthday to You."

Bob Burns serves as pastor and shepherd of Spiritual Growth Ministries, a guiding ministry to church leaders in areas of spiritual growth, and he ministers at Spring Valley Church of God.

Christmas Gifts

"On entering the house, they saw the child with Mary his mother; and they knelt down and paid him homage. Then, opening their treasure chests, they offered him gifts of gold, frankincense, and myrrh." *Matthew 2:11 (New Revised Standard Version)*

Christmas can be a wonderful holiday of family and friends. It can also be an exciting time of anticipating the future and evaluating the past. And it can be a big occasion for giving and receiving gifts. Although Christmas was not celebrated during the time of King David, he liked to give gifts. He even wanted to give a gift to the Almighty: a temple. When the Messiah was born the magi from the East brought their precious gifts to Jesus, paying Him homage.

But what will I give to God on Christmas? I used to be part of a big ministry for God's glory. I am not any longer. I used to make big money (in my opinion) and give it to advancing God's kingdom on earth. Now I mostly receive. I used to feed and clothe the needy. Now I am needy myself. So what could I give to Jesus on His birthday? My heart is sad. I seem to have nothing to give even to my loved ones. How much more my heart is crying, for I truly believe that I have absolutely nothing to give to the Lord!

"Give me your heart."

"What's that?" I ask the four walls startled by the message that seemed to come from nowhere.

"Give me your heart," I hear again. This time it is so gentle and strong that in my spirit I know—the Lord is speaking to *me!*

"Jesus, is that all? Is it enough?"

How little our precious Lord wants from His children! Yet, how much He gives to them not only on Christmas, but throughout their life here and in heaven!

Jesus, we thank You for all the gifts that we receive on Your birthday. Amen.

Yulia Bagwell, Beth Yeshua, is a housewife-caregiver, a writer and a translator for *The Upper Room* devotional magazine.

An Unremarkable Event

"For to us a child is born, to us a son is given, and the government will be on his shoulders. And he will be called Wonderful Counselor, Mighty God, Everlasting Father, Prince of Peace." *Isaiah 9:6*

On November 1, 200, an unremarkable event took place. Our daughter blessed us with a granddaughter. Unremarkable? Yes. From a world perspective, a baby being born is nothing out of the ordinary. It was no different than any of the millions of births that take place every year. However, that unremarkable event has had a remarkable impact on the life of our family. Her presence in our lives has changed us. Things simply are not the same as they were the day before she was born. She is living proof that babies have a way of turning the world upside down.

Children are used as prophetic signs of change in the writings of Isaiah. However, this hymn is not remembering something that happened once upon a time long ago. It is a hymn which looks forward to a future time—a time when there will be no more oppression and no more captivity for the people of Israel.

The first annunciation of Good News did not come to the powerful, but to the oppressed. They were the poorest of the poor in Judea at the time of the birth of Jesus. They longed for the day when the prophecy would be fulfilled and a child would turn the world upside down.

If you are quiet, you can almost hear their whispers as they kneel by that crude cradle, *"He's the one. He is going to do it. He is going to turn the world upside down."* Babies have a way of doing that, don't they?

Surprise us again, Lord, with what You can do through the littlest and the least who surround us. Give us faith to believe that the baby in Bethlehem still has the power to change the world. Then help us to follow Him. Amen.

Rev. Randolph T. Riggs is senior pastor of First Presbyterian Church in Lancaster.

The Savior Who Transforms Me

"For today in the city of David there has been born for you a Savior, who is Christ the Lord." *Luke 2:11 (New American Standard Bible)*

Emotion welled up within me as I listened to the beautiful voices and powerful instruments performing Christmas songs in the foyer of Lancaster Bible College's chapel. Joy was in the air, and it captivated my heart as I considered the fact that Lancaster Bible College is my alma mater. It is a miracle that I have a collegiate alma mater because decades earlier I had to withdraw from college due to severe depression.

Recalling the life that I had lived before becoming a Christian, it is astounding that I would earn a Bible college degree. Frankly it is a miracle that I was graduated at the age of fifty-four. These facts reflect the truth that God has done transformational work within me, all because He sent a Savior into the world to redeem sinners.

My journey with the Savior, the Lord Jesus, has included dark valleys. Although I couldn't see beyond the pain and fear during these times, they would prove to be springboards to spiritual growth and emotional healing, wrought by God's love, grace and skill. In fact, He was performing the activity described in Psalm 51:6, "Behold, You desire truth in the innermost being. And in the hidden part You will make me know wisdom."

One of these valleys was particularly dark and frightening. My husband had needed to take me to the hospital because my emotional state was deteriorating rapidly. When the nurse asked my name, my almost inaudible whisper was "Satan." That lie had been planted deep within my soul during childhood, strengthened each time I had been called a devil or demon, finally came to the surface. Now the lie would be rejected, and my skillful Savior would continue to perform His marvelous and matchless work within me.

Lord Jesus, I praise You for Your willingness to enter this world and my heart.

Susan Marie Davis and her husband Karl are members of Calvary Church, Lancaster.

God in the Cathedral

"For whoever is not against us is for us." *Mark 9:40*

I was bustled, along with my traveling companions, past the statuary and stained-glass windows, memorial plaques and tributes to politicians. I sat down with a hint of irritation and quite a bit of skepticism. This was Westminster Abbey, and I was having nothing to do with it. Yes, it was one thing to admire the artistry or appreciate its role in history: the site of the coronation of kings, a place where "important things" happened. But we were there for Evensong, for worship! How could a low-church Protestant like me, one who helps to provide leadership to a congregation that worships with drums and screaming guitars and video projectors, actually worship God in this overblown monument to hubris and political power?

But we began the liturgy with "Lord of the Dance," of all things, and I found myself, almost against my will, singing praises to that dancing, joyful Lord along with the other worshippers. And then the priest— a dignified, older man (I was sure he was going to be pompous!) shared a brief meditation that resonated deeply with me, for I recognized what he spoke of from my own experience. When he led us in prayer, his voice cracked and he paused to wipe away tears as he prayed for those who were suffering, there and elsewhere. I cracked open my eyes to look at him and knew I was looking at my brother. I knew that the God I worshipped in my home church, the God I encountered on the mountaintop, the God I met with daily in my private prayers, was present there as well. For whatever else humans had done with or for that building, it was first and foremost a place to meet with Him.

Father, forgive me for putting You and Your people into boxes, for the presumption that what I know best or am most comfortable with is the only or preferred way for You to work. Thank You for showing up whenever and wherever Your people worship You. Amen.

Tony Blair is one of the senior pastors of Hosanna! A Fellowship of Christians in Lititz. He also teaches at Eastern University and Evangelical Theological Seminary.

No Digging in the Trash

"Brethren, I do not count myself to have apprehended; but one thing I do, forgetting those things which are behind and reaching forward to those things which are ahead, I press toward the goal. . . ."
Philippians 3:13–14 (New King James Version)

Christmas was over, and we returned home from a trip to find an arduous mountain of mail to go through. Here amidst all the junk mail and bills was my Christmas card with a "Return to sender" stamp on it. "Refused," it shouted in big red letters on the front of the envelope. And apparently, from the postmarks, it had been returned or "refused" twice! It came back from a hurt, angry, unforgiving, disgruntled family member. It was an intentional, deliberate attempt to hurt me, and it did just that.

After some tears, I stood over the trash can and tossed it into the trash, saying this is now behind me, while asking the Lord to bless and heal this person. I asked the Lord to help me move past this hurtful act of rejection, to forget this attempt to discourage me in my desire for reconciliation and to release His Holy Spirit into the situation.

Later that day, after throwing out all the junk mail, I realized that I had inadvertently thrown out a refund check! Now I had to reluctantly go dig thru the disgusting, smelly trash to retrieve it. And there it was again, the returned Christmas card with the big red letters "refused" on it. All the rejection and hurt feelings came rushing over me again. The enemy tried to bring it all back up again. So I said, "No, I have put this behind me, it is done. I am not going there again. This stays in the trash and I am not digging it up again."

Whenever I am tempted to go over and over a hurt memory, or nurse it like a pet, I remember the disgusting trash and I refuse to dig through it again.

Lord, thank You that when You forgive me, You also completely forget. Help me to be like You, forgiving and forgetting the past hurtful things, and moving forward in life-giving relationship

Shirley Ann Bivens serves in the children's department at Christ Community Church. She also does Christian clowning, as Coco the clown, and is a full time grammy.

God's Course

"A man's heart plans his way, but the Lord directs his steps."
Proverbs 16:9

Think back ten years. Does your life now look as you had imagined it then, ten years in the future? Mine doesn't.

Life has a way of taking us places we had never imagined ourselves. And yet, is it really a chance set of circumstances that have placed me in my current situation? Have I failed because I'm not even close to obtaining my dream? A short while ago, I would have answered, "Yes. Somewhere along the line, I really got off course."

If I evaluate, though, how it is I came to this place in life, I can point to specific instances of God's directing that have brought me to where I am today. The conclusion, then, is that I'm precisely where *God wants me to be*, even though it is not at all where *I thought I should be*.

Having the assurance that I am in God's will is just the beginning. While it brings a sense of peace instead of failure, the longing for the dream remains. Perhaps the dream is yet to be fulfilled, or perhaps, it is not the will of God. Either way, it needs to be surrendered. Christians talk about surrendering our lives, our bodies, our gold and silver, our wills (are you hearing the words from a familiar hymn?). But our *dreams*, too? Yes, perhaps our dreams first and foremost. It is our striving after them that will influence our decisions in daily life—how to invest our time, energy, money, relationships, etc. When we finally surrender our dreams to God and say, "Your will, not mine," we can also find contentment. We can rest in the fact that God promises to meet our needs and guide our path according to His plan which will bring far more blessing than anything we could dream.

Lord, help me to trust You with my dreams and be content living in Your good and perfect will.

Rebecca Nissly, Community Bible Church (Marietta), serves at Susquehanna Valley Pregnancy Services.

Year-End Inventory

"But He's already made it plain how to live, what to do, what God is looking for in men and women. It's quite simple: Do what is fair and just to your neighbor, be compassionate and loyal in your love, and don't take yourself too seriously—take God seriously." *Micah 6:8 (The Message)*

Micah lays out a straightforward inventory for us to assess how we've lived this past year and to prepare for the New Year.

1. Was I fair and just in my dealings with others? Did I help the least of these? Who can I bless in the coming year? Is there someone God wants me to mentor?
2. Was I compassionate and loyal in my relationships with others? Was I honest? Was I honoring? How can I show more mercy in the New Year?
3. Did I take myself too seriously? In what ways did I make life about me? Did I experience God's grace through my failures and weaknesses? How can I decrease so that He can increase?
4. Have I taken God seriously? Have I loved Him with my whole heart? How can I revere Him more next year? How can I bring Him more glory?

Father, You've made it clear how You want us to live, but it's easier said than done and it's impossible without Your help. Grace us, Father, to love You more in the coming year and to do better at truly loving our neighbors as we love ourselves.

Lisa Hosler serves as president of Susquehanna Valley Pregnancy Services and on teams seeking God for the transformation of Lancaster County.

Index

Abbie, 284
Anita, 285
Adams, Darlene, 43, 372
Apicella, Vincent, 227
Araya, Mario, 139
Arnold, Grace, 175
Arnold, Sandy, 353
Atkins, Mike, 244
Atkins, Sandra, 280
Bagwell, Yulia 296, 337, 343, 374
Barnes, Linda, 30
Barnett, Nancy, 269
Billota, Peter, 230
Bivens, Shirley, 241, 378
Blair, Tony, 13, 377
Blantz, Sharon, 119, 359
Boll, Brenda, 20
Bowlby, Judy, 300
Bowman, Sue, 127
Bowser, Jackie, 17, 163, 246
Boyd, Karen, 270
Boydell, Bruce, 67, 260
Boydell, Joan, 70, 134
Breckbill, Sue, 57, 148
Britton, Reyna, 11, 357
Brown, Alice, 216
Brubaker, Paul, 56, 351
Buch, Mary, 95
Buckwalter, Marlene, 350
Burns, Bob, 335, 373
Charles, John, 211, 273, 346
Charles, Sharon, 226, 274, 333
Christine, 304
Christensen, Eileen, 265, 289
Clegg, Nancy, 84, 170, 192, 231
Colleluori, Dominic, 44
Colleluori, Peachy, 40, 94, 125, 249, 352

Colvin, Denise, 162, 361
Culp, Brinton, 122
Davenport, Debbie, 267, 290, 309
Davis, Susan, 282, 360, 376
Deb, 283, 342
Denlinger, Pat, 243
Dooley, Ellen, 143, 189, 219
Dorr, Lisa, 263, 302, 362
Dorward, Jan, 19, 46, 96, 144, 355, 363, 367
Doutrich, Donna, 281
Eberly, Sharon, 292
Elaine, 326
Eldredge, Darla, 250
Eshleman, J. David, 89, 171, 294, 313, 330, 344, 369
Evans, Marti, 218
Farner, Jo, 229
Ford, Jim, 141
Gabikiny, Chou, 135, 136, 261
Garber, Cyndi, 341
Gatten, Nichole, 26
Gehman, Grant, 7
Gehman, Jenny, 106, 182
Gibble, Nancy, 120, 268
Givens, Rosalyn, 69
Good, Beth, 212, 334, 365
Good, Kelly, 213
Good, Lisa, 31
Good, Lou Ann, 236, 315, 338
Good, Marie, 194
Good, Seth, 18
Greiner, Bonni, 45
Hameloth, Lynnea, 66
Hamilton, Jennifer, 180
Harsh, Christine, 210, 329
Hassel, Jean, 81
Healey, Cindy, 312
Heim, Tamalyn, 166, 206, 262, 316

Hershey, Steve, 28, 71, 129, 146, 178, 220, 298
Hertzler, Rosene, 35, 238
Hildebrand, Lisa, 64, 104
Hodecker, Terry, 91
Hollinger, Kathleen, 232
Hoover, Don, 73, 131
Hoover, Glenn, 158
Hoover, Ginny, 172
Hoover, Lloyd, 74
Hosler, Lisa, 380
Hurst, Deryl, 248, 310
Hurst, Louetta, 201
Ingham, Linda, 58
Jackson, Scott, 164
Jenner, Helena, 16
Karen, 86
Kaylor, Dorinda, 78
Keller, Karen, 259
Kirkpatrick, Diane, 80, 159
Kirkpatrick, Sandra, 93, 103
Klopp, Ken, 54
Knight, Karen, 29
Kornhaus, Susan, 68
Kramer, Kendra, 222
Kreider, Larry, 107
Kulka, Susan, 299, 320
Kurtz, Sharon, 37, 358
Lanford, Sonja, 251, 340
Lannan, Renee, 34, 118, 370
Lehman, Mary Ruth, 113, 208, 214
Levan, Carol, 77
Libonati, Carrie, 130
Little, Ruth, 245
Martin, Brian, 264, 288, 321
Martin, Nelson W., 200
Masters, Kathleen, 233
McCamant, Sharon, 62
McKelvey, Leah, 99, 165
Medrow, Janet, 41, 258
Mellinger, Jere, 10, 168
Miller, Beaty, 253
Miller, Debbi, 205, 336
Miller, Joanne, 215

Miller, John, 39
Morgan, Barbara, 79
Morris, Ruth, 252, 279, 295, 314, 371
Mummu, Marie, 22
Musser, Wilma, 9, 110
Myer, Ron, 123, 142, 169, 272
Neal, Sharon, 303
Nicholas, Jane, 145, 176
Nissly, Rebecca, 151, 235, 379
Nolt, Gary, 204
Nolt, Joe, 190, 319
Nolt, Kathy, 25, 87
Orsulak, Thomas, 138
Ortega, Joy, 98, 207
Outlar, Sandy, 114, 228, 345
Owens, Sally, 12, 38, 51, 82, 83, 152, 153, 240, 271
Patterson, Joan, 76
Paules, Jenn, 173, 186
Pennell, Karen, 72, 202, 257, 291, 328
Pierson, Anne, 132, 157
Printzenhoff, Jill, 184
Prokopchak, Mary, 278
Prokopchak, Steve, 8, 88, 109, 311
Ressler, Rosene, 247
Rew, Robert, 196
Rhoads, Lois, 92
Rice, Tara, 366
Riggs, Randolph, 234, 375
Riker, Cindy, 101, 203, 324
Riker, Don, 42, 100
Roach, Carol, 277
Roche, Deborah, 140, 209
Robenolt, Ruth, 137
Sabol, Laurie, 23,105
Sanoski, Susan, 112
Sauder, Sarah, 197
Schneck, Jim, 167, 301, 322, 356

Schlicher, Carolyn, 50, 287, 348
Schultz, Ruthi, 224
Scott, Kathy, 177
Sensenig, Naomi, 124
Sentgeorge, Paula, 33
Shaner, Jim, 133
Sheehan, Diana, 179, 275
Sheila, 85
Shiner, Susan, 108, 327
Shirey, Barb, 15, 293, 323, 368
Shirk, John, 48
Showalter, Doris, 305
Siegrist, Dave, 63
Siegrist, Teresa, 155
Siegrist, Wesley, 24, 121
Slonaker, Tracy, 14, 55, 90, 306
Smoker, Marv, 59
Sanoski, Susan, 112
Stanton, Jim, 181, 256, 266
Stauffer, Ruth Ann, 52, 239
Stephanie, 147
Swanson, Amy, 317
Swisher, Kathi, 102
Tina, 354
Toews, Becky, 49
Thomas, Joyce, 193
Van Scyoc, Donna, 331
Van Scyoc, Mark, 325
Wagner, Daniel, 347
Walker, Dolores, 276
Weaver, Jay, 75, 221
Weaver, Jeanette, 161, 242
Weaver, John, 21
Weaver, Sandy, 47, 339
West, Wayne, 254
White, Linda, 188
Wilcox, Patti, 32, 156
Wilson, Kathi, 307
Wilson, Patrick, 27, 111, 195
Wingenroth, Randy, 198
Witmer, Miriam, 53
Witmer, Nancy, 199

Woodcock, Robert, 237
Wrightstone, Phil, 5
Yoder, Keith, 6, 117, 174
Yoder, Marian, 60
Young, Janet, 297
Zeager, Tom, 364
Zeiset, Yvonne, 126, 183
Zercher, Joan, 187
Zeyak, Cindy, 154
Zimmerman, Cynthia, 116, 150, 185, 217, 332
Zimmerman, Kim, 61, 115
Zimmerman, Mike, 308

A Celebration of Partnership

The following regional networks within South Central Pennsylvania partnered in publishing this devotional. We invite you to contact them to learn more about how God is at work to bring transformation in your local region.

The Regional Church of Lancaster County

Keith Yoder, Chair, and Lisa Hosler, Assistant Chair
Box 311, Leola, PA 17540
Phone: (717) 625-3034   www.theregionalchurch.com

We are a network of Christian congregational, marketplace and ministry leaders dedicated to the growth of God's kingdom in Lancaster County through relational partnership.

To attain spiritual and social transformation of Lancaster County, we actively cultivate partnerships to:

PRAY: fill the region with continual united prayer and worship
WITNESS: communicate the gospel of Jesus Christ to every person in each local community and culture group
LOVE: mobilize initiatives to transform our communities with the love of God
PROTECT: promote biblical unity, reconcile relationships and provide spiritual discernment for the well-being of the Church.

Many partnerships; one mission: Lancaster County transformed by the gospel of Jesus Christ.

Reading Regional Transformation Network

Craig Nanna, Director
P.O. Box 8188, Reading, PA 19603
Phone: (610) 371-8386   Email: craignanna@readingdove.org

Reading House of Prayer

Chad Eberly, Director
Phone: (610) 373-9900 Email: ChadE@rhop.net www.rhop.net

Uniting leaders together in strategic kingdom relationships for the purpose of transformation in the Reading region. Our priorities include advancing the kingdom of God in the Reading region through relationship, the unity of the body of Christ, the house of prayer and strategic initiatives that will produce transformation.

Transforming Ministries: Coatesville Regional
Bill Shaw, Executive Director
643 East Lincoln Highway, P.O. Box 29, Coatesville, PA 19320
Phone: (610) 384-5393   www.QuietRevolution.org

A catalyst in the movement for church unity and community transformation. Generated out of humility and united prayer the mission of LTM is to feature the Lordship of Jesus by being a conduit for the development of trusting cross cultural relationships and incubator of collaborative ministry initiatives.

Lebanon Valley Prayer Network
Stephen J. Sabol, Executive Director
825 North Seventh Street, Lebanon, PA 17046
Phone: (717) 273-9258

This Network exists to lay a foundation of worship and intercessory prayer for the purpose of birthing transformation in the Lebanon Valley.

Lebanon 222
Jay McCumber, Director
515 Cumberland Street, Lebanon, PA 17042
Phone: (717) 279-5683

The Lebanon 222 Team exists to discern and implement God's heart for the Lebanon Valley.

Capital Region Pastors' Network
Dave Hess, President
P. O. Box 9, Camp Hill, PA 17001-0009
Phone: (717) 909.1906   Email: c.reg.pastors@pa.net

We are a network of pastors in the Capital Region of Pennsylvania committed to Christ and to developing relationships among pastors, rooted in prayer, which lead to partnerships in ministry bearing the fruit of revival.

For more copies of this book
Visit www.theregionalchurch.com